Digesting India

PRAISE FOR *DIGESTING INDIA: A TRAVEL WRITER'S SUB-CONTINENTAL ADVENTURES WITH THE TUMMY*

'Part memoir, part travelogue with lashings of history, literary references and unbridled fun, this collection of eight essays takes the reader on a whirlwind ride through India and the food (and alcohol) it holds... *Digesting India* will leave you chortling and hungering for more.' —**Preeti Zachariah, *The Hindu***

'You really do not have to be a foodie to enjoy Zac O'Yeah's *Digesting India*...this Scandinavian-born author, settled in Bangalore, who has been exploring the sub-continent for over three decades now never ceases to surprise himself, and the reader with the everyday magic of India. This time, he discovers it through food.' —**Sukant Deepak, Indo-Asian News Service**

'*Digesting India* is in-depth and immersive, filled with anecdotes that many readers will be delighted to come across.' —**Anjana Basu, *Outlook India***

'A droll and deeply researched new book by Zac O'Yeah reveals to India the food, booze and culture of its backstreets' —**Samar Halarnkar, *Mint***

'O'Yeah brings a lot of knowledge and research to his writing, but wears all of it lightly—the tone is light, the puns keep flowing...All through the book I felt like immediately booking myself a ticket to the place he was writing about and at the end, wanted to undergo the same adventure—try the foods, learn about the place, see the landmarks and talk to the locals.' —**Sidharth Bhatia, *The Wire***

'O'Yeah's writing is humorous, insightful, and delightful, tempting the reader to binge on this country's delectable, sometimes unknown, offerings on each page...*Digesting India* is unputdownable.' —**Sharmistha Chaudhuri, *India Today***

'Zac O'Yeah's new book, *Digesting India*, harks back to the good old times when travel writing was about slow journeys, memorable encounters, subtle observations, tongue-in-cheek humour, deep dives into a destination, and more.' —**Avantika Bhuyan, *Mint Lounge***

DIGESTING INDIA

A Travel Writer's Subcontinental Adventures with the Tummy

(A MEMOIR À LA CARTE)

ZAC O' YEAH

SPEAKING TIGER

SPEAKING TIGER BOOKS LLP
125A, Ground Floor, Shahpur Jat, near Asiad Village,
New Delhi 110049

First published by Speaking Tiger Books 2023

ISBN: 978-93-5447-506-1
eISBN: 978-93-5447-507-8

10 9 8 7 6 5 4 3 2

Typeset in Dante MT by SÜRYA, New Delhi
Printed at Printworks, Delhi-92

For Mita & Rahul, and the great life!
I hope this book will tickle like a pickle!

'What, for instance, could hing mean
to your salt-and-pepper accustomed tongue,
of what do lichees taste to you?'

—*Food of Love*, Anjum Hasan

CONTENTS

Prologue

It's one meal I'll never forget. Ever. About to catch a bus to Nepal the next morning, I celebrated a successful tour of India. I was a rather inexperienced backpacker so I had reasons to be happy despite the fact that I munched on an only slightly dubious tandoori chicken in a somewhat seedy drinking den in Patna. I bet you can guess what happened next. Yes, exactly that.

Illustration: Paul Fernandes

At 3 a.m., I made a desperate dash for the commode where the resulting World War I-class bombardment of poison gas was so explosive that the toilet door flew off its hinges. As is well known, travellers' stories evolve as one grows older, but this is exactly how I remember it thirty years later as a mature, responsible tourist.

Wishing to put that ignoble moment behind me forever, get it off my shoulders so to speak, is one good reason why I wrote this book. In fact, I've never told anybody of my discomfiture, not even my wife, but in hindsight it is a hilarious episode to throw into a travelogue to raise the stakes.

Like I told you, I wasn't as experienced then. In retrospect, my theory is that the chicken, before turning zombie on me, had been entombed in putrefying marinade for too long. Perhaps a week, maybe even a month—maturing extra rapidly from young chick to elderly hen thanks to the lengthy power cuts that were common back then. It might have been waiting for me for a year, considering how well it had been marinated, until all hell broke loose…motion. But did I make the bus to Kathmandu? Yes, thanks to about 1 kg of Imodium that turned my intestines into a solid block of concrete.

A decade later, around the turn of the millennium, I had become a hardened professional travel writer, flying across the world on assignments. One sunny day I was being taken by a stubborn, officially-appointed guide to every single batik shop in Sri Lanka. He seemed hell-bent on getting me to buy enough hand-printed textiles to clothe the entire generation of 1967 in hippie fashion. Just then, I experienced tell-tale eggy burps reminiscent of that night in Patna; only this time it was evidently a gastric malfunction derived from dicey seafood at the previous day's five-star hotel. The only reason I continued to go along with my guide was a feeble hope that the next shop might provide me with a customer loo. Ultimately, I found relief in a grimy backyard bathroom. For days afterwards, my tummy continued to feel like a carton of champagne bottles about to self-detonate. As I was checking out on my last day, with the train to Colombo about to leave, the manager refused to let me go as he perused a ledger seemingly forever and kept asking, 'Why didn't you order food from the room service? We have king prawns.'

'Kindly book me a tuk-tuk [as rickshaws are called in Sri Lanka]. I need to be at the station in seven minutes!' I said.

'Sorry, phone is out of order.'

Too late to return to the suite to 'do a number two', I simply threw 1,500 LKR on the counter to cover tips for the room service meals that I never had and ran. I was lucky. As I was jogging towards the railway station, a tuk-tuk stopped beside me. 'Colombo train?' he asked.

'Yes, yes!'

'Train is 8.45,' he said and pointed at his watch. It showed 8.45.

Fortunately, goats were leisurely grazing on the tracks and the train was delayed as usual. I asked the stationmaster for the nearest restroom, because by now my tummy felt pretty much as if the aforesaid champagne bottles believed that New Year's Eve was minutes away.

'It'll come,' he replied.

'What will come?'

'Toilet is on train. It'll come in half an hour.'

Needless to say, a nearby coconut grove got its fair share of fertilising that morning and I wrangled a funny column out of it. A third time, an intestinal catastrophe was caused by one of those oh so delectable fried mussels known as kallumakkai, which are a specialty served in Thalassery, the fishing town in northern Kerala. Out of culinary curiosity, I had been snacking on them all day and one individual must have been in a sour mood at being deprived of its shell and thrown into sizzling oil, only to see its life pass by in agonising reminisces of happier days playing water polo with other mussels.

It clearly didn't like what it saw inside my bowels and knocked on all emergency exits at 2 a.m., sending me out of bed to projectile vomit into the wastepaper basket. Afterwards, considering that we had been on such intimate terms, I decided to name it Fred to pay homage to that exotic Franco-Cajun turtle soup served at the Galatoire's in New Orleans where, as per tradition, after setting down the tureen the waiter always leans forward to whisper, 'Its name was Fred.'

According to scholars there are world records in this specific field among tourists, with the highest known score so far being 37 t.t.b./h. ('trips to bathroom per hour'). In three decades on the road, I've occasionally felt like I'm about to breach that impossible limit, but it's never gotten that bad. By now, you're obviously wondering why I am going on about such farty aspects when you bought a supposedly arty book. This collection of travel memories isn't in actual fact about unsavoury experiences. The larger point is that I've had thousands of astonishing meals ranging from fried silkworms in Shanghai to the national dish of boiled super-hot chillies in Bhutan, from the weird rotten shark delicacy so treasured on Iceland to curried goat intestines in Zimbabwe, from the primeval pizzas of Naples to the raw meat sandwiches of Denmark, all of which gave me tons of ideas for stories.

And it follows that since 50 per cent of my writings are about local delicacies, I've naturally suffered as many forms of tourist diarrhoea as there are dishes in the average cookbook, ranging from 'Delhi-belly dancer-tummy', 'Calcutta-chromosomes' and

'Kathmandu killer-craps', to 'Beijing-burps', 'Istanbul-intestines', 'Moroccan motions' and 'Zimbabwean zumbas' as they form an integral if annoying part of travel.

On the one hand, if I played it safe, I might not have suffered inconveniences but would have had no stories to tell you. Some backpackers tramp on for years without snafus, spending their lives on the road eating yoghurt and nuts, starved of any destination's gastronomic heritage. Here, I'm reminded of a guide published in London in 1911—*A Handbook for Travellers in India, Burma and Ceylon,* which complains that: 'As a rule, the food supplied in hotels and railway refreshment rooms in India is not very good. Outside the really large places and cantonments, the meat, with exception of bullock hump, is often lean and tough, the fowls are skinny, and the eggs ridiculously small.' The helpful handbook warns prospective tourists: 'Bread is fairly good, but this cannot be said of the butter, and milk is not free from danger. Aerated water should be drunk in preference to plain water, even in private houses; and the water in hotels and refreshment rooms should be absolutely avoided. If the traveller leaves the beaten track, he should have a tiffin (luncheon) basket, containing knives, forks, and other simple fittings and supplies; and, as a matter of fact, whenever any long journey is undertaken, it is well to be always provided with such a basket of potted meats, soups or bovril, biscuits, jam, tea and sugar, some spirit, and soda-water, which is good and cheap in India, as this renders one immune against the accident of detention, or of failure to obtain an eatable meal at a railway refreshment room.'

The same attitude prevails even today, 112 years later, among foreign visitors to India. As for me, if it weren't for Fred and his bacteria-infested friends, I wouldn't have written this book, in which eating habits become an essential and deeply intertwined part of the larger narrative of places and culture. The above examples, distasteful as they may seem to dignified readers who would rather spend money on a decent poetry collection, illustrate three important aspects of successful voyages:

a) The need for preparation (never go on the road without Imodium);

b) Ditto for adjustment (learn to use coconut groves creatively);

c) And to be human (give even the most painful memories a name like 'Fred' or 'Donald' or something suitable).

For me, travel has always been about exploring—be it cuisines or cultures. After having munched on alligator sausages in Louisiana and barbecued kangaroos in Australia, I've been looking to expand my horizons with the aid of books like *They Eat That? A Cultural Encyclopaedia of Weird and Exotic Food from Around the World* and, not to forget, *Dinner with a Cannibal: The Complete History of Mankind's Oldest Taboo.*

A crucial aspect of travel, one that not everybody keeps in mind, is the importance of analysing oneself and one's reactions—both physical and mental—to what happens on the road, and in so doing learn new things. What have my tummy chronicles revealed to me?

a) The best-laid plans don't always work;

b) One ought always to make the most of the situation.

In other words, we could for instance rely on catching the ferry from Calcutta (as it was called once) like the chivalrous Phileas Fogg in *Around the World in Eighty Days*, but our train might run out of railway tracks somewhere in Central India. In Jules Verne's 1873 novel about those early days of tourism, this unforeseen change in the plan results in the memorable scene where Fogg rescues a virtuous maharani from a sati pyre and later weds her. A dire situation with a happy end! Not every trip needs to result in marriage, even if it has happened to me once, but the idea is to be prepared for the unexpected.

The art is therefore about learning to adjust when conditions change and, for example, courteously accommodate another passenger when the bus is overcrowded. Mistakenly assuming that the day before Friday the 13th ought to be safe for travel, I was once robbed of all my money, VISA card, valuables etc., by miscreants on a train in Assam, while I was engrossed in Rohinton Mistry's novel *Such a Long Journey*. When I reported the crime to the ticket-collector, he offered me rice and curry on the house. Seeing my plight, the other passengers fed me chai and ciggies that I gratefully chain-smoked to steady my nerves, until I got to Delhi where the hotelier recognised me from previous visits as an unfussy guest and offered me free accommodation until I got my situation in order. He also uncorked a bottle of Bagpiper and poured me a drink. I stopped tearing my hair out and after a few pegs, I knew I had a great feel-good story to sell to a travel magazine. At other times, when I've had no such luck, I've slept on railway platforms in Salt Lake City and rural Punjab, or flea-infested bus stations in Africa, or under a bush in some Copenhagen park.

Discomfort is the price that a frequent traveller pays in the hope of a bonus at the end. And, after all, minor disasters are merely *minor*—when compared to the many journeys of a lifetime. There's indeed something ridiculous about expecting everything to be 100 per cent glitch-free. Staying and eating five-star is not necessarily a safeguard against everything bad, so one may as well dive right into the adventure.

Situations where one negotiates the unexpected and manages to retain an optimistic approach, rather than boarding the next flight home to sulk, are the moments when one's resolve is tested in order to make it possible to reap rewards later—hopefully. At least in theory, these instances enable us to understand more about ourselves (and how to deal with life crises) and other people (humans are essentially kind and social). Incidentally, I learnt the art of patience in the Himalayas when I reached a bus stop on a winding mountain road and asked the uncles hanging about if the semi-deluxe limited-stop express was expected soon.

'Yes,' they agreed.

I waited with them but nothing happened.

'Is it coming today?' I asked an hour later.

'This week for sure,' said one of the men who knew a bit of English.

'This week! Why didn't you tell me it may not come today?'

'Or next,' he replied coolly.

I walked to the nearest village to find lodgings until a slow bus eventually came, but I also realised that these uncles by necessity spent much of their lives waiting for transport that might or might not show up—while I was free to move on. That was my first real trip anywhere in the world, but it was followed by much more learning through travel. The moral implication is that we should interact with strangers (who are actually the real people, we're the strangers who pass through) roughly in the same way that we interact with our own friends. Of course, to call ourselves genuine artists of tourism presupposes that we have backup plans—scans of important documents in the Cloud, sufficient insurance coverage, a global SIM and, don't forget, that mandatory Imodium to bring up the rear—because the solutions we think up on our feet are only as useful as they turn out to be.

Nonetheless, the moment you make it down alive from a steep peak after having lost sight of the trekking path in the mist, or talk your way out of a tricky situation in which desert militia are about to pepper your taxi with machinegun fire and you reach the coast of the Red Sea, it will seem that no matter what absurdities you've gone through, the trip was so worth it that you immediately want to do it again. At least I did. As with most art forms, the end thus justifies the means. You're feeling richer and spend hours at the backpacker café in Dharamsala or sit in a pub in Britain bragging about your exploits. Like Baron von Munchausen's legendary feats, your travails and triumphs grow with each retelling. If you sell your story to a publisher, you might even get your travel expenditure reimbursed.

The final step, then, of any trip is its dissemination or else it will lose its meaning. The click-and-go generation might be satisfied with WhatsApping selfies, but that is no long-term solution because as the saying goes: Elephants have memories, humans only Facebook. For older generations, holiday documentation was about embellishing one's trophy display case with Russian dolls, German schnapps glasses with the names of different cities printed on them, and porcelain plates where the mouth of the British Queen grins at the spot the *chateaubriand* should sit. I too have stocked up on fun objects to use in daily life—a Greyhound thermos mug on my desk reminds me of an American overnight bus journey, an empty pack of Maghreb brand cigarettes reminds me of smoky nights in Marrakech bars, a soft silk shawl from Antakya takes me back to the Mediterranean end of the Silk Road the same way the polychromatic T'ang porcelain camel with broken legs on my windowsill transports my mind to its other end at Xi'an.

As we know from thousands of years of human experience, the primary form of documentation is the written journal. Julius Caesar kept a belligerent one when he tried to conquer Britain and Germany in the first century BCE, jotting down notes regarding the weird habits of the Celtic and Teutonic races. The scholarly monk Xuanzang (also spelled as Hsien-tsang in mustier tomes) did so too when he toured India in the seventh century CE, noting how far it was to walk from one Buddhist monastery to the next, searching for the origins of faith. His *Journal of West Countries in Tang Dynasty* is perhaps the best 1st millennium guide to backpacking in India and remains in print as a valuable source of information for archaeologists. American humorist and author Mark Twain, ditto, on his trips round the world in the nineteenth century. Their writings are now invaluable records of locations and how these appeared back then, knowledge that otherwise may have been lost forever.

It's worth keeping such journals for their own sake—whether you publish them or not—because they may show their true value when one least expects it. In the case of what you are about to read, these are my finest pre-pandemic experiences from the road. So this might turn out to be a memoir of a lost world, but I'm hopeful that if things work out well—and the corona virus that had disrupted our lives since 2019, is replaced forever by Corona-beery cheery nights at pubs again—this book will serve as an inspiration to return to the joys of travel.

❖

Speaking of which, the pandemic that hit the planet in 2019 is still an on-going phenomenon as I write this in 2023, resulting in irritating travel restrictions. According to the latest updates, it may take years before things completely normalise. If they ever will, that is. This notion is, to say the least, a nightmare for those of us who enjoy travelling, sampling unaccustomed flavours and exploring cultures other than our own. For someone like me, who has viewed those viral food delivery apps as nothing but culinary malware—clickable edibles and mass-manufactured monotonous meal kits travelling to me rather than me venturing out to look for interesting items to ingest—this so-called new normal was indicative of a stomach-upsetting paradigm shift. It indeed looked like the beginning of a bad, unappetising time.

I'll never forget that moment in early 2020 when I realised to what extent times were about to change. I happened to be walking in Bengaluru's bazaars, when I heard the yells of, 'Corona! Corona!' Momentarily distracted (there had already been talk of a lockdown in the city to stop the virus and so I was wearing my anti-pollution mask to play it safe), I looked around and noticed teenagers dressed like villainous extras in some Kannada gangster flick, pointing in my direction. Then it clicked. *I* was the corona.

I hurriedly headed for the Chickpete Metro station to put distance between me and the rowdy pretenders. Two days later, papers reported on how a foreign tourist, who arrived in town from an ashram in Puttaparthi on 22 March 2020, the first day of curfew, found it impossible to get lodgings in the Majestic area, which, apart from hosting the railway station and main bus stand, is also the hub for budget accommodation.

The elderly foreigner was hounded across the roads by a wild crowd. Alert journalists and policemen rescued the hapless tourist before he was lynched and even fed him, as it seems the only word the starving, panicky man could utter by then was, 'Banana. Banana.'

The normally traveller-friendly area had—virtually in the blink of an eye—turned on visitors in a way one would never have imagined. Sure, one could maintain that these misguided local gents were only indulging in mischievous timepass—what else to do on a curfew day but turn vigilante? Yet it set me wondering how this situation will affect the relationships between inhabitants and tourists in what was hitherto arguably the most hospitable country in the world. As a personal testimony to this, I just have to think about the decades that I've lived in Bengaluru and how I've come to take it for granted that strangers everywhere—in the neighbourhood, on buses and trains, in markets—will greet me with a merry 'Had your coffee?' and be eager to strike up a conversation. Is it all over now?

I realised, when I read in the newspapers about another foreign tourist who had to wait fifty-five days at Delhi Airport before getting a flight home, that the travel restrictions hit too close to home for somebody who has spent half of his life travelling. In my own case, considering how much I had been travelling for my writing work in the previous decades, I was happy to be at home—on one of my occasional breaks between journeys—as a newspaper had offered me an all-expenses paid trip to Los Angeles that spring. For whatever reason I had been tardy about it but if I had boarded the plane, I'd have had to spend the next couple of months sleeping on a park bench in Hollywood. Or until I was jailed for vagrancy.

I was even starting to get wary of myself. Was I touching unsafe surfaces when I closed the gate outside my house? Even my usually helpful pharmacist had been bitten by the mental bug, although we were both masked and he was also wearing protective gloves, and neither of us was coughing and we were separated by the counter—a protective wall of clear plastic and 4 ft of air. When, after doing my other purchases, I asked for cough medicine, he took a step back, looked at me askance and said, 'We don't have any. Why do you need it?' He'd drawn his own conclusions and before he dialled some emergency helpline, I hastened to defuse the situation. 'Simply to have in case the worst happens. Pray god it doesn't.'

Something had definitely changed. Afterwards, I met a lady who worked as a maid for one of my neighbours (so we always greeted each other), but now she was lying on a quilt spread out on the pavement and looked like she was starving. Still, she smiled at me. 'Coffee *aitha*?' I asked, as we do in Kannada, before realising that she could probably afford neither food nor coffee. I gave her the 200 bucks left in my wallet before dashing home.

Our frustration over the pandemic may result in xenophobia, but who will we blame? The Chinese? But as Mahatma Gandhi argued with reference to colonial oppression, one cannot dismiss all Britons as bad merely because some of them upheld an unfair colonial system; likewise, just because the pandemic may have come from a particular food market in Wuhan, we should not stop eating chopsuey. It just doesn't make sense to allow social distancing to become a rabid distrust of everybody, especially since the only way life can go on is if one believes one's fellow humans to be responsible enough to follow the guidelines issued by authorities in a crisis.

Tourism—which earned India approximately $200 billion annually and employed forty million people pre-pandemically—definitely ushered in an interest in what was previously considered alien. When I was a kid in Sweden, there were few Indian restaurants but nowadays, there's a curry house on every second corner (helped by the fact that so many Swedes have holidayed in India and return home realising that the generic curry powder on the supermarket shelf doesn't compare favourably with fresh-ground masalas). Simultaneously in India, even smaller towns nowadays have eateries serving Conti staples. This is admittedly to simplify a complex matter, but the notion can be expanded to encompass, say, other Indian cultural exports such as yoga, Booker-winning novelists and Bollywood dance. Thanks to tourism, the culture of India has thoroughly penetrated the western world, whether we talk of the voluptuous creaminess of korma or mind-altering ideas like karma.

A futuristic non-tourism world, should we imagine it, might be like Disneyland (for kids) and Las Vegas (for adults), where we sightsee replicas of the Eiffel Tower, the Empire State Building, pyramids, Greek temples and so on. In Las Vegas, I ended up in a Roman-themed casino where guests could walk into an air-conditioned piazza of outdoor cafés situated under a perpetually sunset-rosy sky—just like being in Italy, but without the hassle of actually flying to Rome, not to mention the risk of ending up marooned for weeks at Leonardo da Vinci Airport because of all the possible global disasters one can think of.

Some hospitality properties were converted into workation (to break the tedium of WFH) or 'coronacation' hideaways where customers selected their preferred comfort from three to five stars and degree of 'self-isolation', contactless services via QR codes and Apps, vacation packages turned into 'vaccination packages' with immunity-booster cuisine. The general trend was an obvious preference for domestic destinations—rather than falling sick in a downlocked foreign country.

As a travel writer, I observed all of this with ever-deepening puzzlement. What were they doing to the world's hotels? Was my next hospitality industry reality check going to turn into a tedious hospitalisation? Or worse—as hotels increasingly attracted work-from-homers and turned themselves into office suites, I apprehended that the next time I was going to take a break from work, I'd find myself in a smaller replica of my own office instead of a relaxing room far from any desk. Scary thought.

Or perhaps this was the end of tourism as we know it because cyber-tourism took off in a big way at the same time.

App- or web-casting guides walked you through sightseeing itineraries for $30-40 and you didn't even have to put on hiking boots. Foodaholics learnt to fry *okonomiyaki* from Japanese chefs, how to boil Turkish coffee in an Istanbul café, or fast with meditating Buddhist monks, a Dharavi-dweller showed foreigners how to make perfect vada-pav online and Bengaluru foodies convened on video-conferencing apps to gorge on home-delivery biryanis. Dating went virtual with cafés in cyberspace serving signature Non-Fungible Token-tea—not to mention non-fragrant, non-caffeinated. And the nibbles may look Instagrammable, but in the metaverse they won't taste of anything. So, are we finding ourselves in a world where, if we cannot go to the Taj Mahal, that monument of love comes to us—in a virtual form to be viewed through sterilised 3D-glasses, downloaded as a software simulation which, if it has viruses, will only be bugs in the programme? The signs are already there considering how much online services benefit from the real world coming to a physical standstill.

Big questions. To look for small answers, for the first time ever I went to a palmist who answers vital questions—love-life, afterlife—at Rs 101 a pop. My query? *When will I again travel the world?* Possibly I was getting desperate, for I had strange nightmares about eating my camera. But I didn't tell that to the chiromantic practitioner, lest he think I'm weirder than his ordinary clientele.

After studying my palm, he instructed me to shake cowries while praying to any god of my choice, and then chuck the shells onto the table top. Unfortunately, he said rolling his head 180° this way and then 360° that way, envious sorcerers in my immediate social circle had engineered a black magic spell which is why I hadn't travelled. Unless I hired him to search my home for hidden hoodoo jujus, there was no prospect of journeys. At that moment, I snapped back to my senses because a year before I had lived in a different house, which was demolished months back, so any jinxed hex would have to be in some landfill. Yet, my problem remained—for a travel writer, I'd travelled unusually little since the end of 2019.

❖

Writing this book, I had my Hamlet moment as I walked past a spot that used to be crowded with snack hawkers. Now there were perhaps two, with few customers in sight. It seemed as sad as a Shakespearean tragedy. But the moment I dug in my pockets for loose change, I felt the stirrings of comorbidity. I carried on. Repining, I reverted, then changed my mind for the umpteenth time. Seeing a couple of fearless youths enjoying spicy snacks, masks down, I gave in to my inherent herd mentality, praying for herd immunity, and...*shabash!* Whatever it was, I forget exactly, probably a greasy roll stuffed with curried goat liver.

Years from now, the nexus between Wuhanese wet markets and gluttons' wet dreams may seem like a trifling conundrum, but had I foolishly put myself in mortal danger or was I merely giving in to a wholesome urge to enjoy life again? What's healthier: To go on existing indefinitely in a state of paranoia or to redevelop an appetite for existence? For isn't it true that the French word 'restaurant' originally meant a soup kitchen where one went to be physically restored to health?

But after the exquisitely brief pleasure of having fast-food again (it took me under seven minutes to gobble it down) after seven long months I worried for seven days that I might get COVID-19. I heard the clock of death tick like Edgar Allan Poe's tell-tale heart through the next nineteen nights, had nightmares about eating nineteen barbequed pangolins or two kilograms of bat fritters in a Wuhanese chophouse, yet as this goes to print, *I'm still standing* (two inches taller than Elton John).

It's worth remembering how, about 111 years ago today, Mahatma Gandhi debated 'whether the profession of a clerk or book-keeper is better or more respectable than that of a hawker. A hawker is an independent man. He has opportunity of studying human nature which a clerk slaving away for a few pounds per month can never have. A hawker is master of his own time. A clerk has practically no time he can call his own. A hawker, if he chooses, has opportunity for expansion of his intellect which a clerk cannot dream of.' Food hawkers aren't necessarily doom-bringers, because those that I personally observed were stricter about wearing masks than the common people I met. So I told my paranoid mind to focus on something worth worrying about instead.

Street-food may not be the healthiest option, but it can't automatically be equated with junk-food. Luxurious restaurants apart where patrons peer into kitchens behind glass walls, vendors with pushcarts are among the few chefs that customers can see in action. Wherever you go in India, if you are unexpectedly hungry, your easiest choice is street-food. Competitively priced, available at most hours, usually made fresh to order, it is what locals love to eat—so, a great way to befriend a new place. Furthermore, paying attention to the where and what also helps: Does the snack look like a petri dish?

In Kolkata? Grab a kathi roll near New Market. Mumbai? First thing to do after alighting from the train is to head towards the vada-pav stalls outside the station to get the yummiest pick-me-up of potato dumplings in a crusty bun. Delhi? Take the Metro to Chawri Bazaar and head up-street to Shyam Sweets, a kiosk dating back to the 1910s, for their legendary bedmi aloo.

And here, I'm not only thinking of India for in many other countries like Taiwan and Turkey, roadside cuisine has reached the highest possible epicurean echelons too.

In fact, the world over travellers encounter tantalisingly pocket-friendly short-eats: Meze in the Mediterranean, tapas in Hispanic lands, and in the country of XXXL T-shirts there's even a saying that, according to my American friend James, goes something like 'every candidate for US President is required to show their face and eat a Philly cheesesteak sandwich to prove that they are one of the common people. This is an election year qualification ritual.' So, after visiting the White House in DC, I obviously had to take the Amtrak train to Philadelphia and try out the most calorific 'Born in the USA' meal-on-the-go. Essentially, this is a hashed steer steak with plenty of onion smothered in gooey cheese, stuffed in a sub and preferably had at Pat's (where it was invented in the 1930s). Bill Clinton, Humphrey Bogart and Frank Sinatra all sampled it there, and it's the reason why cabbies are fatter in Philadelphia than elsewhere. The scariest junk I've ever eaten was at Whiz, a temple of terrifying tuck in San Francisco, whose 'corndog' is an indigestible cornmeal-battered hotdog on a stick, deep-fried until it becomes positively lethal. A suicidal treat that swiftly turned into a heartbreaking threat as my left arm tingled like a kathak dancer's ghungroos. Soon afterwards, I was diagnosed with high blood pressure. But eating it felt as deliciously sinful as having a Maggi-noodle Schezwan paneer dosa or chai-Maggi (tea cooked with instant noodles) in Bengaluru.

Even if it might be bad for my health, I sorely miss the *choudoufu* or 'stinky tofu' that's been fermented until it trumps the most matured of European cheeses in terms of olfactory orgasms, cooked in porky lard and served with a drizzle of garlic soy. If that's not your scene, then the *bao*—as the name implies a Cantonese cousin of the Goan pav (but in China we're talking steamed pork-patty-buns stuffed with slurps of crab roe broth)—should hit the gastric G-spot. The only things I found hard to digest in China were oil-fried scorpions, skewered chicken sphincters and animal genitals in general, but at least I tried.

So what if it's not the optimal fitness diet? One Bengaluruan foodie friend asserted that the grubbier the grub, the better it'll taste—because decontaminated squeaky-clean canteens can only serve tasteless nourishment. In the US, I asked a connoisseur why he loved corndogs and the expert retorted, 'We're not meant to live forever. We do our best to prolong our lives with medications, but Mother Nature dishes up temptations to curtail our lifespans. Every species understands this. Just look at lemmings, that don't have to eat corndogs to commit mass suicide.'

If one were to analyse this from a spiritual aspect, junk-food is divisible into junk (evil) and food (necessity): The necessary evil. After reaching that conclusion, I felt pretty much alright with my relapse to wayside cookery. Because there's nothing that beats the real deal, those spicy sauces blending with one's drool as one devours up hot snacks. Even if the world is full of museums dedicated to our collective memories of edibles, including a recently opened one in Tamil Nadu where Indian food traditions are traced back to 13,000 BCE, an Instant Noodle Museum in Japan and two Museums of Pasta in Italy, travelling in a hurry to where the next curry awaits is at the top of my post-pandemic agenda. Oh, and there's actually a Curry Museum, in...wait a minute...Yokohama?

Salivating, I search for its webpage to find that Yokohama's curry-themed exhibition was created to honour reinterpretations of Indian dishes—such as curried chocolate and curry cocktails—but has now shut down. Interestingly, curry arrived in the port town, with its large expat community of foreign traders, when Britons sailed eastwards from Calcutta in the late 1870s, packing Indian food in their tiffin-carriers. Once transferred into bento boxes, this became a Japanese staple. It seems the Japanese got hooked on curry's British avatars because their imperial aspirations led them to perceive it as sophisticated food fit for a global empire. *Kare*, as they call it, is milder and sweeter than its Indian prototypes, and remains the topmost comfort food in Japan. Coincidentally, the English word curry is an Indian loanword—its origin seems to be the Tamil 'kaari' which may be translated as 'black-peppery vegetarian broth'.

Another example of curry being adopted abroad was exhibited at the Currywurst Museum in Germany, celebrating Berlin's bizarrely beloved curry-ketchup-spiced pork-sausages that fuelled the labourers who rebuilt the city after each World War. Until the pandemic hit the food business, some seventy-three million currywursts were sold annually in Berlin alone, with another billion portions being eaten across the country! Come to think of it, even in Scandinavia where I grew up, no feast was complete without a jar of curry-pickled herring on the table and those scrumptious *smørrebrøds* of Copenhagen, topped with piles of *karisild* (curry-pickled herring), are as Danish as it gets. Appetisingly enough, the Indian tourism organisations cashed in on the country's foodie fame by modifying the monumental 'Incredible India' campaign which took place around two decades ago, into an 'Incredible Tiffin' drive in the 2010s.

I suppose you've guessed by now—since you probably picked this book up as you think a little like me—that I too prefer to have my curry on a plate before me rather than in a museum, relish the intimate feel of stepping into welcoming eateries (rather than having to masticate ambience-deprived delivery-food), and love looking at what's cooking if there's an open kitchen (instead of 'representative' web images). Furthermore, despite incongruous touchlessness being the new F&B menu card rule, India is the original finger food-country and will remain so, or to quote the magisterial culinary critic Pushpesh Pant from his epic *India Cookbook*, 'an Indian gourmet does not use knives, forks and spoons: the fingers, assisted by a variety of breads, are best to fully enjoy the temperature and texture of the food.'

When the British high commissioner visited Bengaluru and made the mistake of tweeting an image of himself eating a masala dosa—that quintessential and iconic southern quick tummy-filler referred to as 'the world's best pancake' in international food and travel magazines—with fork and knife, the Twitterati blasted him with comments like 'Ayyo, karma, how to teach you guys about civilisation only! Eat with hand saar, holistic sensory experience will be!' as reported by *Deccan Herald*. After thousands of Tweeters petitioned him to stop applying cutlery to South Indian food, His Excellency ate another dosa the next day—by hand—and admitted that 'it tastes better'.

Ayurvedic experts and yoga masters will any day enumerate the innumerable health benefits of using elegant mudras—essentially shaping one's fingers into whichever piece of tableware that best fits the food—to tuck into grub. The tactile feel of food against the fingertips is said to improve digestion and whilst the rest of the world relies on cutlery, we who eat with our right hand (and not the wrong one, mind you) can at least be sure that the fingers that fondle the roti are properly sanitised. As the ancients always said, hand over those forks and fork it in with your hand. What may be considered bad table manners in another country is the supreme sophistication in the Indian tradition as it was at ancient Rome's banquets.

It also requires elaborate cooking techniques to match—softer meats, suitably cut vegetables and breads that can be used to mop up gravies.

Anyway, to get on with the show as they say, here's my panegyric to Indian hospitality, to eating and travelling and to enjoying food on the road in a post-pandemic World 2.0 again...oh, and one last thing—the sharp-eyed reader might wonder how come I mostly write about old places, time-tested restaurants, antiquated watering holes and the glory of the past. There's an easy answer to that: It would be futile to even think of writing a book about restaurant culture in the present when the present becomes the past three weeks down the social-media timeline, but the slightly older past—the one we may cherish, the one that existed up to three years ago—doesn't necessarily have to change as long as we write and read about it.

—Zac O'Yeah

Bengaluru, 2023

I

A Town Called Beershop
(Regarding Bengaluru)

'Verily, thousands of visitors, from other parts of the State as well as the country and from abroad, pour into the city every day; aeroplanes, trains, buses and cars bring visitors of all classes and from all walks of life.'

—Old tourist brochure (that was new
when I first came to town)

Author in Koshy's Cafe, Bengaluru.
Photo: Raghav Shreyas

Whenever I tread down the lane where Premier Bookshop once stood, my face turns into a sentimental emoticon. Sitting behind a cluttered counter, the proprietor T.S. Shanbhag—always dressed babu-style in his trademark semi-synthetic half-sleeves and polyester pants—was quick to recognise regulars and knew what we wanted, whipping out the latest arrivals of interest from the unruly stacks packed three rows deep, throwing in whatever discount he felt I needed to be persuaded. No haggling was expected.

It was always exciting to lose oneself among the books, as long as one remained slim enough to fit between the shelves that, in their own way, were a healthy incentive not to consume too much beer in pub city. Despite there being barely squeezing space inside the shop, it is a well-known fact that back in the 1980s, the proprietor caught celebrated history writer Ramachandra Guha getting pre-maritally kissed by his wife-to-be—as confessed in Guha's essay 'Turning Crimson at Premier's'. As we see in that revealing passage, it was possible for two people to fit in there, once upon a time, but as the collection grew it seemed increasingly doubtful that one could have romantic encounters in the narrower and narrower space. Only intellectual.

'Even in the old Bengaluru known for its hospitality, grace and charm, Shanbhag stood out for these qualities. He was personally acquainted with his customers and his books,' writes Suresh Menon in his memoir on booklove, *Why Don't You Write Something I Might Read?* Premier's well-stocked selection was intelligently put together, so more than a shopkeeper one could claim that Shanbhag was a curator of literature and, hence, in charge of intellectual developments in the city in those days—and, for me, crucial as an ally to build up my home library. But he shut shop in 2009 because CBD rentals were becoming impossibly high even for as tiny a shop as his. Besides, he was well past retirement age and he told me that he felt like calling it quits anyway after running it for nearly four decades. Fans of the bookshop held a function to felicitate him for his service to them. Sadly, he passed away from COVID-19 in 2021, I learnt, as tearful local newspapers paid tribute to the premier bookseller to Bengaluru's bibliophiles.

The loss of this legendary shop was a big blow to culture. At that time, when everybody ordered books online, it looked like the city centre was becoming illiterate. Thankfully, the Raj-era Higginbothams (74, M.G. Road), after having been boarded up for years, revived, smartly renovated back to its former glory. The chain was founded in south India in the 1800s, branding itself as 'official booksellers to His Royal Highness'. As one of the city's original bookshops it remains something of a hallowed relic.

Higginbotham's neighbour, the venerable Gangarams, founded in 1965 and once the biggest bookstore on M.G. Road, was not so fortunate. It shifted to a smaller space in 2013 and became less eclectic. Strand Book Stall, related to the Mumbai bookshop of the same name and specialising in lavish art books and remaindered imports, as well as Fountainhead that pioneered the trend of bookstore book launches with Arundhati Roy's *The God of Small Things* back in the late 1990s, and the smart Sankar's Book Stall, all went out of business and vanished without a trace. Even the beloved Variety Book House & Magazines Shop shut down both its showrooms. Their model had been to sell magazines from all over the world at discounts; this was the shop for cultural journals and comic books; whether one wanted years old copies of *The New Yorker* from New York or the most recent issue of *Rock Street Journal* from New Delhi, they always delivered. But increasingly, people accessed online magazines, which lead to a slump in sales.

Even the pavement booksellers were getting scarce. A lone book pirate occasionally pushes his cart along M.G. Road still, but the uncle who used to spread out an array of non-pirated books on a ledge hasn't been around in years.

To cut a long story short—browsing offline appeared to be doomed and the main reason why I fell in love with the city seemed lost. But then the other day, I decided to survey the scene and down Brigade Road, I slipped into the first alley on the left. At 71, Brigade Road Cross there is a secret treasure untouched by modern commerce: Select. Founded in 1945 by the passionate book collector K.B.K. Rao and run by his 92-year-old son K.K.S. Murthy today, its survival seems nothing short of a miracle.

Originally, it was run from a garage owned by a British bibliophile in nearby Museum Road, but as the stock grew with the inclusion of collections left behind by departing ex-colonialists, it moved into a bigger space. Luminaries who frequented this quirky repository include the Nobel laureate C.V. Raman, author Ruskin Bond, playwright Girish Karnad and the afore-mentioned Ramachandra Guha who eulogises the shop in his essay collection *The Last Liberal*, declaring it to be his 'favourite of all India's second-hand bookshops'. So, what is this celebrated shop like today?

Downstairs are a few impossibly crammed chambers while a locked storage hall upstairs holds the rare books with an estimated 70,000 titles—and also lithographs, maps and other collectibles—which apparently have included autographed copies of Rabindranath Tagore's Nobel Prize-winning *Gitanjali*. Bibliophiles can borrow the key from Sanjai Rao, grandson of the founder, and if a book isn't available, he'll try to track down a copy—this time he offers me two out-of-print books on Bengaluru that I've been hunting for. One is still plastic-wrapped and unused; the other is in fine condition despite being fifty years old—he tells me that he recently unearthed it from the bookshelf of a person in the older parts of town. I'm aware that one can buy it online for Rs 5,000 which is way above my budget, so I ask how much he wants for both.

Rao thinks for a moment and suggests, 'Let's say 1,650, shall we?'

I agree immediately, but I ask him why he doesn't demand more.

He says, 'It wouldn't be correct, because now the books have found the right owner.'

I celebrate my good luck with a pitcher of draught at Pecos, the retro rock & roll bar in another nearby alley that also serves up mean tacos and makes you feel that John Lennon might be alive and chanting mantras in the loo. There's reason for cheer as some newer bookshops are thriving so well that Church Street is again becoming a regular tourist destination for Gutenberg-worshippers.

One trendsetter is Krishna Gowda. Gowda's has been a remarkable journey for somebody who once peddled books on the M.G. Road pavement. Founded in 2002, his Bookworm gradually expanded to four branches in the area, out of which one was exclusively dealing in children's books. Once the pandemic lockdowns ended, in 2021, he consolidated his empire into one outlet in an old colonial era bungalow down the street, which gave him even more display space. The bungalow also has a garden where he will set up a book café. On my first post-pandemic visit, I suggested to him that this must be India's biggest bookshop. Humbly, he answered, 'Blossoms is bigger.' Having visited every significant bookshop in the country, I was about to correct him, but then again if Gowda prefers to be humble, then who am I to argue? Apart from a huge second-hand selection, he also sells the latest titles at an attractive 20 per cent markdown—which results in spectacular sales figures that

Ramachandra Guha with Rajmohan Gandhi at the launch of *Gandhi: The Man, His People, and the Empire.*

Photo: Zac O'Yeah [All images except where specified: Zac O'Yeah]

in turn make authors love the welcoming Gowda, who usually greets every writer he recognises with, 'We've sold a thousand copies of your books, please sign another fifteen today.' It is also a haunt of journos from the nearby editorial offices because whoever lingers long enough is served free coffee and as for me I left with Rs 4,000 worth of books, but paid only Rs 2,500 and that complimentary cuppa was thrown in, too.

The other major store that has, for decades, been specialising in an eclectic mix of new and used paperbacks is Blossom Book House, just a few steps away from Bookworm. I was introduced to it some twenty years back by renowned bibliophile Pradeep Sebastian when it had just been opened by Mayi Gowda (not related to Krishna Gowda) who gave up an engineering career to fill a minuscule cubicle at the back of a shopping complex with around 1,500 books. Business took off and it has since then, true to its name, blossomed into two gigantic stores diagonally across from each other, making Blossoms (as fans calls the shop) probably the biggest second-hand trader in India, selling on an average 1,500 books a day—a feat that has earned it listings in tourist guides from the *Lonely Planet* to *Frommers* as one of the city's must-dos. The main branch (84/6, Church Street) sprawls across three storeys—the ground floor showcasing the latest sold at discount, plus travelogues, cinema and philosophy; upstairs, one finds fiction (with a substantial Indian selection); and the top floor is exclusively for non-fiction (great collections of biographies, dictionaries, handbooks, self-help, you name it).

A special feature of Blossoms is a framed letter written by Rabindranath Tagore in 1931. The unique document was found, by chance, tucked inside a book. Their newer outlet (2, Church Street) is a veritable supermarket of literature with graphic novels aplenty, yards of non-fiction, tons of novels, plus free mineral water dispensers and loos, so one can technically go on browsing forever as there's basically no need to leave the shop. The combined retail space of both Blossoms is approximately

750 sq m, holding nearly half a million books, which is quite an expansion from the original 18 sq m hole-in-the-wall premises. This phenomenon has even inspired a fan-page that collects quirky conversations called 'Overheard at Blossoms':

Guy 1: Why are you going there, da? That's romance section.

Guy 2: Yeah, I know, dude. I want to see if they have one book.

Guy 1: Full romance books you're reading? Are you Romeo or Devdas?

Guy 2: No, dude, I saw one chick in my bus reading some Nora Roberts book. I thought I can say I also read it if I get the chance to talk to her.

Guy 1: Dude, you're my guru from now, da!

The spirit of Church Street is best illustrated by the fact that new independent stores, such as The Bookhive owned by the enthusiastic young Keshava R who loves to source difficult-to-get titles for his devoted customers, keep opening to give literature more and more space in this marvellous place. All the proprietors I chat with suggest in their various ways that they're not into it for huge profits, but a love for books as products and a deep engagement with the trade is at the heart of the matter. Also, the fact that there are so many of them, makes bookshop-hopping more fun than trying to find something readable online.

After loading up on literature the best thing to do is, at the end of Church Street, to cross Saint Mark's Road and spend the rest of one's afternoon at the bohemian Koshy's. Run by the always cheerful Prem Koshy, this 1950s multipurpose breakfast-to-dinner café-cum-bar is a culinary-literary landmark that wears its patina of timelessness lightly. It inspired literary sensation Vivek Shanbhag's globally bestselling Kannada novella

Ghachar Ghochar in which much of the action takes place in a fictionalised Koshy's. The novel's title apparently means 'tangled up beyond fixing'.

Koshy's other habituès include, apart from aspiring Hemingways and alleged CIA agents who eavesdrop on thinkers, intellectuals such as Ramachandra Guha who has been a regular for more than fifty years and in his essay, 'Café, Memories of Lime Juice and an Owl on a Moonlit Night', calls it 'an always-welcoming place in a chaotic and ever-changing city'. Hence, one might consider Koshy's an oasis for bibliomaniacs who live in the slow lane, as compared to all those cyber czars in the fast lane of gastropubs in Koramangala and microbreweries of Indiranagar. If one is to believe their motto: Top people have something more in common than an entry in Who's Who—they always think of Koshy's, when they think of dining out.

Some say this was where political dissidents convened during the Emergency in the 1970s (perhaps mistaking the Saint Mark's Road address as Marxist Road?). Curiously, the café is often filled with legal professionals (due to the high court being a stroll away) while at the same time, members of the LGBT community used to meet at a nearby table in those days when it was illegal to be nothing but a heterosexual. Before the Internet was invented, newspaper editors caught up with the news here—*Deccan Herald, New Indian Express, The Hindu* and *The Times of India* have their offices within walking distance. And it seems that even the late Queen Elizabeth of Britain came here to eat roasted chicken back in 1961. So all things considered, their motto does sound quite accurate.

Here, beer is cheap, coffee even cheaper—ah, how can one ever stop thinking about that powerful smell of the old-fashioned 'cream tray' with its concoction of tar-strong decoction with pewter pitchers of hot milk and cold cream that resurrects even the brain-dead, unlike the chicory-laden adulterations at most vends? Chicory is something that I expect in a salad but not in my cuppa. After a sip, life begins afresh; the loose wiring of the mind hooks up; random dots connect into words; untangling, they paint poetry…all thanks to coffee. No wonder then that an estimated two to three billion cups are consumed daily in the world, making coffee the second biggest business product after oil.

Koshy's is, as the crow flies, situated just 200 km from where the beans grow in the Western Ghat hills, guaranteeing its freshness. Statistics suggest that in the US people spend no more than the two minutes it takes to grab their decaf-to-go in a takeaway shop, in the UK folks sip theirs for twenty-five minutes on an average, but at Koshy's, nobody drinks up in less than two hours because they talk so much between sips. Whereas in many countries—say Italy, the typical café is like a bar where you get your caffeine shot at the counter because sitting down involves surcharges, here, we are talking of a living room where you can spend your life leisurely.

Other than that, the chaotic menu is a motley ledger of colonial-style Anglo-Indian standards such as spinach-au-gratin, non-south-Indianised North Indian dishes, Asian odds and ends, a special Kerala curry-and-rice section, plus off-menu options that only those in the know may order (like organic wild mushrooms or grilled pig's brain, and once I even scored a rare treat of tasty testicles).

Sorting through the day's booty and already regretting that I gave some tomes a miss, I know that next month, once I've read what I bought today, I'm going to do this same tour all over again—because even if Church Street has no church (well, actually, tucked away behind Koshy's one will find the town's oldest cathedral, Saint Mark's, inaugurated in 1816), it certainly is the place for book adoration.

❖

At the time I settled in town, I had published a few novels in my native Swedish language, but mostly made my living off travel writing. Due to my interest in other cultures, I searched for Bengaluru books, but after a good decade in town, I hadn't seen a single local thriller. Until fairly recently, indeed, crime fiction used to be dominated by British and American locations and concerns, but nowadays we read globally bestselling detective novels set in places like Botswana, Japan or—somewhat surprisingly—in Sweden, which is otherwise believed to be one of the least crime-ridden parts of the world. So why not Bengaluru?

My favourite bookshops did stock Asian crime stuff—I remember finding Japanese thrillers by Keigo Higashino at Bookworm, at Premier I bought *Bangkok 8* by John Burdett, translated Bengali detective story collections and *The Blaft Anthology of Tamil Pulp Fiction* are always available at Blossom Book House, as are sometimes second-hand copies of out-of-print 1970s pulp classics such as the 'Jaz Zadu' series by Shyam Dave about an IMFL-guzzling James Bond-character who 'attracts beauties and bullets with equal ease'. But nothing typically Bengaluruan, at least not in the first decade of the 2000s (later on, local writers have addressed this lacuna).

Anyhow, one day in 2008, I sat down in my favourite dive (it was located in the Majestic area of town if you must know but has, thanks to the ongoing gentrification, been demolished since) and wrote the first lines of what was to become the 'Majestic Trilogy', a project which was to occupy me for a decade until the third and final book was published in 2018. People sometimes ask me about my audacity, to even think that I as a foreigner can write novels set in Bengaluru, by and large without using foreign characters as an alter ego through whom to view events and cover up my ignorance. It was admittedly a gamble, yet the fact that I've received movie offers both from Kannada filmmakers and Bollywood suggests that many think it works. But the truth is that I was just having a beer in Majestic and after several beers too many, I strongly felt that every self-respecting city ought to have a library of detective novels dedicated to it.

In Sweden, for example, there are villages like Fjällbacka, home to approximately 1,000 souls, which have been the setting of serial-killer hunts in novel after novel. Realistic? How many semi-professional killers would it take to decimate 1,000 villagers? It defies logic, but you read the books (or stream the movie versions) because Fjällbacka is depicted as quaint and yet appears to have a darker side. That, in a nutshell, is the success story of crime fiction and why it is a global sales phenomenon, keeping publishing houses alive and kicking. And one thing led to another, the first idea spawned the next, and soon the matrix of my novel began to unfold.

A fictional detective is something of an urban explorer, so writing (or reading) such books can be a way of getting to know a place better. The detective character, be it logic-fixated amateur sleuth Sherlock Holmes of the late nineteenth century, the professional gumshoe gunslinger Philip Marlowe in the early twentieth or feminist icon Lisbeth Salander with her super-IQ in the twenty-first, has always been a bit of a misfit; obsessive and neurotic, constantly probing what goes on in cities after sunset, the stuff that most of us remain blissfully clueless about—whether made up or real, fiction or fact, who can tell? Does it matter?

Yes and no. I go to New York and buy an Ed McBain paperback or Paul Auster's 'New York Trilogy' to land in town; in Stockholm I pick up a Sjöwall-Wahlöö novel for local colour. Before going to Mumbai, *Sacred Games* by Vikram Chandra does the needful. It doesn't matter so much that McBain fictionalised the Big Apple as Isola, or that much of Chandra's city can't actually be found on maps. It's deep atmosphere us readers are after. A pioneering crime writer when it comes to using exotic locations, H.R.F. Keating became notorious for having largely written his 'Inspector Ghote' series without visiting Mumbai, where most of the books are set—just like Walter Scott based his war drama *The Surgeon's Daughter* in Bengaluru, 'this fine and populous city' where the 'rich pavilions of the principal persons flamed with silk and gold...' Several of Scott's relatives and friends had served in India, while Keating too had his methods, but I'll return to this matter in detail later. For now, we may note that in his how-to manual *Writing Crime Fiction*, he states that all the world's exotic hotspots are open to the plot and 'it is not altogether necessary, if your mind is constructed that way, actually to visit your chosen locale'. I beg to differ.

The attractiveness of 'crime fiction guided walks' grows organically in the footsteps of the booming thriller industry—whether it be Sherlock Holmes tours in London (to his mock-up home at 221B Baker Street, 'the world's most famous address') or Philip Marlowe bus rides in Los Angeles. (The late Raymond Chandler, incidentally, loved showing visitors the settings for his plots.) Trailing fictional heroes and villains is a global pastime. From this follows one important conclusion: Place, milieu and atmosphere are oh so important for a fictional sleuth. In the case of my own creation, the semi-heroic wannabe hero Hari Majestic, the hallowed ground is the aforementioned Majestic area.

Furthermore, I wanted to avoid creating a stereotypical literary detective—the overweight, middle-aged, divorced cop (if male) or the nosy spinster aunty (if female), or any of the other varieties of 'classic' investigator characters. Hence, the Hari Majestic of my novels was a week-old orphan when found under a seat in the third row at Majestic Talkies. That's how he got his surname. In his late twenties in the first book, he is a reformed tout who has turned into something of an unofficial trouble-shooter, a Mr Fix-It. People come to him with their problems—missing siblings, cheating spouses, suspected scams—and since he knows Bengaluru like I know my own nostrils, he's the perfect private investigator.

A reality check was required to understand what proper detectives were like. So one day after a few beers as I was literally cart-wheeling towards the Majestic bus stand, spotting a sign for a detective agency, I dropped in. Already on the staircase, I got the vibe that I wasn't going to find chain-smoking private eyes with brandy bottles in their shoulder holsters. Instead, a notice stated that job applicants must be well-groomed, freshly-shaved and with a proper haircut. I touched my own chin and realised that I should have visited a barber first.

It turned out that an Indian detective bureau is like any other open-plan workplace; this could be, say, an accountant's office or even a low-end call centre, if it wasn't for all the staff looking so ex-army. They also didn't care much for PR, I found, when I asked for a public relations person. After several unanswered questions, I was ushered into a glass cubicle where the head of the bureau sat behind a desk covered in spiritual promotion materials rather than beer ads.

Brimming with excitement, I asked my first question: 'What do real detectives work with?'

The boss replied, 'That I can't tell you, because it is secret.'

I tried again: 'If I wanted to hire you, what could you do for me?'

He stared out through the window and his all-detecting gaze was fixed on some enigma in the distance. 'Supposing you wanted to buy that house over there and needed to know who owns it, we could find that out.'

I glanced at that very same house, but no, there were no suspicious criminals lurking on its terrace—and if I really wanted a house, I might go to a real estate agent rather than a secret agent, but I found it wiser to say: 'So, is that what detectives do for a living?'

He shook his head vigorously. 'Not at all; I simply said that supposing you wanted to know.'

'And how much would it cost me to hire you to do that?'

He looked at me doubtfully and said, 'That I can't say, it's a secret.'

So instead I googled and found out everything I needed to know, watched plenty of Kannada action flicks of the so-called 'Machchu Longu'-type (named for the elongated machetes used in gang wars before handguns became popular) and became a fan of the wacky ones by Real-Star Upendra, the king of cool one-liners, and his closest rival at the time, Challenging-Star Darshan. I wondered what a literary equivalent of such films might read like. After all, Indian cinema follows a different logic from Western, so shouldn't that colour the literary plot and its protagonists as well? A typical Indian action movie includes elements of comedy and romance, song and dance, without being self-conscious about it; likewise a comedy will have romantic scenes and action sequences; and a romantic movie may be comical as well as action-packed. This has obvious roots in that ancient theory of dance, theatre and music, the

Natya-Shastra, which states that any artistic work must have a dominant mood, rasa, without neglecting the eight *bhavas* (emotions) such as for example *hasya* (comedy), *rati* (love), and naturally, also *vira* (heroism) juxtaposed with *bhayanaka* (terror).

By contrast, Hollywood (and Western storytelling in general) seem to follow the strictures of 'the dramatic unities'—propounded from Aristotle onwards and refined in the era of French Classicism: Credibility in theatre is created by avoiding mixed registers and hybrid art forms such as, for example, tragicomedy. This tendency remains very much alive today in the West. But India is too diverse for anything so simplistic. I therefore set out to write a romantic tragicomic thriller in Bengaluru.

The private eye became my key to unlock the city's geography and chronicle how crazily it changed. When I observe Bengaluru, when I meander through town, it's like I'm hiking through a magical manuscript forever in progress, a poem that will never be completed but will always remain in flux. Like no other place I had known, this city appears to follow a will of its own. In a street corner adorned by a colonial-era bar's lazy verandas, there would be a glass-and-steel shopping mall topped by a food court coming up before I emptied my beer. This kaleidoscopic urbanism intrigued me. Just when I thought I knew my whereabouts, the kaleidoscope shifted and everything tilted.

Writing books is, in fact, a little bit like trying to stay alive here: A chaotic activity; you must kill your darlings; tear into pieces what you've previously written and rewrite upon the ruins of your earlier ideas; stretch your limits to conquer new ground; attempt the impossible—just like the city itself does each day.

Some people complain about the uncontrollable growth,

how Bengaluru swells at an impossible pace, the lack of heritage awareness and how everything old-worldly is torn down. This may be contrasted against the pride of provincial newspapers as billions of venture-dollars flow into the city. The other day I saw this stressful headline as I was leisurely enjoying my pilsner: 'Bengaluru is now the world's fastest growing tech hub, Mumbai sixth.' London was #2 on that list, after pubtown, and it made me worry that ale might soon become more expensive in Bengaluru, charged in sterling pounds or perhaps bitcoins instead of Indian currency. Yes, I too do regret the loss of the past, as rapid change can be unsettling, but as an author I also find it incredibly stimulating.

When I was writing the first novel in the trilogy there was that heritage cinema hall called Majestic (which lent its name to both the area and my hero) but as I was writing about it, real estate developers tore it down. It was insane, but I didn't take tension—after all I had immortalised it in my novel, which is all I could do to preserve it. Around the same time, the Central Jail which was conveniently located at the edge of Majestic and where ladies used to line up at lunchtime to bring tiffin-boxes to their incarcerated husbands, a sight which featured in my novel, was reformed so to speak—into what is now the twenty-acre Freedom Park, a site for public meetings.

It felt as if I was writing local history at the same time as history was being erased around me. The eternal construction sites, the suburbs pushing city limits another kilometre out with every passing year—art produced in a place like this might, I reasoned, defy ordinary imagination, the way that Bengaluru itself does, to all appearances expanding fast enough to swallow the entire world. And here I was, right in the middle of it.

As a matter fact, if I hadn't broken journey at Bengaluru City Junction in the early 1990s, I don't think I would have been a novelist today. It takes a little luck, and much cheap beer, to help us find our true callings.

It is strange how cinematically I recall, in vivid Technicolor wide-angle, that morning when I got off the train, filling my lungs with the nippy but peculiarly brownish-beery and somewhat sambar-flavoured Deccan air, and crossed the footbridge above the roar of the Majestic bus stand where the humongous BMTC fleet of battering rams on wheels was revving in unison, preparing to take on the potholy streets. According to statistical calculations, there are more potholes per kilometre here than anywhere in the solar system.

The buses seemed to be breeding more buses like randy rabbits as I watched them (6,771 municipal at last count), but once I left them behind I was in Majestic—a peculiar interzone, which not only catered to a floating populace but was the traditional home to the film industry: India's fifth largest, the so-called Sandalwood that produces a hundred features per

Majestic, the area in Bengaluru with most cinemas per sq km—a classic movie poster.

year. Despite geographical shifts over time, even today Majestic remains home to production houses, shops that rent out filmy equipment and sell props like fake handguns and duplicate police uniforms, and trade in DVDs both genuine and pirated, not to forget cinema halls seating over a 1,000 each (in this age of increasingly smaller-screen movie-viewing), which makes it any cineaste's joy…and it was like coming home.

Little did I know at the time that this town was to be a vital part of my future. Long before I planned on becoming a writer, I'd been journeying for months through the harsher north of India—and had my encounters with the usual tourist traps in Delhi, Varanasi, Agra and Rajasthan—so by then, I was battle-hardened and my only concern was how to survive on less than a shoestring. The boarding and lodging house in Majestic that I checked into wasn't the best in India, but at the rate of Rs 85 a night I wasn't complaining. They even had running hot water in the mornings. There were no special tourist attractions nearby, therefore no need to carry out any sightseeing agendas. I spent my days in those bookshops around Church Street as well as in the nameless second-hand bookstalls that used to proliferate due south of Kempegowda Circle.

Browsing through piles of always dusty and often mouldy tomes was sure to leave one's throat parched. This phenomenon poses serious health hazards to any bibliophile. Mercifully, the distance between these intellectual havens and the nearest dimly-lit ramshackle pub was rarely over fifty steps, so as day turned into night my brain would be further stimulated by cheap 650 ml bottles of UB lager. With a faintly mildewed paperback in my hands and a bladder designed by the almighty bladder-designer to harbour a six-pack, I read for hours.

Having decided to break journey for a bit, I ended up spending a month or two in Majestic, which also had the maddest bazaars for basically everything a traveller might need—an enchanting place where temples stood next to cinemas with their larger-than-life cut-outs of cine gods; separate mythological universes cheek by jowl.

Later, I realised I liked it because Majestic is large-hearted enough to accommodate pretty much everybody and as if to prove it, I came across a thriving migrant food culture. The back alleys featured modest Malayali eateries serving the world's coconut-oiliest chicken fry, extra-spicy Andhra biryani joints and Bengali canteens cooking authentic mustard fish like the tiny Babu Moshai hidden in the maze of narrow lanes, and the area has even lent its name to a local variety of Chinese cuisine, 'Mejestic' style, famous for its chowmein-stuffed grilled sandwiches and Schezwan bhelpuri. Just being there was like doing a culinary tour of India and I'm reminded of R.K. Narayan's words in one of his rare travel stories: 'In any big road, apart from the Bangaloreans themselves, it is always possible to pick out men of other provinces—the South Canara man, the Bombay merchant, the cooly [*sic*] from Telugu and Tamil land, the long-shirted Bengalee [*sic*], the Parsee, and the Sikh driving a military lorry. It almost looks as if Bangalore were a junction of all the provinces in India.'

It was love at first sight, or smell. It's hard to explain how one can fall head over heels for a few tumbledown city blocks and a fistful of alleys like Majestic. But the sudden, unexpected homely vibe that's provided by easy-on-the-purse food, affordable accommodation, jolly people and an abundance of beer came as a pleasant surprise. Or perhaps due to some karmic coincidence, I was a South Indian in a previous lifetime who had found his way home. For years to come, I kept bouncing back like a malfunctioning email. Hardly a year went by when I didn't, for some reason or the other, find myself in

Bengaluru. If it wasn't a literary festival, then I was writing for a travel magazine, or just coming to see friends, and in the end, I wasn't particularly surprised when I got wedded to a Bengaluru-based girl in the year 2000.

Even then, living as a happily married man in a salubrious suburb and accustomed to the brain-rattling spice spectrum of Indian morning meals, I end up getting on a bus to good old Majestic once in a week or so, to revisit those haunts and wallow in my private urban nostalgia.

Only after settling down in the city did I learn that Majestic, which I was so backpacker-sentimental about, was something of a terra incognita for the average upper-middleclass city-dweller, where people simply didn't go unless they were after pirated films or other illicit fun. A bad place. Years later, as I was writing my detective novels and reading about the underworld, I learnt that rowdies planned gang wars over plates of vada-sambar-dip ('curried donuts') and tumblers of filter-coffee in the very Kamat Hotel that I habitually ate at.[1] Several Kannada gangster flicks had taken their inspiration from the area—including a 2002 blockbuster starring Challenging-Star Darshan in his debut lead role—titled *Majestic*.

But to be truthful, regarding crime, I've experienced very little first-hand. During my first sojourn in the early 1990s, I went to the Thomas Cook office on M.G. Road to exchange traveller's cheques (this was at a time before ATMs) and carried back Rs 10,000 stapled together into a brick. It was in my pocket when I, sauntering towards my lodgings in Majestic, was accosted by six to seven local gents who all had the build of large Old Monk rum bottles.

I instantly knew they represented the underworld dons who had instructed their staff to perform shakedowns on naïve backpackers, collect contributions towards their 'social work' and add 'tourist tax' to their development fund. After surrounding me, one said, 'Give us twenty bucks.' I was prepared to give up my whole stack of cash, but when I heard that request the only thing I could do was laugh. My merriment confused them and I took the opportunity to sneak off even as they shouted after me, 'Come back!'

My second run-in was more recent and grimmer. As I stepped out of a pub feeling humane, I noticed a fellow customer lying on the pavement, which has always been considered natural behaviour in Majestic. Only this time, I witnessed three urchins rifle through his pockets and snatch his wallet. Which again is only to be expected, but when they pulled off his pants, I felt an urge to object because, in other circumstances, it could have been me and what would my wife have said had I come home undressed from the waist down? As I gently pointed out the wrongfulness of their deed, the ringleader (who must have been about eight) pulled a switchblade and suggested that I mind my business if I wanted to retain my own garments. Times had clearly changed.

With plenty of cash dispensing machines, today's prospective robbers would typically have taken me to one of these, forced me to surrender my ATM card and key in my PIN so that they could help themselves to my bank balance (therefore I always leave debit cards at home when I go to paint the town red). Travellers are nowadays also advised against many of the deceptive bargain tourist experiences to be had such as cheap massage offers at shady 'spas' that can be fronts for activities that result in jail-sightseeing for purchasing erotic services.

Those days are clearly over when lodges were cute and resembled The Best Exotic Marigold Hotel—in the feel-good flick starring Dev Patel as an hotelier taking care of retired Britons like Judi Dench in a Kiplingesque environment. Not many know that even if it was filmed in Rajasthan that's so much more colourful with its camels and palaces, the novel that the movie is based on, *These Foolish Things*, was set in Bengaluru. Its sobriquet used to be, as everybody knows, 'Pensioner's Paradise' and the retirees in the book (should you read it) are being taught to communicate in Kannada, rather than Rajasthani. For lunch, there's no laal-maas but a 'coronation chicken' typical of the town's Anglo-Indian heritage and the hotel in question is a spacious colonial cotton-trader's bungalow from 1865, 'with flowered bedspreads and mismatched, cream-painted furniture' and there's 'an air of somnolence about the place: ticking clocks, creaking ceiling fans and, from the kitchen, the distant clatter of pans.'

'The longer you stay in India, the less you know,' thinks one of the protagonists, a feeling I sometimes share. The author Deborah Moggach appears to have actually visited town but many local references are misspelled: Puttaparthi is for some reason called Pattipurnam, Cunningham Road is fictionalised as Cunningham Street, the obviously Catholic Saint Patrick's Church is labelled as Anglican, turkeys are bought from Gandhi Market which is an unlikely name for a slaughterhouse, Bengaluruans speak Hindi to one another…and which lodge that fictional one was modelled on—purportedly near the crossing of Brigade Road and M.G. Road—I'm not quite sure of, as the Dunroamin Retirement Hotel obviously is a figment of the author's imagination, though it reminds me of the long gone Victoria Hotel. Some descriptions of Bengaluru are amusing such as when one of the retirees 'walked past the United Ice Cream Parlour and Khan's Video Rental, past the Hideaway Pub—The Hot Spot That's Really Cool—a throbbing den into which he had once unwisely ventured, to find its customers of kindergarten age. The road was being dug up in the torpid

Indian manner; one man squatted with a bucket while another man, clutching a spade, listlessly tipped in teaspoons of rubble.'[2]

Even if tourists can't check into this hotel, there's plenty of lodging houses in Majestic including one named after the biggest ever local movie star Rajkumar who kick-started the golden age of Kannada cinema. And that is why Majestic once had the greatest number of cinemas per square kilometre—an incredible twenty-two of them (though only a handful remain)—and remains the place to go if one prefers, rather than streaming at home, a single-screen hall and the company of other wild fans.

What more does a writer need in life? Ah, yes, there's the matter of beer.

❖

'Where did they go?' I gently lament as I stagger like a camel crossing a desert with the high-altitude Deccan sun augmented by global warming and shrinking green cover, hammering down on my balding pate.

The name Bengaluru is, according to folklore, slang for 'beer galore' that harks back to the colonial era. And it isn't far off the mark. If you were ET and landed anywhere in town, like I did, in the 1990s, there'd be a handy watering hole next to your UFO as attested to by statistical data (three per square kilometre was the norm). Therefore this city attracted lots of aliens who wished to get 'Bangalored' as it was called in those days. Slide in through the darkest door in sight, find a comfortable seat away from the sun, and within seconds an unfussy waiter brings a 650 ml lager while other clients mind their own bad habits.

With the outsourcing boom resulting in a hike in disposable

income, those jolly yesteryear pubs were torn down. Today, if I happen to be thirsty, I must locate the discreet elevator that takes me to a mall rooftop where, invariably, there's a hoity-toity cocktail lounge, where fruit-infused beer-on-tap is misspelt 'biere' and hard-selling waiters force me to sample overpriced, over-perfumed microbrews.

Being an aficionado of unfashionably seedy taverns where 'beeru' is served by the 'pintu', I'm unapologetically backward-gazing these days. For example, I spent so many years lounging in the cane chairs at Dewar's in Bamboo Bazaar that drunks mistook me for the portrait of Queen Elizabeth that hung behind the bar. The come-as-you-are, become-as-drunk-as-you-

Bengaluru's most nostalgic bar—Dewar's, Bamboo Bazar.

must Dewar's, born in 1933 and gone in 2010, was like a caring mother, a seafaring father, a homely bungalow where labourers in loincloths mingled with us khadi-clad intellectuals and everybody felt safe as the sturdy rosewood tables were too heavy to be used in bar battles. And the rattan chairs too light to cause harm with. The beer snacks were excellent, too. According to the grapevine, the extravagantly generous breadcrumb-coated fish fillets and other dishes like mutton balls and dry brain fry were introduced by an Irishman; after a few pegs to clear the historical haze, regulars recalled his name as Mr Dinky, but he went home to Dublin some years after independence, maybe in the 1960s.

Sarovara in Lavelle Road was another unpretentious beer hall. Across the street from the Bangalore Club where non-members were not welcome, it offered a passé ambience and great prawn fry to go with the chilled brew. Ultimately, the building was sold to some random luxury hotel and today one can only revisit it by watching the gangster epic *OM* (1995), the Kannada equivalent of *The Godfather*—its larger-than-life 'Machchu Longu'-type bar fight directed by Real-Star Upendra was shot at Sarovara and its gardens. Yes, in those days pubs in the Garden City used to have lavish gardens.

Others that vanished post-2000 include the already-mentioned Victoria Hotel that had cool verandas for an afternoon beer, overlooking its vast green grounds (nowadays occupied by Central Mall), and the nearby Carnival, half-garage, half-dive catering to the pub city's trademark drunk drivers—get a fix and get your two-wheeler fixed at the same time. Less known but equally stunning watering hole Kishore (picturesque gingerbread bungalow at 95, M.M. Road) recently reopened as the non-boozy but charmingly named Beerappa's Foodcourt while others are most likely awaiting demolition such as the art deco Highway (40, Broadway Road), which used to be a favoured drinkery among ruffians who conducted their wheeling-dealing in the Russell Market's so-called thieves' bazaar.

An era of gold-coloured inebriation is simply over, its legacy more or less lost. It all began with a Scotsman who founded the Castle Brewery in 1857, giving Bengaluru's beer an over 160-year-pedigree. Ale was an expensive cargo to ship from England, not to mention that 'old Blighty beer' sometimes went bad on the way so that whatever reached Indian shores had frequently turned fairly foul. One report calls imported beer 'thin and sourish' and therefore it made sense to start breweries across the country. At that time, the town's population had just crossed 130,000, half of them living in the Cantonment's infantry camp, (half in its neighbouring walled old city,) making it the biggest 'English' town in southern India, which was enough to warrant a beer industry. As the demand for potable drinks grew, another called Bangalore Brewing Company was built to cater to army needs in the 1880s on the spot where UB City shopping mall sits today. These, and another three, including the famous Nilgiri Brewery that had been set up some distance away in cooler climes at Ooty, merged into the United Breweries in 1915, known for its classic UB pilsner which remains a perennial favourite. Business thrived and huge barrels of beer were carted across south India.

Initially, brewing was a medical strategy to provide the troops and populace of the 'Civil & Military Station' with a health drink—a mildly alcoholic, bacteria-free beverage, which could be drunk like water and wouldn't be as harmful as the cheap hooch they got from illegal hawkers who peddled spurious concoctions outside their barracks. Despite the many virtues of coconuts, when distilled to arrack it ruined their gastric systems that were already under assault from exotic bacteria. Getting over-drunk was also a first step towards immoral recreational activities with the outcome that the troops 'filled the veneral wards' as one academic paper puts it. In the 1860s, the India Office issued cautionary orders 'to prevent the soldier from getting access, by surreptitious means, to the more fiery and deleterious spirit to be found in the Native bazaars'. Instead, they were given sufficient money to cover a daily beer ration and a fistful of hangover pills. Around the same time, corroborating this so to speak, *Allen's Indian Mail* (in an article on brewing) calculated that there were at least 200,000 beeroholics in the country—armymen, merchants, planters, Eurasians, Parsees, etc—in need of daily pints which worked out to 120,000 hogshead barrels (equalling a total of 25½ million litres). Remarks the editor: 'The question of supplying ourselves with beer becomes, then, one of great economic importance.'

If the above numbers are correct, it works out to 350 ml, or a very small pintu per punter—which is way less than, say, the daily Czech per capita consumption of 500 ml. The actual quantities required would probably have been much larger if ale was indeed the safest beverage in the tropics. The popularity of 'Bangalore beer' as a brand spread quickly all the way to Madras, Hyderabad and other English settlements where the climate was too hot for brewing—though even this beer did risk spoiling and was occasionally pronounced 'to be as bad as ever' so that for example, in the year 1900, brewers had to undertake 'to turn out high-class beer' instead of yucky gunk.

It is estimated by experts that their brews would have resembled British IPA (a strong beer) rather than lager, i.e. nothing like the modern-day dainty Kingfisher but rather what is labelled as Superstrong, with an alcohol content of 7-8 per cent similar to that of punchy Knockout which is beloved by hard-drinkers in downmarket joints even today.[3] Apart from 'English beer', they also brewed a 'Native beer' with the difference that it contained a very small quantity of malt while jaggery was used as its base, producing more acidic beer (according to colonial reports) that kicked like a mule so that one got tipsy cost-effectively.

Over time, the military personnel got many neighbours—like missionaries, who tried to save their souls after settling down around the Cantonment in areas still commonly known by colonial names such as Benson Town, Cleveland Town and Richmond Town—and for obvious reasons, few could live without the #1 tropical health drink, namely, beer. An 1875 government gazetteer refers to 'Public Rooms' (i.e. pubs) located south of the military barracks, between Saint Mark's Cathedral which was born as the garrison chapel and Trinity Church (where Winston Churchill used to go when he lived in town), basically in the area where Koshy's stands today. Although Koshy's itself is only seventy-plus, it remains the go-to place to understand what colonial taverns looked like—for example in the fine-dining hall a slightly elevated corner space may be what remains of a stage where a jazz orchestra played dance tunes and their kitchens still cook the colonial staple of Fish & Chips. Interestingly, the adjacent building, which now houses the Hard Rock Café, used to be Blighty's Tearooms, a posh hotspot for teetotallers.

In the 1890s, another gazetteer listed four exclusive beer taverns—huge halls for sinking tankards in and old maps locate these more specifically on Brigade Road, towards the corner of Residency Road, and where Resthouse Road reminds us of the presence of one large colonial hotel—identified on an 1885 survey map as Mayo Hotel—that would have been surrounded by these 'public rooms'. Newspaper ads from back then promote 'invigorating' Indian Pale Ale from the Nilgiri Brewery on sale from godowns at 5, Brigade Road, 'strongly recommended by the Medical profession'. The Opera House, formerly a cinema and now housing a mobile phone store, was then a British event venue and party hall. Fazlul Hasan in his seminal *Bangalore Through The Centuries* lists three of these turn-of-the-previous-century Brigade Road watering holes as Adelphi Shades, Elysium and New Inn, where colonial bohemians supped and guzzled, and paddies got plastered after attending service at the Saint Patrick's Church down the road—which is still standing even if those pub-crawling Irishmen are long gone. Also, I glean from memoirs by Bengaluruan elders that there was a Ye Olde Bull & Bush at the bottom end of Brigade Road when they were young (so I'd guess that would be in the mid-1900s) and many also refer to a popular hangout near the corner of M.G. Road that may have been named Bascoe's.

By the time I settled in town, Old Vic was the last genuinely antique bar in that area, but tragically the Victoria Hotel it was housed in was demolished and replaced by a mall. The bacchanalian Chin Lung now rules the beer scene attracting youthful alcoholics from the nearby colleges.

However, the aptly named Funnel dance hall on South Parade (repurposed as a newspaper office in the renamed M.G. Road) seems to have been *the* place to drink the night away. An article on partying in town, *The Boogie Woogie in Bangalore* (published in *The New Yorker* in 1943) praised the unbelievably good local beer while the correspondent described his attempts at hooking up with loose women at 'Funnell's' [*sic*] where 'the chances are good' to pick up a Danish or Czech chick, so after some rum for lunch at the dance hall the correspondent fast-forwards to 'two o'clock in the morning [when] you start learning the Boogie Woogie dance' before, jump-cutting to the next morning, waking 'up laughing and with no hangover'. Obviously, the beer was breathtaking.

While that delightful drink was brewed, as already

mentioned, in the compound now housing the UB City Mall, southwest of the Cantonment, a distillery came up to produce what in due time became known as IMFL, an acronym said to have been coined by booze manufacturers at the time of independence to differentiate industrially produced 'Indian-Made Foreign Liquor', essentially neutral sugarcane spirits coloured to appear like brandy, gin or even whiskey, from artisanal hooch. Judging by maps from the 1850s, the Central Mall was where the city's official 'Arrack Godown' stood with a convenient bar right across the street, where Mayo Hall now stands. One may hence conclude that things were really beginning to look better for city-dwellers.

These establishments were mostly geared towards the English and Anglo-Indians but people from the walled town, a mere kilometre and a half away, also benefitted from their existence as Janaki Nair notes in *The Promise of the Metropolis: Bangalore's Twentieth Century*, to 'many from the old city area, they spelt an unmatched social freedom' because apart from non-veg and alcohol, these were public spaces where women and men co-mingled without social taboos. 'Cantonment people were alcoholic in a mostly harmless and very euphemistic way,' adds Peter Colaco in his memoir *Bangalore: A Century of Tales from City & Cantonment*. According to Wikipedia, which always makes me think of a bar where every drunkard has something to say about everything, a scholar (writing as early as in 1853) observed that 'Drunkenness was also common in the Bangalore Petah, across all classes of people.'

Going to the 'Cant' to drink was something different from hooching on moonshine in a quaint, or creepy—depending on one's mental makeup—bazaar hut; it was a celebration, limitless fun, a liberal ethos suited for romantic occasions, something that to an extent still holds true except that one needs more cash to satisfy one's cravings for fun and sin as the price of a beer at Koshy's is somewhat costlier than the Rs 2 it was back in the mid-1900s.

I've been reliably informed that wining and dining in the 'Cant', even if conservatives deemed it a den of debauchery, was seen as a crash-course in cosmopolitanism before one's first foreign trip. Meals came with knives and forks and one was expected to order beer in English rather than, like I habitually say, *'Ondu pintu kodi.'*

These were the pub city's roots, then, growing parallel to the first half of the twentieth-century's temperance movements, almost as if synchronised. Mahatma Gandhi recommended in 1946: 'Every bar or, failing that, a place next door to it, should, so far as possible, be utilised as a refreshment and recreation room.' And post-independence, when parts of the country obeyed the Gandhian diktat—for as he pointed out already in 1938, 'our freedom will be the freedom of slaves if we continue to be victims of the drink and drug habit'—and went for prohibition, it was never an option in this city where the various brewers and distillers owned schools, hospitals, newspapers, cinemas, cricket teams and, ostensibly to mark the creation of Karnataka state in 1956, one of them patriotically launched what was to become the country's top beer: Kingfisher.

What we know as today's archetypal Indian pub was invented as late as in the mid-1980s after draught came around and two booze giants faced off. Ramda's was backed by the Khoday distillers and The Pub, by United Breweries. Draught beer cost Rs 5-7 a mug in 1987, by when another fifty pubs had joined the competition, serving an estimated 35,000 mugs a day. So when I finally set foot in the city just a few years later, there were innumerable dives that called themselves pubs, no matter if they poured from the keg or out of a bottle or just shandied together a concoction of brandy-flavoured soda that looked like beer. Already on the train heading south, in the early 1990s, a Mumbai businessman excitedly enquired what the difference between a pub and a bar was since he was going south for the first time in his life. It took me time to explain but, in the end, he was enlightened when I told him that jolly pubs focused on beer-cheer and camaraderie, sleazy bars on getting sloshed and anti-social. It was at that moment I understood how important Bengaluru was to civilisation.

According to a 2011 census there were 1,330 sit-down bars (out of which 300 were what one might call, strictly speaking, pubs proper) and 830 stand-up-drinking-dens in town, yet very few genuinely prehistoric—'first-generation pubs' in businesspeak—remain. The Pub, which by when I drunk there had turned into the city's earliest theme-pub, NASA, designed to feel like being inside a space shuttle, has been replaced by a Mumbai-*ishtyle* cocktail disco. Who even remembers Underground, once an M.G. Road institution made to look like a tube station and thus a precursor to Namma Metro, the city's rapid transit network? And did you ever go to Black Cadillac where the johns were named, respectively, Olivia Newton-John and Elton John? I miss them all. In my quest to live in the past, I never ever go to the microbreweries of Indiranagar and Koramangala—no matter how hep they are, even if there were (prior to the pandemic) over sixty to choose between, all cooking beers on site. I prefer the traditional entertainment district of Majestic any day.

The area is rather congested nowadays but nicely compact, so it's better to ditch one's rickshaw and enter on foot. I habitually get off outside Janatha Bazaar, once the flagship department store in town, now looming forlornly, vacant and fenced-in as if it too will be demolished notwithstanding being a most astonishing heritage building—it effortlessly blends royal Mysuru dignity with colonial architectural details such as Tudor arches. Apparently, the complex with its lavish teakwood and wrought iron staircases was known as the Asiatic Building back in the 1940s. In due time, it was taken over by the Public Works Department and turned into a shopping complex in the mid-1960s. At the time of writing, the demolition has been stayed as the conservation organisation INTACH is trying to rescue it.

Out of the aforementioned bars, a majority are concentrated in Majestic where the lion's share of the city's annual consumption of 455 million beers takes place and which seems to have put India (where hard liquor and hooch are way more popular generally speaking)—on the #23 spot globally when it comes to beering. In dicier dives corks are popped as early as 8 a.m. in order to fulfil the day's quota. Bills are usually settled in advance, perhaps the bartenders still recall Winston Churchill famously skipping a bar bill of Rs 13, approximately the cost of fifty-two pegs at the time, as he hastily decamped at the end of the nineteenth century—lugging only his 'campaigning kit I sped to the Bangalore railway station and bought a ticket for Nowshera.' Wherever that is and what he drank there isn't known, though at that time he despised whiskey, 'the main basic standing refreshment of the white officer in the East', but regarding brandy and soda 'there was much respectable warrant'. So presumably it was fifty-two brandies that he never paid for.[4]

More significantly, while living in a rented bungalow which stood near Trinity Metro station (on the north side of M.G. Road) he picked up his reading habit that eventually resulted in a Nobel Prize-winning writerly career, self-educating for up to five hours a day to make up for being 'an uneducated man' as he himself put it: 'So I resolved to read history, philosophy, economics, and things like that; and I wrote to my mother asking for such books as I had heard of on these topics. She responded with alacrity, and every month the mail brought me a substantial package of what I thought were standard works.' He was awarded the Nobel for Literature in 1953, the only Bangalore-inhabitant to ever receive that particular honour (although the IISc professor C.V. Raman won a Nobel in Physics in 1930), and it is believed that Churchill spent the prize money mostly on booze.

Most bars in Majestic are invariably of the 'stand and tank up' variety where patrons aren't encouraged to linger if they can no longer stand on their feet, but there are also several decent sit-down joints for a more meditative mug. Life here

Majestic Drinks—starring in a typical Kannada comedy flick.

is still very be-who-you-are and no bouncer will look twice at your bathroom slippers. Bars match this blatant lack of dress-code with a limited menu, sometimes the chef stands in the street frying the preferred bar nibble of heavily marinated cauliflower (a vegetable introduced by those colonials) in the 'manchurian' manner (a dish so essential to bar culture here that criminals have committed murders because of it), but most serve nothing more elaborate than 'congress'—the quintessential Bengaluruan roasted split peanuts spiced up with curry leaves, chopped onion, cut chillies, shredded carrot, tangy masalas and a squeeze of lime. This was apparently invented by the Iyengar community, which consists largely of teetotallers but operate many of the city's bakery counters and condiment vends. Ah, the name? Well, it was invented in 1969 when the Congress party split, which makes sense in the Bengaluru kind of way.

Talk of the Town (2nd Cross) may to the uninitiated look like an average fast-food counter, but open the discreet door behind the open-air grill section and you will find yourself in a rather gorgeous if shabby, dimly-lit bar that dates back to the 1970s and is decorated with replicas of the jovial Paul Fernandes's drawings of vintage Bengaluru. I habitually line my tummy with piquant chicken and too much beer, before exploring other backstreet drinking options.

I've heard from friends in the film industry that the bestselling whiskey in Majestic is Director's Special, usually to be followed by a spot of casting-couch-surfing. A well-known filmy bar is the cavernous Green Hotel in a quiet B.B. Naidu Road backyard. It was inaugurated by a superstar in 1990 and its board is still adorned by the motto: 'Film Industry's Favourite Place.' I doubt the celluloid stars drop by for afterwork pegs anymore because they've moved on to five-stars with plush lounges, yet the cobwebby heritage décor and cheap drinks make one feel like the good old days aren't over yet.

For one last port of call, I stop at the next corner where Port of Pavilion (1st Main Road) rules the nightlife. It was once a cultish Karnataka coastal eatery, which still cooks up a mean fish biryani, but has over the years grown into a versatile nightclub spread across several floors. I prefer the relaxed beer hall on the covered roof and after seven beers (I know, I know, that's too many), I am admiring the perfection of their chicken ghee roast and decide I must spend the rest of my life here. But there's one jarring note: I hear loud music thumping and there seems to be a party going on to which I hadn't been invited.

I ask the waiter. He does a nudge-nudge type of movement, and reveals that there's a 'ladies' bar' hidden behind an unmarked downstairs door. I suddenly lose interest in the chicken at the prospect of seeing real-life chicks. For a detective novelist, any experience like that is grist for the mill.

As soon as I enter the secret bar, we talk entirely different prices for drinks. Yet the sofas are crowded with men who are happy to pay through their noses to ogle the twenty or so girls in tight blue sweaters and jeans. Mind you, this is not a dance bar. Dance bars—local euphemism for 'striptease without removing garment'—were banned long ago. The ladies stand smiling, holding bill folders, pretending to be waitresses and the lads seem satisfied with that. Despite the far from raunchy entertainment, I read in the papers that it gets raided by the police regularly.

The phenomenon strikes me as surreal, but then there's lots of strange stuff going on in Majestic. The very next morning newspapers report that the police had, that night, descended upon two lodges around the corner, seizing cash and arresting fifty-nine gamblers who had booked rooms to play teenpatti over the weekend. It appears their luck ran out. But having fun in Majestic doesn't necessarily end with a jail sentence, especially if one doesn't break many laws. I've downloaded the Penal Code App to my smartphone and check before I do anything it might advise against.

❖

There are two eyes on my plate. They are not ogling ghoulishly or anything like that, because they're nicely covered in dark gravy and I bite into one…hmm, unusual. Experiences like this are only to be expected when one visits Shivajinagar, home to the slaughterhouse area of Bengaluru. My guide, Mansoor Ali who is devoted to exploring everything edible in town, is unwavering in his resolve to have me try all the 'sparepart items' available—otherwise known as offal.

Semantically speaking, offal encompasses every non-muscular, edible part of an animal's carcass, but various cultures have different preferences and taboos about what may be consumed and what can't. In many Germanic languages, such as my mother tongue Swedish, *avfall* means waste, discards or general refuse and basically the word can be deconstructed into 'fall off', i.e. the bits and pieces that fell off a carcass, by-products from when a butcher does his job of cleaning the meat. The word offal came to English through ancient Anglo-Saxon or Viking invasions, like a substantial portion of the English vocabulary that has its roots in Old Norse. And naturally, we Scandinavians love our old-fashioned black puddings—ancestors of Scottish haggis—that are in fact loaves baked of blood and meal, commemorating the times when Vikings ritually killed animals to drink their blood. I suspect the word may also be etymologically linked to ancient Roman cuisine, where the Latin word *offellae* denotes meaty morsels and titbits that, however, were considered much more gourmet than what we call offal. Actually, animal spareparts were known as *lumulus* in Latin.

Indian 'sparepart' dishes being exceptionally innovative, foodaholics are curious to try, to take an example, batti chutney which is not what you'd think—pickled bats—but rather balls of goat's liver and spleen mixed with plenty of chillies and garlic in Andhra Pradesh. Catholics around south India take pleasure in gravies with pig's blood such as Goan sorpotel or Mangalorean kaleesankiti; curried fish-heads are crowd-pleasers in Odiya eateries, while one of the most creative snacks from the inner Himalayas is a sausage made of barley stuffed in sheep's intestines and then steamed—it seems to be party food there and I found it the perfect complement to a tumbler of local apple wine.

All these examples suggest that I am on a mission of historic importance. Our spareparts tour starts at 11 a.m. with the 'sira' for breakfast, served both as dry-fry and in rich gravy in two separate bucket-sized dishes with hot Kerala parathas on the side. Apart from those hypnotising eyes, it contains other parts from the head of a goat (except brain which is made into a separate dish called 'brain' according to the menu card). So there's for example tongue that I find to be quite delicate with a spongy texture like an exquisite shitake mushroom. These dishes are available at New Hilal in a particular street known as Broadway Road—which in its entirety is something of a legendary hotspot among gluttons—lined with grills, falooda stalls and teashops serving suleimani. Everywhere meat hangs on skewers, covered in marinades ranging from deadly red to spooky white and scary green, Central Asian-origin delicacies such as sizzling kebabs on coal grills awakening distant memories of Turkic warriors roasting meat on swords over campfires, while keema samosas splutter in boiling oil.

Not every eatery dares put spareparts on the menu (so as not to scare tender-tummied customers). To get the best, one must know where to go and what to order, which is why a cicerone and expert on local food ethos like Mr Ali comes in handy. So when I heard about this curated 'Sparepart Walk', I jumped at the opportunity to explore the links between cooking and culture in an area where perhaps angels don't necessarily fear to tread, but mortals may feel queasy about.

After the exhilarating New Hilal, we pick our way down an overcrowded street to the huge multi-floor Taj for goat trotters' soup. Then we head to the nearby Saqlain Kebab Centre renowned for its robust chunks of fried liver (kaliji) and barbecued kidneys (gurda). Unlike its neighbours that offer AC or 'family rooms' for their better-quality clientele, this is as grubby as it gets—no tablecloths and instead of napkins we are given pages of *The Times of India*—but the food is truly superb, for example the canteen's nalli soup with its melt-in-the-mouth chunks of gooey marrow.

Over steaming brain masala and Iranian flat breads at Hamza Hotel (our next stop on Broadway Street), I get chatty with my walking companions. Somehow, I had expected to attend a macho jamboree featuring a bunch of hard-core carnivores out to challenge each other's non-vegetarianism. But instead I'm largely surrounded by dainty madams and strangely enough one pure vegetarian sahib who doesn't touch the food—it seems he is accompanying a non-veg friend for moral support like somebody who might buy multiplex tickets for a midnight screening of *Texas Chainsaw Massacre* in 3D without really being a horror cineaste. Another is a food-blogger who's obsessed with disinfecting the utensils. One lad claims that everything reminds him of his grandmother's cooking except that her offal came in semi-gravy as opposed to 'dry-fry' like here in Shivajinagar. For him this is a trip back to his childhood. Yet another turns out to be an Indian-origin nurse based in Minnesota; she has a healthy appetite, but does make the important argument that offal shouldn't be eaten too often. 'Today's lifestyles wouldn't support this kind of diet.'

'So, what would be best from a medical point of view—once a year?' I ask.

'Twice a month is fine,' she says with a big smile.

Before we part, I ask Mr Ali how come, since we've eaten almost every other weird cut, there's no scrotum on the menus? He blushes briefly and says that private parts are not eaten in India; it is a very Egyptian thing. But then the blogger says that she has heard that people in Mumbai actually eat testicles. *Takatak!* Then again people in Mumbai have always been wilder than us temperate folks in the south.

❖

The journey from Bengaluru takes two hours but I feel transported to a weird twilight zone of colonialism, into what old Bangalore perhaps was like in British times. Lavish bungalows—some inhabited and others barely standing—and pretty churches dating back to the 1800s dot the tranquil landscape of Kolar Gold Fields. The mines were given evocative names that contradicted their hellish nature—so there was a Coromandel mine, an Oriental mine and so on.

For a century, KGF was India's biggest goldmine. The area was designed to resemble a corner of rural England and with a population of nearly 40,000 around the turn of the 1900s, it was indeed a thriving idyll, as long as one stayed above ground. A colonial-era guidebook states that The Gold Field 'extends for several miles, presenting a very busy appearance with its numerous tall chimneys, mills, shaft-heads, buildings, and bungalows of all kinds' and even today it could be a major tourist attraction but, strangely, this ghost-town-in-the-making has stayed off the radar.

I first head for Bullen Shaft, the only one of the abandoned mines which, unaccountably, the owners forgot to shut. The others are all fenced in and guarded by watchmen who are least likely to let tourists sightsee. I must fight my way through thorny weeds and before I know it, I almost step into a bottomless pit. It's scary since the KGF is on the top-ten list of the world's deepest mines. Even if I survived a fall, would I find my way out of the extensive tunnels that form a 1,300-km-labyrinth some 3 km under the earth's crust?

'There is a slight heaviness in the chest and my ears are going dull, I can't very clearly follow what my friend is saying. "Are you feeling funny about the ear? It is due to the great pressure we are in...We are now at sea level...We are below sea level now, a thousand feet below sea level,"' wrote R.K. Narayan in a travel story published in 1944, describing a visit to the mines and how he experienced 'a strange feeling: oppressive and light at the same time, and difficult in the ears, nostrils, and chest, and the temperature is around 90° or 100°. Since I am not sure of being able to bear the temperature and pressure further down I have to content myself with seeing the mine at this level.'

Next, I stop at a ghost mansion perched atop a hummock from which the mining boss viewed the goldfields—its ceilings have collapsed and the halls are empty but were once furnished with mahogany tables, upon which butlers set down cooling cucumber sandwiches and the tea boy poured aromatic Darjeeling from a silver pot. Only the fancily polychromatic floor tiles remain in place. To save it from antisocials whose activities (piles of empties indicate alcoholic consumption and a makeshift stove, illicit non-vegging) it now facilitates, this could be turned into a world-class mining museum chronicling a millennium-long gold fever. Some even say it dates back to the Harappan era—or as Pranay Lal writes in *Indica: A Deep Natural History of the Indian Subcontinent*, 'archaeologists believe that the Kolar Gold Fields have been mined since ancient times, perhaps even from the time of the Indus Valley civilisation.' An old gazetteer of the area posits that the Harappans sourced their gold from Kolar, and certainly, India's gold industry was known to classical European scholars like Strabo and Pliny. The latter described how gold-hungry ants 'the size of Egyptian wolves' carried gold out of caves. Because of this, Wikipedia (that global asylum of lunatic facts and fictions) believes that Pliny travelled from Rome to visit these goldfields, but the fact of the matter is he merely noted down hearsay recorded by his fifth century BCE predecessor Herodotus, who never visited India either, and Megasthenes who may have been the first Greek ambassador to north India but his diplomatic affairs never encompassed the south.[5]

Even the bard of Britons, Shakespeare, seems to have heard of Indian goldmines long before Kolar became part of Britain's colonies, as he remarks in *King Henry the Fourth*, 'as wondrous affable and as bountiful as mines of India.'

In any case, the area was considered important enough by the Gangas and Cholas to fund the upkeep of its temples, so Kolar definitely mattered in ancient times.

Mining went on here for centuries using traditional methods like digging by hand (but no ants) to depths of 70-80 m and this is how the process was described by the first Englishmen to witness it around the year 1800: 'The miners extracted the stones (how we are not informed) and they were passed from hand to hand in baskets by the miners who were stationed at different points for the purpose of banking the stones. The women then took them to a large rock, and pounded them to dust. The latter was then taken to a well and washed by the same process as that used when washing the earth for gold, when about an equal quantity of gold was found to that procured from an equal quantity of the auriferous earth.'

Although colonial surveyors obviously knew about the presence of gold, it took a long time before the gold rush kicked off in the early 1880s. Industrial mining was considered unprofitable since the yellow metal was so deep underground, but eventually the fields became a hotspot for venture capitalists that saw an important resource to exploit, which in turn led to Kolar being one of the first towns to get electricity in 1902, long before the rest of India got powered up.

Life was leisurely for the colonial families then, as narrated by a British lady who spent her days cooking and eating: 'I may begin by telling you that we usually rise about half-past six, when the menkind go off to their offices, or underground, as the case may be. We have tiffin between twelve and one, and dinner at half-past seven. Breakfast is generally at about eight…We get mutton and beef from the local butcher, and also good bread from the bakery on the field. Our butter comes from Bangalore, and from there we obtain peas, potatoes, French beans, tomatoes, cauliflowers, vegetable marrow, and lettuces, and also fruit, such as apples, peaches, grapes, plantains, custard apples, melons, and sometimes pine-apples.' As unlikely as it may sound today when the city's population is counted in double-digit millions, Bangalore was celebrated for its orchards—the best European fruits and berries 'all ripen well' and 'are common there' another old colonial visitor stated, which could be how it earned its moniker, 'Garden City'.

These were, perhaps, the ingredients that went into what George Orwell described in his autobiographical novel about India, *Burmese Days* as 'not meals so much as orgies, debauches of curry and rice' and judging from old documents even the tiffin, that supposedly light snack, would consist of the previous day's done-over meats reconstructed into pies washed down with Mulligatawny soups, alongside curries with rice and roasted fowls, cheeses and freshly-baked breads topped by jellies, all chased with a few stiff drinks or at least a bottle of Madeira. Sunday tiffins would be even more overindulgent, often comprising twenty different items featuring up to four kinds of curry, mountains of ghee rice, roast beef with Yorkshire pudding, various egg preparations, steaks or chops or at least a fore-quarter of lamb, prawns and fish, vegetable stews, puddings and fruit salads and beer that had been cooled with ice shipped from as far as Alaska via Chennai in the days before refrigerators. The 1878-printed *Culinary Jottings for Madras, A Treatise in Thirty Chapters on Reformed Cookery for Anglo-Indian Exiles* by nom-de-plume Wyvern provides us latter-day gluttons with twenty-five menus to drool over. It turns out that tiffin, despite being widely used in many Indian languages to suggest a light meal, is not an Indian word at all but a colloquialism for monstrous over-eating coined by the Britons in 1807.

I quite unsuccessfully try to enter the 1890s' vintage KGF Club to fortify myself with a drink, but it opens only at 6 p.m. It is said to be the fourth oldest golf club in India. I spot, through a grimy window, a rotting piano in its decayed ballroom with wooden teak floorings dying to be waxed as I prick up my ears for any ghostly echoes of mildly indecent songs. But there are no ghosts in sight. Everything is allegedly gone, including the English-imported brass door knobs, the sterling silver cutlery with the club's emblem...yet, the distinctly Victorian building could be turned into a tourist attraction with a great dining hall, the way it is said to have been once upon a time—licking my lips outside the windows, I imagine menus consisting of 'bad word curry' (minced meatballs), 'Grandma's country captain chicken', 'dak bungalow chicken', 'devil pork' and 'railway mutton curry'.

Exclusive clubs like this dotted the Cantonments of India and can today provide us with a telling image of the erstwhile empire's soul. Make-believe places simulating 'home', i.e. England, they demarcated a boundary against the India outside of them (a bit like gated communities do today). Typically set in Anglican flower gardens, they had libraries full of mildewed books that fed more insects than intellects, game rooms for shooting billiards (one of the KGF clubrooms still holds a hundred-year-old snooker table), and dusty heads of dead animals rotting on walls above bars where gin and tonic was the choice cocktail as it was believed to prevent, even cure, malaria. There was some truth to this notion, as the tonic water gets it bitterness from quinine, a bark extract traditionally used to treat fevers and inhibit malarial parasites. On the other hand, to offset its bitterness bartenders used a liberal dash of gin and unfortunately this combination of alcohol with quinine severely harms the liver. In *Burmese Days*, Orwell wise-cracked about how colonials returned to Britain 'with a wrecked liver and a pineapple backside from sitting in cane chairs' as he, at the same time, elaborated on how in 'any town in India the European Club is the spiritual citadel, the real seat of the British power, the Nirvana for which native officials and millionaires pine in vain.' A joke at the time went that 'when two Englishmen meet they form a club, if there are three, they form a colony, and if four, an empire.' And so wherever the foreign traveller went in British India, the club was where he met everybody who was anybody worth knowing—of course limited to other Englishpersons, dolled up memsahibs (if he strayed into what was called 'the hen house' i.e. separate bar serving diluted drinks) or more often stiff-lipped gents who sipped their G&Ts with their sweaty legs propped up on the extended arms of wicker chairs variously called 'Bombay fornicators' or, as in the books of Kipling, 'long-chairs'.

I'm told there are still Anglo-Indian aunties, descendants of middle-level mining staff, who breakfast on vodka in their bungalows before heading to this club for G&T nightcaps. Suitably inspired by that, I proceed to assess the KGF beverage situation.

Old-timers recollect that there used to be a KGF brewery which produced a beverage with the simple but striking brand name 'Beer' and that was sold exclusively in a town called Beershop. Life was easier then when things were called by their true names and all of KGF had only one beer shop to supply that essential commodity. Somebody points out its site on B.M. Road but it is now occupied by a nursery school and a small chapel, side by side. My informant is unable to decide which of the two structures used to be the shop (this may be linked to over-consumption-caused memory loss). Basav Biradar, an expert on local history who has made a documentary film on the rise and fall of the mining industry here, clarifies: 'In early 20th century Mysuru princely state, liquor could be sold only through authorised shops. In KGF, there was only one shop called the beer shop, so Beershop became the local name for Andersonpet according to the gazetteers of the time.'

Additional scant facts I ferret out suggest that this shop owned by Anderson & Co was founded in the late 1800s. Andersonpet was then merely a rural bazaar serving the adjacent mines and their staff. Since its prominent feature was the sale of beer the nickname was apt. In 1904, the township was formally christened 'Anderson Market' and whilst that might be a more sober name, it lacks the magical appeal of Beershop.

The Beershop doubled as a tavern and later got licensed to supply liquor ('grog' in KGF's Anglo lingo) as well as the native staple arrack until it developed into a downmarket toddy shop that was most likely shut down when traditional palm wine was prohibited in Karnataka some decades ago. Men still called the town 'Beershop', ladies preferred to pronounce it as 'Bishop' and I imagine the conversations that must have taken place weekly, on Sundays which was the shandy day at the Andersonpet Market: 'Dearest, I'll pop over to Beershop to purchase pig mutton.' Madam: 'Oho, will you ask the bishop for blessings too?'

I find two booze counters around the corner from the defunct beer shop in the O. Daniel Road bazaar—named after the one-time local doctor O'Donnell who is unlikely to have been amused at the corruption of his name. New Lucky Liquors and Littar Flower Wines respectively carry on the Beershop heritage, despite being archetypical stand-up guzzle dives. The beer is no longer brewed locally—it's shipped from Bengaluru. Post-refreshments, one can get entertained across the street at 1920s' picture house Lakshmi Talkies, which miraculously survives in this era of streaming and downloading. When a new blockbuster is released, tickets go for ten times the normal rate and audiences get so excited that they must be mildly lathi-charged by constables before they can enter the theatre and enjoy the film.

One would think that a town called Beershop deserves a pub scene, but truth is its economy was hit hard when the mines shut, and like the legendary beershop, vintage vendors such as the English Warehouse—where everything from Coleman's Mustard and special sauces like Sutton's 'Empress of India', to tinned European vegetables and Atlantic herring and corned beef shipped from Cork, English jams and jellies, bottled Mediterranean olives and jars of Parmesan cheese from Parma were sold—closed in the early 1960s as there were only three Britons left in KGF by then, with the last European mining superintendent retiring in 1964. According to a report in *Deccan Herald*, the ex-mine workers have it hard since then and, as of March 2022, there were '30,000 families living in British-era sheds without roads, drains and other infrastructure.'

But as recently as twenty years ago, Anglo-Indians gathered for New Year's barn dances with ballroom orchestras playing tunes of the past. However, today, KGF serves up none of the Eurasian cuisine that nostalgic foodies wax lyrical about such as fishy kedgeree for breakfast ('mess of re-cooked kippers' curried along with hardboiled eggs in chicken broth, i.e. a non-veg permutation of khichdi), no dinner rolls with masala chops, no aubergine bakes or devilled chutney, none of what I read about in Bridget White's evocative *Kolar Gold Field: Down Memory Lane*. But this otherworldly place could revive—imagine if instead of flying to say, Scotland, one took the train to KGF to eat scones at bungalows-turned-heritage-B&Bs, followed by a round of golf (yes, there's still a golf course) and if craft pubs housed in former clubs offered potted ox tongue. Indeed, KGF could be a goldmine for the leisure industry.

Eventually, I stop at the New Imperial Bakery which used to deliver hot-from-the-oven loaves every day at 4 p.m. and is possibly the only remaining shop from old times. Back in the day, flour would be imported from America to avoid the local variety which was often adulterated with sand to weigh more. These days demand is down, so the jolly baker fires up his huge oven only occasionally to prepare items like the fabled Kolar muffin or seasonal hot-cross buns. The great grandson of the bakery's founder is understandably proud to show off the interiors where firewood is stacked neatly ahead of the next baking-day. A lazy cat lounges between glass jars on the hundred-year-old counter, but there are no more stick-jaw toffees or curry puffs, so I make do with a plastic bag full of orange and pineapple biscuits. For a bite of that bread, the only souvenir that a tourist can carry home of the golden age, I will have to revert to KGF another day—preferably a century ago, as soon as time travel becomes possible.

II

Looking for Malgudi

(The Imagined India)

'Green of several shades we saw, mountainsides lightly coated with verdure and fern, the dark foliage of trees rising hundreds of feet from the valley, light green, dark green, pale green, evergreen and every kind of green shade, were offered for our delectation...'

—*The Emerald Route*, R.K. Narayan

R.K. Narayan's home in Mysuru, now a museum.

Lyrical descriptions of food, hunger and eating in novels can go on echoing in one's head—or stomach—just like gushing depictions of nature. In my notebook, the most unforgettable lines are from R.K. Narayan's *The Guide*. 'He had a craving for bonda, which he used to eat in the railway station stall when a man came there to vend his edibles on a wooden tray to the travellers. It was composed of flour, potato, a slice of onion, a coriander leaf, and a green chilli—and oh! How it tasted—although he probably fried it in anything; he was the sort of vendor who wouldn't hesitate to fry a thing in kerosene, if it worked out cheaper. With all that, he made delicious stuff...'

Counted among the world's great writers, often mentioned in the same breath as Balzac, Chekhov, Dickens, Faulkner and Gogol, his many admirers comprised the likes of E.M. Forster, Graham Greene, Somerset Maugham, John Updike, Germaine Greer and even the exigent V.S. Naipaul—but, being Naipaul, with reservations. In *An Area of Darkness* Naipaul noted that the 'virtues of R.K. Narayan are Indian failings magically transmuted. I say this without disrespect: he is a writer whose work I admire and enjoy.' Essentially, Naipaul's grievance was that Narayan's fictional India hadn't prepared him for the factual India that severely culture-shocked him during his first visit to the country of his ancestors—suggesting that his own shock was made worse by Malgudi.

One of the less studied aspects of his writings, by the way, is how Narayan employed food to great effect in his stories. *The Vendor of Sweets* has edibles in its title; *The Man-Eater of Malgudi* suggests that humans can be part of the food chain; the protagonist in *Waiting for the Mahatma* suffers from a gnawing craving for freshly-cooked South Indian dishes, but is instead offered stale short eats: 'Kara sev, vadai and potato bonda…' In his short story, 'The Martyr's Corner', the focus is exclusively on junk-food—the protagonist being one of those hawkers who peddle goodies from the roadside every evening: Narayan's olfactory imagery excels in describing the dosai 'looking like layers of muslin', and chapattis with free-flowing chutney, duck's eggs 'resembling a heap of ivory balls' for those in need of protein, a sight so tempting that 'even a confirmed dyspeptic could not pass by without throwing a look at it'and to top it all there's puffy melt-in-the-mouth bondas too.

Ah, those lethal bondas! Salty and deep-fried, they mess with my BP, my medication must be upgraded, I burp from undigested chillies, the spicing drives my guts nuts. And it is in *The Guide* that Raju, the reluctant guru, is forced to undertake a fast by his devotees. He gets hungrier and hungrier by thinking of that bonda which used to be on sale at the station where he once worked as a tout, until it takes on hallucinatory powers. It heightens the dramatic tension unbearably as we approach the story's culmination.

It is an ironic tale. Initially, Raju benefits from the meals brought by villagers to the temple ruin he's squatting in (they think he's a holy man), but when drought strikes the land, there are no more free lunches coming his way. This forces him, eventually, to turn into a genuine saint—to conjure up rain through self-mortification. He goes along with it even if he knows that he has no supernatural powers. In the process, he's transformed from an egocentric crook to a self-sacrificing altruist, from being a tout (or, as he preferred to call himself, a *guide*) he turns into a guru by accident. But this story had a curious side effect on me. For years, I was unable to pass one of those deep-frying roadside chefs with their vats of boiling oil—probably spuriously recycled like Narayan suggested—without buying a piping hot globular bonda. These deadly globoids always came with lashings of mint chutney which may well have been churned out of greenish gutter water. I knew bonda wasn't healthy to binge on, but whenever I saw one I recalled Raju's starvation and had to eat it, as if to support his cause.

Interestingly, Narayan wrote *The Guide* not at home in Mysuru but in California—where his productivity was hampered by one singular disagreeable factor: The lack of vegetarian fare. Back in the 1950s, vegetarianism hadn't caught on there, nor were there any South Indian canteens unlike today when Bengaluruan IT experts rule Silicon Valley. In those days most menus in the Bay Area featured nothing but beefsteaks. Americans would question (as described in *My Dateless Diary*):

'Are you a vegetarian by conviction or religion?'

'I am a born-vegetarian. I cannot eat anything except rice, greens, and dairy produce.'

'Extraordinary! Wonder that you are alive.'

Eventually, in order to endure, the novelist bought a hotplate and lived on curd rice (his favourite dish, always had with lime pickle) until he finished the manuscript. His predicament is clearly mirrored in the hungry protagonist of the novel.[6]

The choice of bonda as a literary device is apt, considering that this Udupian dish has been a part of Karnataka's culinary legacy since at least the twelfth century. Food scholar K.T. Achaya terms it a variant of vada but historically speaking, bondas must have been stuffed with other vegetables because potatoes originated in Peru and are a distinctly colonial-era addition to the Indian pantry that only gained widespread acceptance as a household ingredient in the late nineteenth century.[7]

I was eventually cured of my addiction by climbing the colossal cliff at Sravanabelagola, known for its massive monolith of Jain saint Bahubali who starved himself to death about one millennium ago—on that very spot—after realising the vanity of hungering for power. The climb up and down the rock made me ravenous, and again, Narayan's lines replayed in my mind—the drooling Raju's fantasy of the ultimate gluttony, to 'eat bonda for fifteen days without a break', and the pain of his starvation heightened by the crowds of onlookers, 'picnic groups enjoying themselves all over the place'. Once I got down from the hill, to the bus stand where there was, as at almost all bus stops in India, a snack-frying man, my appetite for patently insalubrious edibles suddenly vanished. If those ascetics could starve themselves to death, I figured that I could at the very least abstain from bonda-hogging and lose inches from my podgy bonda-shaped BMI-world-record-breaking waistline.

Since then, I've not eaten a single bonda.

❖

Bengaluru has an endless Outer Ring Road. Cars like speed-addicted oversized cockroaches on growth hormones, horny and honking lorries, and buses resembling pregnant dinosaurs whiz past. The noise is deafening as I—the only fool on foot—

share the 'pedestrian space' with the occasional murderous scooter taking a shortcut through the wrong lane, dodging their exhaust and dust tails.

The city's roads are home to an astonishing ten million vehicles including seven million two-wheelers, about 1.5 million three-wheelers, over two million four-wheelers, with more being added at the rate of one vehicle per minute—altogether causing about 200 pedestrian deaths per year. Intriguingly, this is despite the fact that traffic moves slower and slower as it is estimated that the average speed of vehicles in the city was 35 km per hour in 2005, ten years later this had come down to nine per hour, today one shouldn't be surprised if travelling 5 km by car takes an hour. It is the secondmost congested city in the world, after London, and on an average a motorist is estimated to spend 200 hours annually in traffic jams. There's even an expression used by rickshaw drivers for certain times of day when roads get 'doubly-jammed' and if you buy a 'pre-owned' car in Bengaluru, you will notice that the gearbox hasn't been used from third gear upwards, while first and second are likely to be completely worn out. Anyway, I count myself lucky that there are a few inches of space for pedestrians as I'm reminded of the oft-shared joke—'In India we drive on the left of the road. In Bengaluru, we drive on what is left of the road.'

However, I'm not really studying the vehicular mess, but only strolling through Doddanekundi, once a probably charming ancient village by a pond of the same name, 20 km outside the town centre. The name of the locality is generally interpreted as 'jungle full of jackals', but now the flora and fauna have been swallowed up by the ever-expanding city and it's just one more suburb dotted with malls and drive-ins. Curiously enough, despite everything pointing to the opposite, Doddanekundi is nowadays best known for its bicycling culture, with cyclist clubs and the city's first cycling lanes laid out between its IT-parks, to 'tackle vehicular congestion by incentivising non-motorised travel and promote shorter non-motorised urban commutes' according to an article I read.

But that's like more on paper, I'm thinking as I recite to myself Darwin's immortal words—from *On the Origin of Species*—in which he seemingly explains why it is important that I make it alive through this traffic, or how the 'preservation of favourable individual differences and variations, and the destruction of those which are injurious, I have called Natural Selection, or *the Survival of the Fittest.*'

My quest is beginning to seem absurd before it's properly begun. I'm looking for Malgudi, that gentlest of places characterised by a completely different pace of life—quaint bungalows and cheerful bazaars populated by astrologers, printing presses, painters of signs and talkative men. If one googles this fiction created by Narayan ninety years ago, a quick search throws up several modern candidates in present-day India. One Malgudi is a gated community south of Chennai ('inspired by R.K. Narayan's ideological concept'), another is a pharmacy near Mysuru University, a third is a café called Malgudi Junction in Kolkata, and then there's a Malgudi restaurant on Bengaluru's outskirts.

The latter is said to offer delicacies of the four southern states, and a special 'Malgudi menu', which is why I'm searching for it. After a seemingly endless survival exercise on the Ring Road, it appears before me like a mirage—built to resemble a traditional home with wooden pillars, it has a swing on the porch, a tray of help-yourself bananas by the door, and walls covered with reproductions of drawings by Narayan's brother, the illustrator R.K. Laxman. Aunties in saris demolish huge thali meals, sinking their hands into veritable culinary landscapes

Malgudi Days Museum—closed on Tuesdays.

consisting of mountains of rice and oceans of sambar; soft-spoken software techies tank up on non-veg with beers…Non-veg? Beers?

What would Narayan have ordered, I ruminate as I peruse the menu card. The Malgudi section is a mishmash of southern appetisers such as chicken-65 (supposedly invented in 1965 in Chennai), chicken-95 (invented, well, thirty years later I presume) and Malgudi spl. chicken, but much as I've internalised his novels I can only recall two chickens ever being cooked and neither was considered edible…and once chicken pullao is even suspected to be a murder weapon, another time chicken is declared outright disgusting:

'I don't eat those things!' he cried.[8]

Therefore, I flip to the Tamil vegetarian selection. Narayan came from that side—born at a time when Bangalore was part of the colonial Madras Presidency—and towards the end, he returned to his birthplace Chennai where I was fortunate to be invited home by him in the late 1990s. He had stopped giving formal interviews and was unwilling to answer the same questions about Malgudi's symbolic meaning, so I didn't know what to say at first but soon any nervousness evaporated as it turned out he preferred to discuss Tamil food habits. The subject interested me too. Despite that, and considering that it is rumoured that he was twice fielded as India's candidate for the world's highest literary award, I just had to sneak in the question of whether he hoped to receive the Nobel Prize for Literature.

'No, I don't need a Nobel Prize. What would I do with it?' he said and quickly changed the topic. 'So exactly which Indian dishes have you eaten?'

I named all that had found favour with me and he appeared pleased that I enjoyed both dosa and idli, because dishes like these couldn't be had in Europe, he explained: 'The temperature wouldn't allow a proper fermentation.' A Tamilian would know. The constantly warm climate—Chennai's seasons are sometimes only slightly jestingly characterised as hot, hotter and hottest—was used for great effect in creating fermented goodies. (Later, I learnt from a chef in the UK that it usually takes a minimum thirty hours to ferment dosa batter in London even in summer). The less we talked about fiction, the more communicative he became and so we chatted about basically anything but writing. Now and then, the grand master of Indian literature inspected his potted plants with a critical eye but seemed to be entirely unsentimental when declaring that some of them did not seem to be particularly alive—for that is the course of nature.

'I think that all things, humans included, go through a phase of decay towards the end. So this is entirely natural, all this,' he said alluding to his own aged body and the fact that he had stopped giving interviews about his books, only then to ask as one writer might, with comradely pleasure, of another, 'Would you like to see my study?'

It was at this moment that I think he realised how much our meeting meant to me and the moment that I later felt the greatest gratitude for. He made his way slowly through the apartment he shared with his nephew, with the support of a crutch, over to a chamber where he kept a cot and a writing desk. He sat down to sign a copy of his autobiography for me and then rested his hand on a pile of papers.

'Are you writing something at the moment?' I asked.

'No, this is my correspondence. Every now and then, I have a typist write out letters for me, but mostly I let the mail lie here and go through a phase of decay. It's like a natural process. I imagine that if I wait long enough, these will disappear.' He then asked me to write to him sometime, he enjoyed receiving letters. But he added, 'If you don't get a reply, you'll know why.'

In case you wonder, I did post a letter, but I never heard back from Narayan. But our conversation about food stuck in my mind, so Tamil grub it is. Sandwiched between the non-veg offerings there's a short list of veg and I do the usual travel writer thing and order what I've never heard of before, hoping for an exciting discovery.

The munakai soup is a light sambarish preparation with drumsticks and I can imagine it being eaten in Malgudi. Their varthalkuzhambu—supposedly one of the most classic Tamil dishes—turns out to be over-spiced garlic pods pickled in salt, a bitter and sour assault on the bowels. Hmm, Narayan may have opted for the standard meals that seem to be a big draw.

As I empty my plantain leaf, I'm even more determined to find the real deal—the actual Malgudi. There are clues.

Internet sources useful for various degrees of disinformation situate Malgudi near Coimbatore (from where Narayan's wife hailed and where his daughter later settled after marriage).

In Tamil Nadu there are, in fact, several candidates such as Lalgudi, roughly 100 km from Rasipuram which is what the initial 'R' in R.K. Narayan's name stands for. And the town of Mangudi has an even more deceptively similar name. But what if it's in Karnataka instead? I've found evidence for such a notion in the Doordarshan series *Malgudi Days* by playing the video in slow-motion. Recall the episode about the mailman who doesn't deliver an inauspicious letter on a wedding day? The footage of the post office flashes the zip code 577 411 in passing. It happens to belong to a small Malnad town called Agumbe (with a population of 180 joint-families)...Malnad... Agu...Malgu...umbe? It's a 71.4 per cent match.

His cinematic adaptations give hints. When Narayan scripted his first and only feature for the silver screen, the now lost Tamil low-budget satire *Miss Malini*, it was shot in Chennai and portrayed life in that town. But when he rewrote his screenplay into the novel *Mr Sampath—The Printer of Malgudi*, the plot obviously moved from Chennai to his imagined Malgudi. This book was then adapted into the Hindi movie *Mr Sampat* and it was again a Gemini production filmed in their Chennai studios. Despite the Hindi-speaking characters, its sets look distinctly South Indian such as the Hanuman Vilas Hotel, an archetypal vegetarian café that can still be experienced, for example, in the older neighbourhoods of Bengaluru. By the time his novel *The Financial Expert* was 'adopted' [*sic*] into Kannada as *Banker Margayya* it seems that Malgudi had finally been located in geography, in the Malnad ('hill country'). Watching the movie, I spot the name Koppa on a signboard—a town some 30 km from the hill station Agumbe. Another clue that firmly settles matters came when Malgudi made its biggest-budget appearance in the award-winning Dev Anand-starrer *Guide*, for regardless of its box office success, Narayan preferred the humbler small screen televised version simply because the Bollywood version was shot in Rajasthan and Gujarat, which didn't fit Narayan's own image of Malgudi at all—'they had discarded my own values in milieu and human characteristics,' he lamented in his autobiography. But he felt that Shankar Nag's acclaimed *Malgudi Days,* with a stellar cast of senior Kannada actors, largely shot in Agumbe, really did justice to Malgudi.

A clear lead, if there ever was one. But before leaving the metropolis, it must be pointed out that Bengaluru isn't entirely irrelevant in the search for Malgudi, for it was here that Narayan came up with the name. It happened on Vijayadashmi Day in September 1930, an auspicious moment to set pen to paper according to his grandmother (who was very dear to Narayan and about whom he later wrote the biographical novel *A Grandmother's Tale*) and so that's when he began writing his first novel *Swami and Friends*.

Narayan had recently graduated but was unemployed. Staying with her in the big city, he waited for his future to somehow reveal itself, loafing about in the streets, planning, and then buying an exercise book in which to write his novel. 'As I sat in a room nibbling at my pen and wondering what to write, Malgudi with its little railway station swam into view, all ready-made, with a character called Swaminathan running down the platform'. The station had a banyan tree, a stationmaster, and two trains a day, one coming, one going.

In the completed book, the station scene features at the end, as the backdrop to the climax when his friend goes away on a train and leaves Swami devastated. 'All the jarring, rattling, clanking, spurting, and hissing of the moving train softened in the distance into something that was half a sob and half a sigh.'

As for myself, I'm booked on an overnight train that passes Malleswaram station without stopping. Next morning, reaching the temple town Udupi, the nearest railhead to Agumbe, I plan to hire a taxi and, with some luck, I'll find a cabbie named Gaffur, like the driver in Narayan's stories.

The coastal air is as sweltering as if breathing hot steam. Since dosa happened to be one of Narayan's favourite snacks, the first thing I do is to have a gigantic metre-long masala dosa at the Mitra Samaj canteen by the Krishna temple, where the pure-veg Udupi cuisine received its recognisable form 500 years ago as a monastic diet for the area's priestly class. Chefs-to-be train from their teens in any one of the temple kitchens that have perfected the art of high-quality sattvik food (no onion-garlic, no foreign veggies except chillies). To quote food writer Shoba Narayan, from her book *Food and Faith: A Pilgrim's Journey Through India*, dosa originated in this 'small, dusty town, no different from those dotting interior India. Its temple and cuisine, however, hold an outsize place in the local, regional, national and even international imagination.' In an article in the *Hindustan Times*, she brings up the possibility that it was invented so that the devout could 'hide forbidden onions inside the dosa folds'.

Unsurprisingly the holy town's name has become synonymous with the world's perhaps most wholesome and pocket-friendly vegetarian menu. Local, yet global—Udupi serveries were a secular version of refectories, bhojanashalas or temple feeding halls, and they rose to fame in Bombay around the time of World War I, as workers from Karnataka migrated there. With chefs hailing from Udupi, the dishes were familiar, comforting, and—accustomed to mass-feeding—their service was quick. Ten years later, there was an Udupi canteen in Madras (well, Chennai) perhaps much like the one I had seen in the aforementioned film and by the time of independence many towns had Udupi Bhavans, prototypes for the ones that nowadays can be found even in Silicon Valley, California, which is increasingly becoming another suburb of Bengaluru. A joke goes: What did Neil Armstrong see when he landed on the moon? A vegetarian Udupi hotel serving masala dosa!

There and then, life already feels very Malgudi. Once I get into a taxi, the driver's name turns out to be Krishna Prasad, which roughly translates as 'food consecrated to god' and which isn't bad at all considering that the Udupi Krishna temple is the main tourist attraction in these parts. He is exceptionally efficient, too, and drives up the narrow ghat road so fast it is like bungee-jumping uphill.

The 55-km journey to Agumbe, which sits at the top of a pass connecting the Deccan Plateau with the coastal belt below, is a tunnel of emerald greenery, areca nut plantations and rubber-tree nurseries. When he first visited Agumbe in 1939, Narayan described the view towards the ocean as 'a spectacle which is worth travelling a thousand miles to watch.' On the ascent up the serpentine road, we run into a cloud after the third hairpin bend and as we drive into Agumbe, following another dozen increasingly scary bends, the mist is so thick that it's like entering a fading photograph of a town...or hamlet, as this turns out to be.

Ah, finally I'm in Malgudi! Everything looks like the TV series but less crowded. There are barely any people. No cars. It's so quiet it is magical. Central Agumbe is essentially a T-junction, called 'circle', with a post office, a bus stand, some shops and canteens such as the roomless Hotel Kubera, as well as a bank and a school with a faded board outside—I decipher the name 'S.V.S. High School'—could this have been the Albert Mission College featured in the TV series?

A winding side lane, Car Street (where I still see no cars), takes me to a village square with the Srivenugopalakrishnaswamy temple that appears familiar and a primary school where kids like Swami and his friends crowd the classrooms, and a ruined pilgrims' hostel built in 1906—the year of Narayan's birth. People use the ruin to dry coconut husks.

Everybody I speak to, from the postman to the shopkeepers, remembers *Malgudi Days* which was filmed in 1985-86. When asked whereabouts the shooting happened, they all say: 'Everywhere.' Most villagers got walk-on parts, doing cameos in the series that transformed Agumbe into a bustling small town if only for the duration of the shoot. The film's crew and cast numbering more than a hundred were all lodged with the villagers. Apparently, an 18-ft equestrian statue of the British resident, Sir Frederick Lawley (cheekily executed in the form of a caricature by Bengaluru-based artist John Devraj), was put up at the T-junction that was turned into a proper 'Circle' for a time.

The key location, where the filmmakers spent months on end, is Doddamane ('the big house') in the main street.[9] This private home, erected in the year 1900, has a grand front veranda adorned with pillars and a central courtyard. The first episode that took place in the house was 'Maha Kanjoos', the memorable story of a miserly grandfather and his mischievous grandson.

Kasturiakka is the matron of the house and sits on a cot in the inner veranda, in the company of two other ladies. Before I quite know how it happened, I have a steaming tumbler of kashayam in my hand: A milky, lightly-spiced (with basil leaves, I think, and something else I can't quite put my finger on) health beverage trusted in these hills. Kasturiakka's hospitality is the stuff of legend. Visitors to the village can stay in an upstairs room and pay as they like, but she doesn't allow filmy folks anymore. She talks about how the shooting turned everything upside down. Listening to her, it is easy to believe that one has indeed stepped into a different world. The family is proud of how clean Agumbe is and claim it hasn't changed at all since the eldest among them were children in the 1930s. When I step out again, I get a funny feeling that the slow pace here really does adjust one's inner biorhythms to Malgudi time. The air is fresher, dreamier than elsewhere, remarkably so. Or maybe it's because of the fluffy wet clouds that wrap themselves around everything including my toes.

Whiling away Malgudian days at Dodda Mane, matrons with Kasturiakka in the centre.

But however close to an ideal village Agumbe might seem, with its kindly, unhurried, educated inhabitants, there are things missing. Where, for example, is the railway? Arasalu station, a 77-km drive north, on the rather obscure line from Shivamogga to Talguppa, was used for the TV shoot. Its abandoned colonial-era station building was recently developed into a charming Malgudi museum, housing props and memorabilia, well worth a detour if one happens to be passing nearby. And there's no clock tower in Agumbe. There's also no Lawley

Extension, suburban living belongs in Agumbe as little as traffic jams do.

The station at Arasalu has been renamed as Malgudi Station—confusing for passengers wishing to get off at Arasalu—but should you happen to buy a ticket to the Malgudi Express, one of the slowest trains in Karnataka, you will end up over 200 km due south, in Mysuru where Narayan spent much of his life.

Indeed, the Malgudi map drawn by Clarice Borio and reproduced on Narayan's request in one of his books, if tilted to the right, and then a bit to the left, bears a striking resemblance to a map of Mysuru. The river Sarayu for one is quite obviously based on Kaveri, south India's great sacred river. Green Hotel on Hunsur Road used to be part of the Premier Studios that was renamed the Malgudi Film Studio in his novels. The fictive Market Street with its Bombay Anand Bhavan, feels much like Sayyaji Rao Road with the real-life Bombay Tiffanys sweets and snacks shop (limited seating on two metal-topped benches) in the factual market building, which is surrounded by any number of places that remind me of, for example, Malgudi's Regal Haircutting Saloon and other sundry enterprises. The Palace Talkies resembles the genuine Prabha Theatre. While many other theatres have shut down, it survived the pandemic lockdowns in its futuristically upgraded avatar as Prabha UFO Digital Cinema. And the imagined clock tower must have been inspired by the nearby genuine clock tower, a few hundred steps north of the palace.[10] Sampath—the printer of Malgudi—is said to be based on a real-life printer, who printed Narayan's own *Indian Thought* publications (cheaper editions of his writings for the Indian market), and it is a curious but little-known fact that Narayan, at the Metropole Hotel near the railway station, observed a tout or tourist guide in action one day, which triggered his bestselling novel *The Guide*.[11]

In short, Narayan didn't bother to hide his tracks. And for sure, Lawley Extension could well be a portrait of Yadavgiri, a suburb behind the station where Narayan, in the winter of 1947-48, purchased a 55x36 metre plot worth about Rs 5,000 and over the next four or five years built his graceful two-storied home. If one didn't know, one would pass without a second glance as it is dwarfed by its posh neighbours. But a useful landmark is the Paradise Hotel, where Narayan and his brother Laxman dined in the 1980s and which stands across the street. Writing this, I sample bisibelehulianna, a Mysuruan VFM all-in-one-dish that is part veg biryani, part fiery sambar gravy and part mystical puree of hot-hot spices. And so I find that much here in Mysuru fits my mental image of the world of Narayan.

The house had shockingly enough been sold to a builder and was about to be demolished a decade ago, in 2011. Waking up to this cultural calamity, booklovers demanded that this irreplaceable legacy be rescued, so since 2016 it's been a museum where visitors may check out the author's library which includes a big fat biography of his mentor Graham Greene, his shirts, muffler and grey jacket. Before the pandemic struck in 2019, already 17,000 fans had taken the opportunity to pay their respects.

It's strangely moving to see the old-fashioned kitchen and imagine him making himself a cuppa—a fastidious caffeinist, he apparently had an impressive collection of eight percolators. I recall publisher David Davidar mentioning, in a preface to a collection of Narayan's stories, that 'after offering me some superb home-brewed filter coffee, he showed me around the house that he'd had constructed to his specifications, especially the many-windowed study on the top floor from which he could look out upon the town which had provided much of the raw material for his stories.' Although he generally ate meals and slept in the joint-family home in nearby Lakshmipuram, he used come here to write in his 'office'. The study that Davidar refers to, is a sunny bay-room with eight windows that offer panoramic 180° views of the entire city, plus playful birds and squirrels.

R.K. Narayan in his study (in Chennai).

Eventually, I find a conclusive clue in Narayan's essay 'Misguided "Guide"', where he talks extensively about the aforementioned Bollywood movie *The Guide*. The film team (that included the Nobel Prize-winning scriptwriter Pearl S. Buck) apparently came all the way to Mysuru to see the setting of the book—and Narayan writes, 'I showed them the river steps and a little shrine overshadowed by a banyan on the banks of Kaveri, which was the actual spot around which I wrote *The Guide*. As I had thought, nothing more needed to be done than put the actors there and start the camera.'

So there, he admitted it! He also took the moviemakers to the top of Gopalaswamybetta, the highest peak in the Bandipur National Park, up a steep jungly road where one might encounter tigers or elephants. 'At the summit I showed them the original of the "Peak House" in my novel, a bungalow built fifty years ago, with glassed-in verandas affording a view of wildlife at night, and a 2,000-foot drop to a valley beyond. A hundred yards off, a foot-track wound through the undergrowth, leading on to an ancient temple whose walls were crumbling and whose immense timber doors moved on rusty hinges with a groan. Once again I felt that here everything was ready-made for the film.' It is easy to imagine his disappointment when *The Guide* was shot in Rajasthan and Gujarat instead of his beloved Karnataka.[12]

It is a well-known fact that Narayan liked to saunter about in his hometown for inspiration and socialise with the various characters he met on the streets (talkative men, printers and vendors of sweets, and other oddballs), which he thought of as part of his 'office hours', or at least that's what he once told fellow writer Ved Mehta. In an obituary, Khushwant Singh described his own visit to Mysuru and how 'being with Narayan on his afternoon stroll was an experience. He did not go to a park but preferred walking up the bazaar.' There, Narayan stopped 'at shops to exchange namaskaras with the owners, introduce me and exchange gossip with them in Kannada or Tamil…' which gave Singh an insight into how Narayan got 'material for his novels and stories.'

Without Narayan to guide me, I spend a day walking in his footsteps, from his childhood's Bojanna Lane where formative experiences took place, to the family's house in Lakshmipuram, a fancier area with a clear Tamil vibe. And I recall how he typed his first stories on a second-hand typewriter. To get his friends to listen, he treated them to coffee, running up such a long bill that he had to sell the typewriter to clear his dues. But it must have been worth it, as he remarked, 'the cup of coffee blunted the listeners' critical faculties and made them declare my work a masterpiece.' Without a typewriter, he had a typist hammer out his handwritten manuscripts on demi-sized bond paper.

Following clues in *My Days*, I next walk to where his typist lived by the Jaganmohan Palace. Narayan made it a point to reach the house before the man could finish his breakfast, to follow him to his stall, Venus Typewriting Institute, through the narrow alley by the temple on the corner, now the ostentatiously named Srisribrahmatantraswatantraparakalaswami mutt, to Santhepete Bazaar behind the Hardinge Complex.

Leaving the typist to his work, usually Narayan walked up to the market, opposite which still stands a bookshop he frequented in the hopes that it'll stock his books one day—but when I ask for Mysuru-related literature, the proprietor only shows me expensive, lavish books on the maharajas. When I specify what I'm interested in, it turns out they have a single thin paperback by Narayan tucked away at the back. After I pay for it, I continue to a nearby stationery shop, R. Krishnaswami, which was another of his hangouts. The proprietor remembers him and says they kept a chair out in front, where Narayan sat down to watch people and take notes. I ask what pencil he used and am shown their enduring bestsellers.

The local Apsara brand is cheap at Rs 6 so Narayan bought those when he was short on money, so I buy a packet, but when he could afford it he'd upgrade to Staedtler pencils. 'A hundred years ago we were one of only three shops in India to stock these, the others were a shop in Bombay and another one in Madras' I'm told.

And as I get myself a luxurious Rs 625 set, I hope they'll bring me Narayan's blessings.

❖

Apart from being a hub of literary tourism, Mysuru is renowned as a foodie fairyland with its reputation resting primarily on the local variety of Karnataka's most world-famous dish, namely the 'Mysore masala dosa'. Like the Russians who have their blinis with vodka, the French who have their creamy crêpes, the Swedes who have...well, don't really have anything comparable as R.K. Narayan discreetly hinted during our conversation about dosas when I had travelled to Chennai to meet him.

It's interesting how, if one eats one's way from coast to coast, dosas mutate. They can be as thick as pancakes but with a smaller-than-Udupi diameter in Tamil Nadu; softer with spongier centre but crisper edges in Kerala (appams); on the east coast in Andhra Pradesh zesty dosa-like pancakes are known as pesarattu with the spices mixed into the batter, in contrast to which Tulu Nadu on the west coast has its gossamer-like non-spicy neerdosas ('water pancakes') and then there are the utterly buttery bennedosas of central Karnataka. Elsewhere on my trips, I've chomped on non-veg egg-coated dosas stuffed with minced mutton, or had stacks of them alongside Malabari chicken gravy; in Bengaluru's bazaars rice pullao-stuffed dosa is the stuff; while faddish experiments have spawned the Punjabified butter-roasted paneer dosa, but then again thanks to health-conscious restaurateurs, one also gets 'olive oil dosa'—just to mention some varieties on Indian tables.

Of all the notable Mysuru products that attract tourists, the dosa is perhaps the most emblematic yet most impossible to carry home as a souvenir. More easily packaged mementoes include the GI-tagged Mysuru silk (from a factory founded in 1912 by the maharaja himself), GI-tagged sandalwood oils and soaps (world-famous since 1916), likewise GI-tagged Mysuru incense, or sinfully sweet ghee-laden Mysore pak (also GI-tagged and best had at Guru Sweets whose owner invented this home-grown chickpea flour fudge in 1935), and last but not least, the GI-tagged Nanjangud-rasabalehannu which is a special variety of tiny bananas superior to all other plantains anywhere in the world, with matchless aroma—as I bite into one, it reminds me of sweet, ripe, juicy strawberries (India is the world's #1 producer of the sweetest bananas).[13]

There may be a deluge of burgers and pizzas on the contemporary Mysuruan fast-food scene, but the dosa remains the city's greatest bestseller and is, now and then, fielded as a 'national dish' whenever matters of gastronomic symbolism is debated. A global poll has put it at #4 on a list of 'Top 10 Dishes to Eat Before You Die' and for its Indian market, the conservative McDonalds junk-food empire, realising that they can't ever hope to beat local fast-food, found it necessary to introduce a McDosa masala burger.

Another great place for dosas in Mysore—this is where the maharaja goes when he craves a dosa.

Every good canteen in Mysuru prepares its dosa the same way (well, almost): Urad dhal and rice batter must be mixed in the exactly right proportions, then soaked and fermented overnight after which it is shallow-fried at the ideal temperature until its surface becomes perfectly golden brownish, crusty on the outside but fluffy within. An added signature smear of flaming-chilli-garlic-onion 'disco paste' for heightened tastiness is the hallmark of Mysuruan dosa. It is finally filled with the correct stuffing known as 'palya' that is basically curried potato mush. Narayan's own favourite came from a 'hotel' near his Lakshmipuram residence, a well-known eatery that was regularly frequented by late Kannada cinema legends Ambarish, Dr Rajkumar and Vishnuvardhan. When Dev Anand visited Narayan's 'office' in Yadavgiri, the Bollywood hero was plied with these fabled dosas 'and other South Indian delicacies' brought by Narayan's nephews. Known until recently as Ramya Drive-In, the eatery was recently shut down due to the pandemic.[14]

My first stop whenever I arrive at Mysuru by rail is unfailingly the neat Hotel Ashoka (Dhanvantri Road), a short walk from the station. A traditional eatery, it transports me to a gentler Mysuruan era and their dosa is top class, no doubt. Also, it isn't as crowded as the touristy hangouts. One noteworthy detail about the orthodox dosa is that it is folded into a half-circle, such as at Ashoka, and never rolled like crêpes or twisted into a cone (like elsewhere). The turmeric-yellow filling is a buttery melange of smashed spiced-up potatoes and fried onion lightly seasoned with mustard seeds and chillies.

Even if the potato stuffing isn't an old concept, some form of dosa has been in existence for 1,500 years according to the scholarly K.T. Achaya who found mentions of 'dōsai' in ancient Sangam literature—which means that the dish is as old as Mysuru itself.[15] It's generally assumed to have developed its modern shape in Udupi, as noted, but the enigma that scientists can't quite crack is whether it's a fried, flattened idli or if the idli is a compact, steamed dosa![16]

However that may be, the Mysuru dosa developed into

what we eat today when public eateries became a rage in Karnataka during the first half of the 1900s. As compared to the traditional set dosa—a stack of pancakes with veg gravy or palya on the side—stuffing a dosa with masala was seen as progressive as it speeded up serving and eating, and it could at a pinch be parcelled as a travel snack by wrapping it up in a banana leaf (though it does get soggy rapidly); hence an optimal snack.

Despite being the preferred bite to break a busy sightseeing schedule, for some strange reason one cannot eat dosa whenever one craves it. It's only served as 'tiffin'—and this is generally true across the south—in the mornings until about 11 a.m. and then again from 3 p.m. until when dinner service commences. However, some unorthodox holistic joints geared towards foreigners do cook dosa for lunch, as with multiple yogashalas and mystic research centres to pick from, Mysuru has become the hub of yogic holidays in the world. The local gurus teach a range of Hollywood heroines in search of that perfect physique and burnt-out pop stars; and following in their footsteps, a couple of thousand foreigners join the city's 150 or so yoga studios *every month*. In 2016, yoga was even recognised by UNESCO as an 'intangible cultural heritage' of global importance.

For these yoga tourists, dosas are stand-ins for crêpes when they feel culinary homesickness. They contain only about 350 calories but are nutritious, high in carbs and protein, rich in amino acids and probiotic qualities thanks to the fermentation process, and being fully gluten-free they're the perfect repast for today's increasingly gluten-intolerant health freaks.

So, to sample yogic dosa, and that too for lunch, I check out Dhatu Organics & Naturals (Adipampa Road), a combined ecological grocery store and café in the Gokulam area known for its upmarket meditation centres, kombucha juice bars and sourdough pizzerias. A couple of English girls sit at the next table, eating grilled veg platters and discussing their course in ashtanga it seems from the snippets of conversation I overhear. Although ashtanga is another Mysuru invention, in this case, the girls worship a Mysuru-based Spanish yogi! At another table, a health-conscious yet overweight techie works on his laptop. As I browse the menu, my attention is caught by a millet dosa served with sprouted green gram curry. Yummy!

It is a non-greasy, fibre-rich energy booster. At this moment, if it sounds like there's a deficiency in my personal health consciousness I have a small confession to make. I occasionally practice breathing techniques like pranayama along with friends, but as a person whose natural circumstances consist of unthinking non-veg hogging and brain-numbing beering, I doubt that any veggie utopia can reform me or steer my 'journey of self-discovery' in a more preferable direction. I tried staying at an Ayurvedic retreat once. Deprived of red meat and without even a single espresso in sight to accompany the ciggies I had smuggled with me, there was nothing to do other than observe myself—'witness' as the hypnotic guru with a twenty-five-year-long-CV of ashram-hopping put it—but which only served to freak me out. After doing his best to improve my sordid life via chakra-cleansing-cum-balancing, he asked me how it felt.

'Terribly hard,' I blurted out. 'Whenever I try to think about what you tell me, my mind thinks of something else.'

'That is because your mind is like a drunken monkey. It jumps whichever way it fancies.'

'Oh, that is good to know, it explains a lot,' I replied, thinking that's fine, I just have to learn to live with a tipsy simian jailed within my skull, and squeeze in the odd banana through my ears to keep it calm. During the morning yoga, my creaky bones felt irreparably damaged and the one time I performed suryanamaskar in the yogashala, I fully appreciated how poorly equipped my body is to manhandle anything more complex than a computer keyboard. So I've kind of decided to hope against hope that karmic laws have some paragraph that might let slack souls like me off the hook.

In a world where food is becoming increasingly complex, Mysuru is sheer bliss for the authentic down-to-the-roots preparations on offer and so eating dosa in excess gives me a strong sense of upholding cultural values, even if I feel stuffed like a dosa by late afternoon. Within marching distance east of the bus station stands the somewhat nondescript Mylari Hotel (Nazarbad Main Road), which interestingly enough has been certified by China as the 'best dosa hotel of Asia', if not in the entire universe. Their opening hours are tricky, so one must time the visit well—they fire up the dosa grill at 7.30 a.m. and again at 4 p.m., but shut whenever they run out of batter, which doesn't take long. The establishment seats maximum sixteen, so being early is being wise.

Their dosa is spongy, thick and almost as soft as idli—perhaps constituting that missing link between the two?—and its cloying nature is enhanced by how they cook on aromatic wood-fire rather than gas flame, and it comes not with thick palya or tangy sambar but a mild mix-veg masala typical of Karnataka cuisine, and chutney which I believe is made from fresh coconut lightly seasoned with just some chillies, black mustard seeds, curry leaves and maybe some other top secret ingredients. I order two more because the first was so velvety that I could go on eating until the shop runs out of batter!

Eventually, I force myself to stop, my conclusion being that the Mysuru dosa will feature on my list of five essential things that I would take to a desert island—the other four being beer, Bengaluru, books and my wife's phone number.

III

South by Southwest
(A Passage through Kerala)

'What on earth were you doing with yourself in India for five years?' said Isabel.

'Playing about,' he answered, with a smile of kindly mockery.

'What about the Rope Trick?' asked Gray. 'Did you see that?'

'No, I didn't.'

'What did you see?'

'A lot.'

—*The Razor's Edge*, Somerset Maugham

Toddy shop in Kumarakom.

You know you're in Kerala when you step off the train, walk right into the nearest shack and are served smoothly soothing and slightly sweetish appams accompanying a sublime fish curry—for *breakfast*. Now that's what I call a hospitable attitude! But actually, fish curry is considered a completely normal thing to eat the first thing you do as you open your eyes. And my eyes do open wide and water a bit...because, typically for Kerala, the fiery curry is packed with flavours ranging from chillies, coconut, coriander, cumin, curry leaves, garlic, ginger, mustard seeds, pepper, tamarind, turmeric and many others I can't tell apart, yet without being too spicy to enjoy for breakfast.

A breakfaster's self-combustion is prevented by those delicately plump and spongy palm-sap fermented rice flour batter pancakes called appams, that are sweeter than their dosa relatives, and which have curiously cushioned centres encircled by lacy edges. Appams, also anglicised as hoppers (which presumably is how the colonials pronounced the word), are sheer food artistry, 'perhaps the most beautiful of Indian breads' to quote food expert Pushpesh Pant. The appams are cooked in a special wok-shaped cast-iron appachatti—an implement that accounts for the appam's unique structural features. Widely consumed since time immemorial, they seem to have special links to Kerala's Christians, with varieties such as pesahappam or 'INRI-appam' prepared exclusively for the pesaha that commemorates the crucifixion (it is even embellished with a palm leaf cross). Hence these are said to have originated in that community, which blended ancestral Syrian influences with adopted Indian habits—an intercourse that gave birth to the omnipresent appam.

This shack has no name that I can make out, the owner speaks only Malayalam, but what a fishy welcome! Still peckish, I order fried fish with the delicate scent of coconut oil and go on munching until it's almost lunchtime: A perfect start on a day of sightseeing which immediately makes me forget the long train ride to Kozhikode.

It is a historically known fact that people travelled from afar to shop for spices here—the ancient Greeks and Romans, the medieval Arabs and Chinese, and later, the who's who of colonials whether Portuguese or English, French or Dutch, all came and sampled Kerala's flavourful pantry. Therefore, I dream of culinary fireworks as I follow evocative street signs: Sweet Meat Street is where the city's trademark dry fruit halwa has been on sale for over 600 years and where I also buy chunky pepper-and-jaggery coated banana chips. The Silk Street is the more or less official 'Food Street' lined with scores of enticing eateries—including The Chinese Factory, which isn't as old as one might wish but a modern pan-Asian fusion diner where Japanese *teriyaki* squids effortlessly rub their rubbery shoulders with pepper-grilled paneer and chicken fried rice. Halwa Bazaar needs no explanation because that's where the good stuff is made. Finally I arrive at the narrow, winding, cacophonic Big Bazaar where truckloads of spices are being unloaded into impossibly tiny shops. Everywhere a melange of piquant scents hangs heavy in the air. Not for nothing is Kozhikode known as 'City of Spices' and prowling through Big Bazaar it gets quite easy to imagine what things may have looked like 500 years ago when foreigners traded Portuguese silver, Italian velvet, English woollen fabrics and whatever else Europe produced, for spices.

Coincidentally, one of my favourite English writers, novelist Somerset Maugham, loitered on the city's beach in the 1930s—at a time when a tourist handbook describes the town thus: 'Facing the sea are the houses of the European residents and the custom house, and also the club. There is a great appearance of neatness and comfort in the houses even of the very poor in Calicut; and the whole place is rendered very picturesque by the fine trees and groves of cocoa-nut palms in which it is embowered.'

The 'beach' isn't particularly conducive to swimming but it's rather a quiet neighbourhood where I stay at the Beach Hotel, something of a landmark that was originally built as the British club back in 1890. Luckily it hasn't been significantly modernised since the town's name was Calicut and it oozes antiquity out of every creaky floorboard. I had requested the suite where Maugham plotted his novel *The Razor's Edge* sometime in 1938, but the staff didn't seem sure of who Maugham was. 'Your mom? What's her name?' In any case, the 75-sq-m room I move into is bigger than my compact flat in Bengaluru. Then again, Maugham was a bigger writer than I'll ever be. So I am not complaining, especially since the ex-club retains the most exciting bar in town.

The only kitchen to have survived long enough to have served Maugham, at least in theory, is the French Bakery in Kooriyal Lane. Set up in 1932, when there was only one Frenchman left in town (a watchman assigned to guard a colonial shed), it was nevertheless beloved by other colonials.

Unfortunately, it retains none of its 1930s' character—it looks like any other canteen that does bakes and snacks, with nothing strikingly Parisian about it. Whatever they serve, however, like fish fried in sweetish coconut oil, would approximate what Maugham sampled of Kerala cookery during his sojourn. And being a hardcore Francophile (Maugham had migrated from Britain to the south of France in 1928), he'd obviously have gyrated towards this bakery to pick up some 'hot cross buns' whenever he felt peckish.

Besides, he was a steadfast 'breakfast man'—who wisecracked somewhat ambiguously that 'to eat well in England you should have breakfast three times a day'—though I'm not sure if he would have considered fish curry to be a substitute for traditional English breakfast. Although this three-month sojourn was his first and only visit to India proper, he'd earlier travelled widely in Asia (including Burma which was then part of British India) and so must have gotten used to Asian food. Yet the only meal he describes taking pleasure in, according to *A Writer's Notebook*, is a freshly-shot peacock, which he feels bad about in a moral sense but on the other hand, its 'flesh was white, tender and succulent; it was a welcome change from the scraggy chickens which are brought to the table evening after evening in India.' As we see, he wasn't thrilled by Indian culinary skills. Touring across Burma in the previous decade, with a fulltime Telugu cook in his entourage, he wrote how he was served 'bony, tasteless fish; if not, [tinned] sardines or tunny; a dish of tough meat, and one of the three sweets that my Indian cook knew how to make.'[17]

I like to imagine that the spiritual-minded Maugham tried meditation cross-legged on the floor of the room at the club. And at the bakery, I buy a slice of cake with the word 'Coffee' piped onto it in cream as I consider how Maugham, for the rest of his life, fancied returning to write more about India. Up to now 'the shadow of Kipling lurking over the country' had inhibited him, he told another India-inspired novelist colleague, E.M. Forster, in a letter. But here, he met a different India from the one in Kipling's nineteenth-century stories and regretted not having come earlier.

Apart from entries in *A Writer's Notebook* (1949) and an essay about Hinduism, 'The Saint', in his last book (*Points of View*) that was triggered by his encounter with Ramana Maharishi, India formed the backbone of *The Razor's Edge*, perhaps his greatest masterpiece in which a long lost friend turns up after ten years and is full of mysterious stories from when he 'knocked about the East for a bit' including two years at an ashram in Kerala, 'a beautiful country of green hills and valleys and soft-flowing rivers. Up in the mountains there are tigers, leopards, elephants and bison, but the Ashrama was on a lagoon and all around it grew coconuts and areca palms.'

It is quite certain that he based the ashram described in *The Razor's Edge*, which he located at some distance by train and bullock-cart from Thiruvananthapuram, on a brief visit to Ramana Maharishi's abode in neighbouring Tamil Nadu.

On his travels, however, rather than roughing it out at ashrams he lived comfortably as a government guest, or was 'sumptuously entertained' by many maharajas, or stayed at posh clubs in cities like Bombay where, to his irritation, at the Yacht Club—where Indians weren't allowed—he was pestered by pompous colonials, 'doddering old fools' as he called them in a letter posted from there. Before coming to Kerala he had seen churches in Goa and after breaking journey in Kozhikode, he peeped into the Library in Thiruvananthapuram, where he was pleased to spot his own novels in the collection. He liked Kerala a lot: 'It is green, cool and quiet. You get a very curious impression of pastoral life, peaceful and primitive, and not too hard.'

Next he toured Tamil Nadu where he most likely celebrated his sixty-fourth birthday by the temple in Madurai (on 25 January): 'People talk all day long at the top of their voices, but in the temple they talk more loudly than ever. The row is terrific. People pray and recite litanies, they call to one another, vociferously discuss, quarrel or greet one another. There is nothing that suggests reverence and yet there is a vehement overwhelming sense of the divine that sends cold shivers down your spine.' Then he had his darshan of Ramana Maharishi when he famously fainted. The truth was that after 'a dull, hot drive along a dusty, bumpy road', he demolished a 'picnic luncheon' which, half-way through it, made him swoon. Once he came to, he was too sick to get up for the darshan in the ashram, so the Maharishi came to Maugham. 'He asked me whether I wished to say anything to him, or to ask him any question. I was feeling weak and ill, and said so; whereupon he smiled and said, "Silence also is conversation."' After fifteen minutes, the Maharishi smiled and walked away. Of all the spiritual masters Maugham met, and who gave long discourses, this encounter made the greatest impression.

'I heard later that my fainting had given rise to fantastic rumours. The news of it was carried not only to various parts of India, but even reached America,' he reported in *A Writer's Notebook*. 'When I was asked about it I was content to smile and shrug my shoulders. In point of fact that was neither the first nor the last time I have fainted. Doctors tell me it is due to an irritability of the solar plexus which presses my diaphragm against my heart and that one day the pressure will continue a little too long.'

Another meeting that didn't go according to plan was

on his visit to Mysuru, as a guest of the maharaja, where he wished to meet R.K. Narayan. He'd published three novels in England by then, but when the maharaja's secretary made enquiries no local intellectual knew of him as Narayan was not yet commercially successful in India. Hence Maugham was told, 'There is no novelist in Mysore. We may, however, find you one in Bangalore.' Ironically, Narayan's home stood less than two thousand metres from Hotel Metropole where Maugham stayed. He planned to return the following winter but, as we know, World War II blasted off in 1939.

During the next week, I lunch my way through the town's menus and in the afternoons, I pop into shed-like toddy shops where the drunks wait out the hot day. As per government rules, Kerala doesn't have many bars, but there's always a toddy 'shaap' or 'shappu' around the corner where fish is frying from morning to evening. One drunkard I have a heart-to-heart tête-à-tête with turns out to be a Malayalam writer who calls himself 'God's own poet' and he pulls out a sheaf of printouts to prove it. He makes me read the manuscript of his collected works in English translation as we sip our toddies. Is he perhaps Maugham's reincarnation?

Other highlights include the art deco-eatery Deevar (near the south end of Sweet Meat Street) where a hand-written menu on a board offers all kinds of tempting seafood. I order a kingfish steak and succulent prawns, pronounced 'frowns' by the waiter, cooked to perfection, aromatic, and the total bill comes to next to nothing. The chefs of Kerala realised long ago that what works best with seafood (or in fact, any food) is the oil of *Cocos nucifera*—the humble coconut. It has blessed Malayalam cuisine since the beginning of time by adding a mildly nutty fragrance that enhances the briny nature of marine creatures. It has many miraculous functions apart from the aromatic cooking oil that is extracted from it. Coconut also provides a nutritious, re-hydrating and refreshing juice; its sap can be fermented into wonderful toddy, a single tree producing up to 30l per day, or turned into vinegar, or distilled into arrack (believed to be the mother of vodka). Freshly-grated coconut makes the perfect base for chutneys, desiccated, it thickens gravies and moderates spice levels. It also yields palm sugar (jaggery); flour to make cookies from; coconut cream and milk that can become ice-creams, custards and sweets. It supplies coir to make rope; fronds to construct huts with; and its wood is perfect for carving kitchen utensils out of…which is why the coconut may be called 'God's own nut' if you know what I mean.

When I ask locals, they all recommend the Mappila biryani with date chutney—evidence of those past Arab links—at Bombay Hotel (Court Road), which has nothing to do with Mumbai. In 1949, when it was founded, 'Bombay' simply meant modern or 'fancy', but nowadays it is one of the more timeworn and plainer eateries in the upscale beach area. It has no ambience whatsoever, but is packed with lunch-goers throughout the day and is considered to be the second best option in town. Its snack counter is a snacker's heaven and for dessert, my eyes zoom in on the chemmeen cake which turns out to be not sweet at all but a medium-spicy seafood pie. It is amazingly amazing!

Ambling randomly, I happily stumble upon the town's classiest seafood restaurant, Kingsbay (Customs Street), down an alley towards the northern end of the beach. Housed in a grand building, it sports an eclectic menu. I order their house special, prawn-stuffed crab cheese bake, but the crabs haven't been fished out of the sea yet. So instead I ask what's freshest and the maître d'hôtel calls out to the kitchen. Someone yells back in Malayalam. It turns out that a consignment of mussels is being offloaded, so I order a plate—rich ghee roast is in vogue—and have it with another plate of luscious squids stuffed with spinach and cheese.

Eventually, all foodies will find themselves at Paragon (Kannur Road) in a bizarre location under the Red Cross Road railway over-bridge, and somewhat far from the beachfront. It opened in 1939 (sadly Maugham missed it by a year), and is known as the town's #1 restaurant, without a shred of doubt. This mini-empire with its hyperbolic slogan of 'best seafood in India' and three dining halls (seating 240 eaters) is always thronged by patrons hogging monstrous amounts of biryani. But there's much more on the menu which showcases everything that's fresh in the fishing harbour and I'm spoilt for choice. My order hits the table surprisingly fast considering the complexity: Tawa-fried prawns in a chilli-red masala, pan-fried mussels with caramelised onion, and kingfish in a creamy mango-coconut-milk curry which appears to be something of a specialty. It is a meal that I shall return to, again and again, in my sweetest dreams. And I'm proud to report there was no burping or indigestion that night.

But being a certified tourist, I must push on. About an hour's train journey north from Kozhikode's edible joys, lies a nine-square-kilometre-fragment of the French territories in India—Mahe. A so-called 'factory' or warehouse-cum-residence was built in 1722 in which exportable commodities were stockpiled—but this historic patch of Parisian outreach might today appear to someone passing through as nothing but a busy stretch of highway lined with countless cheap bars. But the moment I turn into a leafy by-lane I'm on a different planet. Vintage bungalows, check; church, check; spooky graveyard, yeah it's right there; and following a charming riverside walkway, I even chance upon a boathouse from where folks are taking catamarans for a spin.

Mahe recently got its first heritage hotel. The meticulously restored colonial-era Villa De 1945 brims with teakwood fittings and stained-glass windows. With only fourteen rooms it's terrifically exclusive and I spend leisurely evenings sipping tea on a huge balcony overlooking the town's quiet boulevard, peculiarly spelt as 'Bulu Ward Road' on street signs. In the dining hall, I sample chemmeen kizhi (shrimp steamed with

French colonial grandeur at Villa De 1945, Mahe.

coconut and circumspectly selected spices), roasted mussels (to die for unless one is already dead), and oh-so-light-fried veggies. For breakfast there's puttu, a tubular steam-cooked loaf of ground rice seasoned with coconut shavings—I've seen it translated on English-language menus as 'steamed rice cylinders' which rather makes it sound like an engine part—typical of the

Nairs, the warrior caste of Kerala, who used to cook rice this way in bamboo tubes known as puttukutti. It is normally served with curried legumes. Not exactly *Français* fare, but a deadly diet all the same.

It is believed that these colonisers' only significant contribution to Indian menus is *le omelette*, a fifteenth-century concept that translates into omelette. French fries may also be of Parisian origin, but they reached via the Brits, hence they are commonly referred to as finger chips in India.

There aren't any grand sights, no Eiffel Tower or Notre Dame, which means one spends one's days simply chilling. Even the government museum must be the smallest in the world—it's the very opposite of the world's largest museum, the Louvre—displaying a random table from colonial days, a couple of swords and a gramophone recording of 'La Marseillaise', but nothing that sheds light on how their Indian entanglement may have affected the Francophone culinary cosmos. Of local spices, I know as much that the occasional pinch of pepper may go into a *sauce béchamelle*, whilst *le curry poudre* is added cautiously to their aromatic palette that is more reserved than Latinate people's in general. They rely more on herbs to collude with the innate sapidity of raw materials or as the *bons mots* go, 'cabbage soup should taste of cabbage', which obviously no Indian diner would agree with.

Nevertheless, the *Larousse Gastronomique* encyclopaedia contains unthinkable 'Indian' dishes such as *cari de poulet* (chicken curry with ham!) and *choux de bruxelles à l'Indienne* which translates as 'Brussels sprouts moistened with curry sauce'! In this context, it is noteworthy that they are the only ones to ever have proposed a law to regulate curry: Apparently in the 1880s it was decided that curry powder must be mild and cannot contain more than 1.7 per cent pepper! Primarily, this weak blend is used when stale leftovers need a makeover. Today, a beloved spice mixture goes by the name of *vadouvan* adapted from Tamilan vadavams (sun-dried masala balls) they came across in south India, to make mildly Indian-flavoured soups, seafood preparations and, especially, duck stews.

Part of a bas-relief based on M. Mukundan's novel *On the Banks of the Mayyazhi.*

Although turkeys don't originate east of Turkey, but are American, they were christened *dinde* which stems from *coq d'Inde*, 'Indian cock', demonstrating how mixed-up the lingua franca is—if you pardon my French. Yet it shouldn't be forgotten that in other colonies, Creole connoisseurship gave birth to *rasson*, a rum-spiked savoury soup clearly derived from South Indian rasam which colonial adventurers carried with them to the Americas. In fact, many bars south of the Vindhya Hills serve a shot of rasam alongside drinks so the pairing isn't as crazy as it seems.[18]

Between meals, I watch the slow action at a laidback harbour where fisherfolks mend nets and check out a rustic temple complex notable for Mahatma Gandhi having visited it in 1934, telling the people that 'whether it is French India or

British India it is one and the same country. The same blood flows through my veins that goes through yours, the same soil, the same atmosphere, the same manners and customs and many things too numerous to mention are common to all of us. But for the difference in the uniform of your police and the French language I read here and there I would notice no difference whatsoever.'

At Tagore Park, an open-air bas-relief depicts the plot of a Malayalam novel on colonial tribulations—*On the Banks of the Mayyazhi* by local author M. Mukundan—set when streets still had names like Rue de I'Eglise and Rue de la Residence, and where the 'half-French would continue to play a role in the life of Mayyazhi, but they were never to achieve the same measure of greatness and nobility. Poverty and its attendant evils were to force them to lead mean lives. Beggars and prostitutes were to be born amongst them.' Speaking of fiction, my next stop is the riverside Le Café in the hopes of sampling something like a *café au lait* with a Proustian madeleine cake to bolster my mental faculties. But they have none of that, no turkeys *à la Cordon Bleu* either—no, they only serve Indian filter-coffee along with tapioca fritters. These are tasty though: kappa or cassava as it is also called, is a regional staple also eaten as chips or as mash—but seem like a completely fictive Continental café snack. It's another matter that in reality Marcel Proust didn't eat the madeleine either, though he propelled it to worldwide fame in his autobiographical novel, *Remembrance of Things Past*, but he rather gnawed on dry rusk that inspired him to write the immortal passage on how memories are triggered—'No sooner had the warm liquid mixed with the crumbs touched my palate than a shudder ran through me and I stopped, intent upon the extraordinary thing that was happening to me.' Personally, I get a bigger kick out of mashed tapioca drowning in something fishy.

The town's self-appointed patisserie on Railway Station Road is merely another typical bakery-cum-cakery, which offers no baguette (the elongated breads that Napoleon supposedly designed thus so that his soldiers could carry their lunch in their pant legs—not true), nor *brioche* (that Marie Antoinette suggested the starving plebeians should eat before getting herself guillotined—true). I'm ready to give up my frenzied search for Romantic flavours when I come across the cool diner Café Eiffel (near Tagore Park), which has quotes by Napoleon on the walls and where I munch on a halal chicken cheeseburger and, what else, French fries?

And thanks to having been part of France until 1954, Mahe follows different excise and licensing regulations, hence the bars offer tremendous value even if some resemble Dickensian nightmares: Drinks are sold at Maximum Retail Price though sometimes a nominal 10 per cent is added if one elects to sit in their dining halls, where snacks include fresh prawns fried golden—in what else but coconut oil?—or plump mussels pan-seared with onion, chilli, coconut chunks and curry leaves. Everything is uniformly mouth-watering.

Bar-hopping classics include Cee Cee's in an oldish bungalow with a huge kitchen and the day's almost-alive catch hiccupping in a well-lit fridge, but I personally prefer to frolic at the Foreign Liquor Palace which, despite its name, has no *château*-trained sommeliers on duty. But it's a friendly enough dive towering right by the Mahe Bridge with priceless views all the way to the azure-coloured Arabian Sea. The banter is good-humoured in a slurry mix of Malayalam and another language that might be English, only occasionally getting semi-aggressive. Within moments of the first sign of belligerence, a drunkard stomps over and says, 'Sorry.'

I say, 'Okay.'

He says, 'No problem?'

I repeat, 'No problem.'

Then he says, 'Nice to have met.'

That's French manners in Kerala for you. Chilling totally, I ask for another super-strong beer and watch the sun slowly set over the Mayyazhi River estuary (jokingly known as the English Channel). However, barflies should be aware that Mahe gets sleepy by 9.30 p.m., so last orders are served at 9.23 p.m., giving drunks approximately seven minutes to drink up that final beer before doors shut. On the other hand, they open early, so the party restarts with wet breakfasts at 9 a.m. Stepping out at 10 a.m., I run into mildly inebriated gents who beg for money to pursue sunrise binges. I suggest to them that coffee might be healthier at such an hour.

A couple of kilometres further up the coast, my feast continues as I get my first kick right after stepping off the bus plying on National Highway-17. I've been in Thalassery (once anglicised as Tellicherry), for approximately three minutes and am already having a salivating seafood experience.

The Shabna Tea Stall isn't the world's fanciest café, but they do 'stuffed mussel' or ari-kadukka which is the town's #1 snack. Best described as a shellfish married to a plump idli, the whole mussel is first filled with rice paste and steamed, then the resulting cake is pried out of the shell and fried with various spice powders.

What a miracle! I have two. Then three. All washed down with oversweet instant coffee. After checking into a room with a balcony at the Paris Presidency, which is part of the Paris Restaurant founded in 1942 bang in the centre of town, I find that it has over the years branched out into four establishments—all standing side by side in Logans Road. Skipping the fancy 'multycousine' section, I track down the original in a heritage building around the corner, at the back, which used to house one of Kerala's first newspaper printing presses a long time ago. There's no proper menu card but it is always crowded, open from morning to early evening, dishing out snacks and meals at a laidback pace.

Despite its name, there's again nothing French about the cuisine at Paris. I guess it's called so because it is 10 km north of Mahe, so the nominal theme is continued just like that only. For starters, I sample their trademark light and fragrant Thalassery fish biryani. It too testifies to the influence of Arabs, but more than merely a mutation of something alien, this biryani is an artwork in itself. Made using short-grained rice that grows in the region, it reminds one of ghee rice but it has actually been baked in a sealed container before getting wedded to the separately cooked aikora whitefish, that translates into 'Indo-Pacific king mackerel'.

I end up ordering lots of this particular fish—curried, fried or any other way it is available—and each time, the result is magnificent. But even if I seem to have discovered the world's tastiest fish, to tell you the truth, I've really come to eat fresh mussels. Having been born and brought up in Scandinavia where mussels are eaten as a snack, in soups, steamed or stewed, in pastas and on pizzas, yes, as practically everything but dessert—I had been for years dreaming of Thalassery, after being told by a couple of Malayalis I once met on a train, that the town is the major mussel fishing port of India. I've never heard anybody rave so much about the delicious kallumakkai (as they call mussels), as those two did, so I added a mental note to my must-go list.

It strikes me as I stroll in Thalassery that two millennia ago Europeans called shellfish *thalassa*—peculiarly enough it's a Greek word meaning, variously, 'ocean' in general, 'seafood' in particular, and it invokes the goddess of the oceans whose name coincidentally also was Thalassa. That gluttonous gourmand of antiquity, Apicius, devoted a full chapter called *Thalassa* to the enjoyment of shellfish in his pioneering *De re coquinaria*, Europe's first known gourmet cookbook commonly dated to the first century. In it, he described how to fry scallions lightly with crushed pepper (imported from Kerala, naturally) or oysters seasoned with pepper and cinnamon, or mussels cooked with ajowan, cumin, mint, pepper and something called malabathrum—the identity of which remained a mystery for the longest time. According to Pliny the Elder, Rome's leading expert on natural science, this was a 'most esteemed' herb with a scent 'superior to any other' and its name indicates that it was imported from Malabar. It is believed to be what we today call tejpat, i.e. cassia, a fairly common ingredient in Indian cooking, but which the Romans willingly paid through their noses for. Anyway, without attempting any too complicated guesswork, the town's name is surprisingly apt, so much that even a mummified Roman mariner might find himself quite at home in Thalassery's kitchens.

Out of the 7,500 tons of green mussels harvested annually in north Kerala, this town is one of the top producers of 'edible bivalve' as these are scientifically labelled. The harvesting is done manually with 'pickers' going out daily in rickety boats to the mussel beds during the season that lasts from September to June, diving as deep as ten metres to scrape shellfish off the rocks where they like to plant themselves. Hence the Malayalam name for mussels—'the fruit on the rock' or kallumakkai.

After lunch, I'm gallivanting on the beach in the hope of seeing my favourite shellfish in its fresh, pre-cooked state. On the way there, I did browse for pickles and condiments in a supermarket at Harbour City Mall, the only shopping complex in sight. They stock seafood pickles, but there are no preserved mussels available. Pepper is another thing to shop for—in Europe the classiest type of pepper is still branded 'Tellicherry Black' even if the godowns of Thalassery, that traditionally supplied this spice to the world, now appear abandoned. (The ancient pepper warehouse in Rome, too, is long gone. I found just a few bricks remaining of it at the Forum, but it was once the perhaps most important building in the city, where pepper was kept

The world's freshest mussels for sale in Thalassery.

under tight security and sold as if it was silver or gold.) Today, foreign buyers bypass Thalassery and do business directly with planters in the hill districts—or buy from countries that produce cheaper but less aromatic pepper, like Indonesia, Malaysia and Vietnam. At the mall, I also chanced upon the Mambally's Royal

Biscuit Factory outlet which practically invented the plum cake in its Indian avatar in 1883 to supply a British spice planter who missed English cakes. Only slightly paradoxically, it was made with French-imported brandy from the colonial competitors in Mahe (maybe as a soft rebellion against British colonialism?). They still bake the same cake though I'm not sure about the brandy's nationality, but it ranks as perhaps the best I've eaten—moist, rich and toothsome.

The fish market is situated right behind the mall where, in the alley leading down to it, geezers sell live mussels out of straw baskets. Seeing those heaps of black-shelled treasures, I'm ready to relocate to Thalassery instantly. A few steps later, I spot the colonial pier at which spice ships docked to pick up pepper and cardamom. Somewhere very near it, the English factory with its godowns and residence of the supervisor, opened in 1683 to facilitate exports. Travel was slower then, so dry items with long shelf lives, like spices, were the ideal trade goods. The boats coasted along the seashore, anchoring at night to catch fish for dinner—but it was no luxury cruise, because apart from abundant fresh seafood, passengers had to carry their own supplies, utensils and bedding. To sail from northern Kerala in say, the 1800s, to what was then Bombay took ten days—and to think that now Mumbai is just a nineteen-hour train ride away.

As per nineteenth-century accounts, there weren't many roads leading into the interior from the ports. Most people trekked through the jungle. Provided that there was some semblance of a track, those who could afford it journeyed by bullock carts—but the bullocks hade to be changed every five miles (i.e. hourly) which made it a slow mode of transport—or somewhat classier two-wheeled carriages known as 'nibs' that were 'waterproof, with Venetians and glass windows'. If the path was very narrow a *manshiel* would have to do, 'a kind of open-sided cot slung to a bamboo pole which projects far enough in front and rear to be placed with ease on the shoulders of the bearers. Four of these men are brought into play at once, while four others run along to relieve their fellows at intervals.' By this latter method one covered 80 km in a day and crossing from Kerala into Karnataka, where much of the cardamom and pepper grew in the hills and jungles, took at least two days—what is now a bus journey of mere hours. And it was brought home to me how arduous travel must have been the time I trekked across the mountainous border on jungle paths: although the forest rangers warned about tigers and wild elephants, pointing out fearfully big pugmarks and so-called 'elephant laddus' (cannon ball-sized poop balls deposited by pachyderms), the worst part for me was falling off the steep track into thorny bushes and cracking four toes. And at the end of the day, I pulled some thirty or forty saturated leeches out of my socks.

Uphill from the old pier stands the 1708 CE fort with an 1830s' lighthouse staring forlornly out to sea. Today, the Brits have been replaced by courting couples whispering sweet nothings, the chicks suitably impressed when dudes boast about future sports careers abroad. Coincidentally this was a base for Arthur Wellesley, the future Duke of Wellington who is frequently credited with having introduced cricket to Kerala—of which there's no conclusive evidence; historians I've spoken with suggest that there may already have been a cricket club or at least a sports ground in existence when Wellesley arrived. Also, he allegedly taught the game to local dhobis, but the first solid evidence of Indians playing cricket in Thalassery stems from some half a century later—therefore all one can say for sure is that the town has been the national sport's Mecca for less than two centuries. Despite having been a heavy-gambling booze-hound in his youth, Wellesley shaped up here and probably lived in what is still known as the Wellesley Bungalow, strategically situated between the fort and the town's cricket pitch. Fighting wars against Tipu Sultan gave him a reputation for being a great strategist—indeed, after returning to England in 1805, he crowned his career by defeating Napoleon at Waterloo. As a gastronomic footnote, he is said to have introduced cocktail cherries to India and his last act was to posthumously lend his name to the pie-like dish known as 'Beef Wellington' which he, weirdly, had nothing to do with (the earliest recipes appear circa 1900). Yet it is possible that he enjoyed a comparable dish here, maybe a kheema dosa, without calling it by any specific name.

Not quite ready to give up my quest for shellfish, I spend the next few days hunting for more mussels in Thalassery. I try the Rara Avis on Logans Road, a fashionable dining option recommended to me by a fisherman no less, but the sad truth is that they make creamy fish molee (with aikora) and soft but firm elegantly bowl-shaped appams fried until the surface gets perfectly crispy…but their kallumakkai dry-fry is done to death.

Then I find the Jubilee Hotel (opposite Old Bus Stand) that celebrates 'the traditional Malabari foods' and rejects the use of MSG or food colouring. The shallow-fried prawns are perfectly executed, but their mussel biryani is made with sadly departed shreds of overkilled shellfish. Not sure who to blame, except myself, when I experience an intestinal catastrophe in the middle of the night, I brush it aside as the price any glutton must pay on occasion.

Things improve at Hotel Adithya Non-Veg which is a steamy joint located by the fort entrance, actually featuring a colourful photograph of mussels on the wall. After I've explicitly explained that I'm not interested in anything cooked in a murderous manner, they rustle up parathas and the very best avial I've had, with lots of diced carrot, chopped drumsticks and beans, sliced plantain, yams and other veggies soaked in mild coconut milk, that perfectly complements a big wok of mussels in spicy gravy.

To properly identity what I've eaten, I ask the waiter, 'What do you call this lovely mussel dish?'

He beams at me and exclaims, 'We call it *Ma-Sa-La*.'

I imprint that on my mind. According to online sources, Mosons Pickle Factory some distance northeast of town, bottles a mussels and dates mixture under its Beevi's brand. My rickshaw drives me to the sleepy Palayad Industrial Estate, and we go in circles until I catch the strong smell of vinegar wafting through the palm trees. It turns out that Mosons doesn't officially receive visitors and there is no such thing as a guided tour, but I buy a bagful of jars with pickled mussels, squid and prawns at wholesale rates. Their stickers say 'Spicy' and I am happy to report that they're correctly labelled—even a tiny sampling sets my nose hairs fuming.

Nearby stands a nineteenth-century bungalow with shaded verandas and a roof of Mangaluru tiles. It is listed as one of the few attractions worth visiting in Thalassery, so I dutifully check it out, only to find that the bungalow is in use as a technical school. To enter the campus requires taking a written permission from the principal. In the compound, the students sit under shady trees and look at me as if I'm some weirdo tourist. Which I obviously am.

It's name is Gundert Bungalow and on its veranda wall hangs a painted caricature of a bearded foreigner, presumably Mr Gundert himself. Suddenly I recall how, in the centre of town on Gundert Road, there's a prominent statue of the selfsame personality.

This encounter with memories of Hermann Gundert—a German who played a significant role in Kerala's cultural development—sets off the strangest chain of associations in my spiced-up brain. It has to do with heavy metal and how that term came to be coupled with a particular form of Western music. And in a way, it all started in Kerala about 175 years ago, when the mother of one of Europe's greatest Nobel Prize winners was born in these parts.

En route to Calcutta in the 1830s, the missionary Gundert fell so much in love with south India that he decided to skip Calcutta and stay put. He ran a school on the porch of this bungalow and when not busy teaching, invited pundits to discuss Indian matters. In the process, he learnt Malayalam fluently enough to become a rather influential writer in the language, publishing a grammar and the first proper dictionary. He was also involved in local language newspapers. Furthermore, Gundert introduced the German model of gymnastics, which is why Thalassery is known today as the home of the best acrobats and circus artistes in India (logically, the bestselling writer John Irving's novel *A Son of the Circus* opens here). All this led to Gundert's appointment as inspector of schools, overseeing an area covering most of Kerala and much of present-day Karnataka as well.

Living in India, Gundert got hitched to a fellow continental European lady from nearby Mahe, and in 1842 they had a daughter named Marie. After the family moved back to Germany due to health reasons, their daughter in turn married a Herr Hesse and gave birth to Gundert's grandson who was also christened Hermann. Little Hermann had free access to grandpa Hermann's vast library, which contained many books on and from India. He was fifteen when grandpa passed away in 1893, which was also the year junior Hesse had his first rebellious drinks and smokes. He had by then gone through a somewhat sad period at the seminary he studied at—he was supposed to become a missionary like his elder namesake, but ended up a manic-depressive misfit who tried to commit suicide. After a stint in a mental asylum, he took a job as a bookshop clerk in the German town of Tübingen (in whose university, incidentally, Gundert's collection of manuscripts from Kerala is housed). He chucked it up at the age of twenty-seven when his first novel was published. What would become his biggest blockbuster appeared in 1927, the year he turned fifty: *Der Steppenwolf.* Some twenty years later, Hermann Hesse was awarded the Nobel Prize for Literature.

One of the main streets in Thalassery is named after German Nobel Prize laureate Hermann Hesse's grand-father.

A Californian hard rock group of the 1960s named itself Steppenwolf after Hesse's novel. The singer John Kay hailed from Germany but wasn't—as far as I know—related to Hesse, except perhaps in a metaphysical way. Hesse's magnum opus was, in those days, gaining the status of a hippie 'Bible' due to its hallucinatory passages that were good to read as one puffed on a spliff, gnawed on peyote and dropped acid, and so it struck the band as a perfect replacement for their much lamer original name, The Sparrows. In 1968, Steppenwolf released their third single on which Kay sang about riding a motorcycle and the 'heavy metal thunder' it made. The song was called 'Born to be Wild' and it went on to become the biggest ever riff-based rock superhit—partly because it featured on the soundtrack of the LSD-infused low-budget road movie *Easy Rider* starring Dennis Hopper, Peter Fonda and Jack Nicholson. And so, in one stroke were born the new musical sound known today as 'heavy metal' and the cinematic genre called 'road movie'.

As a teenager, I was heavily into Steppenwolf and their brand of psychedelic hard rock, so it was the music that led me to read *Der Steppenwolf* and its account of mental self-realisation. And now, many years later, I'm probing Hesse's intellectual roots in this small fishing port. The writer did, before World War I, undertake a journey towards Kerala to trace his own 'Indian' background. Unfortunately, he caught a stomach bug and suffered from heat stroke—the tropics were too much for him—so upon reaching Colombo he took the next available boat back home, without ever setting foot on Indian soil or snapping selfies (like I do) before his grandfather's bungalow. Furthermore, he had met impoverished Hindus and Muslims on the journey and was very upset at the subjugation of Indians under British rule. Yet he was taken by Indian philosophical ideas, which made him write the Buddhism-influenced novella *Siddhartha* some ten years later (and its 1970s film adaptation was shot in Rishikesh and Rajasthan—places the Buddha never visited—by Ingmar Bergman's ace cinematographer Sven Nykvist, with Shashi Kapoor starring as the Buddha).

Personally, I'm quite Buddhistic and never bothered with stomach bugs as long as they bugger off soon enough, so despite already spending one night spewing my guts out, as

I mentioned a few pages back, my seafoodish quest goes on. Hoping to have my karma fulfilled, I ask one waiter where to sample authentic fare. He says knowledgeably, 'You must eat in "kallu-shaaps". They serve the best. Avoid the "shaap" to the south of town, because they mix chemicals in their toddy. Only go to the one on the north side.'

'Kallu' is the Malayalam word for toddy and 'shaaps' were, as the esteemed reader recalls, already explored during my stay in Kozhikode, but this one is said to be the 'shaap of shaaps' in the whole of Kerala.

'Address to tell auto driver?'

'Pen drive!' he exclaims.

I'm sure he's pulling my leg, but later sipping on a musk melon juice in a fancy café, the owner's friend, a knowledgeable chap, sidles up and asks me if I am *that* food writer. I admit I might be 'that one'. He mentions some article I wrote about Kerala ages ago and introduces himself as Biju Aravind—tourism consultant who hopes to put Thalassery on the map. I ask him about a toddy shop called 'pen drive' and it turns out to be well known to him.

'Yes,' he corrects me, 'Pinarayi has the best toddy shop. I'll take you there for lunch.'

So, the next day we meet at the apparels showroom where he's a managing partner and drive 7 km north of town towards Pinarayi, to where the road follows the broad Anjarakkandi River through a hamlet called Kaliyil. A fish stall stands on the riverbank among scattered oyster shells and facing it is a sight for sore eyes—namely the Model Toddy Parlour, an unpretentious whitewashed establishment with a prominent 'non-smoking' sign outside. The interiors are squeaky-clean, airy and—at least in the daytime—very bright.

It's an extremely picturesque location for a bar. The kind

you'd want to spend your life in—like the other customers seem to be doing. Even if it is rather early on a Monday the shack is full of dining drunkards. There's no menu as such but to check what's cooking, we peek into the kitchen where a multitasking lady attends to pots of boiling fish curry, squid 'koonthal' masala and mashed kappa—the typical well-seasoned tapioca purée that goes nicely with fiery curries. We order plates of everything from the bare-chested mundu-clad attendant. The ubiquitous mundu is a national dress for gentlemen in Kerala, akin to the kilt of Scotsmen, and being made of light cotton it provides air-cooling for body parts that shall not be mentioned in a proper book like this.

In another chamber, a huge clay pot is filled to the brim with frothy kallu. I have been sampling toddy before, but this is certainly the best—if toddy was champagne, this would be its Dom Pérignon and I would, after a few bottles, be James Bond. I'm told that the luxurious beverage is harvested every morning at 4.30 a.m. by expert toddy-tappers. Apparently, the toddy industry gives employment to over 50,000 people and if all 'shaaps' were like this Model Toddy Parlour then it should be a good thing—for despite alcoholism being injurious to health (or so they say), the 100 per cent naturally fermented and soothing palm-wine seems to be an organic alternative to industrially distilled hard liquor. More like wholesome sweet-sour buttermilk than booze, it is merely mildly intoxicating, complementing the sizzling seafood perfectly as it moderates its spiciness—tawa-roasted prawns redolent with coconut oil and curry leaves, squid in explosively peppery gravy and tangy fish curry. The zing makes me finish the toddy quickly and so we order more bottles, until life feels unbelievably wonderful.

Before I leave town with my knapsack full of pickle jars, I hit two or three bakeries to parcel ari-kadukka and chemmeen unda—rice-stuffed mussels and prawn-stuffed rice balls—for the road. At the bus stand, as I'm ready to board the '7.1 digital LED smoke effect laser show bus' to my next destination, a drunkard comes up and stares incredulously, as if he can't believe my stupidity: 'Are you leaving?'

I don't know him from Jack O'Bedlam, but he acts as if we're buddies. Is he perhaps one of the 'happy to meet you' guys in one of the bars I've tried out? I say, 'I'm so sorry, but I am.' I'm wondering whether I ought to explain that it is part of my job as a travel writer to always move on. But he merely waves sadly as he tightens his mundu which is on half mast, and says: 'Please come back again soon.'

From here, I'm on my way to Kannur, about an hour's bus ride from Thalassery, and if one googles for grub there one will get many hits on a particular Internet-viral lunch-only canteen called Odhen's, with rapturous rants about the most unbelievably marvellous fish meals.

Furthermore, the prosperous town recently got its own airport and is expected to become the next great tourist hotspot of 'God's own country', although at first glance it looks more like one big shopping mall, like a suburb of Dubai. As it is too early for lunch, I have brunch at the renowned MRA Bakery (Station Road, next to Kannur junction), often suggested as the second-best option if one can't get a table at the fabled Odhen's. Unlike Odhen's, it's open from morning to evening and turns out to be a huge air-conditioned complex with a bakery and confectionary taking up the ground floor, and a vast dining hall upstairs. So, not exactly your standard neighbourhood cake shop.

Characteristically for morning meals in Kerala, there's mulakittath, a violently chilli-red but unexpectedly silky fish curry served with appams, those deadly-yummy pancakes that

I am already thoroughly addicted to. I must refrain from also ordering avial, that lovely coconut-milky veggie stew, as I plan to demolish a lavish lunch two hours later. But I do gorge on their nutty baklava—the best I've come across outside Turkey (the Topkapi Palace kitchen of Istanbul is the native place of baklava though many other parts of Turkey will also claim it as their own) and these are just perfectly flaky, buttery, cardamommy, creamy, cinnamony bite-sized pastries soaked in honey syrup and topped with shredded pistachios. I buy a boxful in case I get peckish.

To rebuild my appetite, I catch a rickshaw to Fort Saint Angelo (a.k.a. 'Kannur Kotta'), situated at the end of a road lined with old colonial churches and cemeteries, about 3 km from the centre. It guards the Mappila Bay with its fish market, which supplies the freshest catch to kitchens in town. The fort is a tranquil spot to roam around in, across manicured lawns, and I skip a museum that anyway seems permanently shut, but trace the cannon-studded red lateritic walls facing the Lakshadweep Sea. This was, namely, established as a Portuguese factory in circa 1500 CE and everything could have proceeded peacefully, if it wasn't for Vasco da Gama. Unhappy with the trading deal the raja offered, da Gama belligerently fortified the site with a palisade and stationed 200 soldiers here to terrorise the populace. Luckily, the Dutch captured the fort in 1663 and initiated cordial relationships with the royal family to whom they eventually sold it. But less than two decades later, power-hungry Britons stole the fort and made it their chief military base in Kerala. So, the eclectic architecture blends Portuguese with Dutch and British elements—including an eye-grabbing skull-and-cross-bone decorated tombstone set in the wall commemorating the Dutch commander's wife Susanna, who died here in the 1700s, aged only seventeen and a half years.

As soon as its staff deem it fit to let in tourists, I check out the comparatively dull Arakkalkettu Museum. It is situated within a cannon shot's distance from the fort in a royal durbar hall by the fishing harbour, but there's hardly anything worth seeing except blurry Xeroxes of faded documents, dusty daggers, vintage telephones and random furnishings. The walls are studded with stern signs yelling, 'Do not touch the antics.' How I wish I had experienced some antics!

Yet I can't avoid imagining an adventurous past when the medieval Moroccan globetrotter Ibn Battuta—pioneer among travel writers—in the 1340s sat in one of the chairs on display, perhaps used one of the antique telephones to phone home (like ET, you know) for some Moroccan takeaway, as he munched on spice-laden Malayali food and gossiped with the lord of the house who owned a fleet that sailed to Oman and Yemen; 'one of the most powerful sultans', noted Battuta of him. South of town, Battuta visited orchards crammed with coconut trees, pepper creepers, and as for bananas, 'never have I seen any place in which they are more numerous or cheaper.' He sampled many different varieties here.

The food-obsessed Battuta also gave an account of a feast served to him further up the coast in Honavar, in present-day Karnataka, where he found the men peaceful and women uncommonly handsome. The food was served to him on a plate 'which they call *ṭālam* [i.e. thali]. A beautiful slave, clad in silk, comes and causes to be placed before the prince saucepans containing the food. She has a large spoon of copper with which she takes a spoonful of rice and serves it on the plate; she pours ghee on it, and places some pickled pepper in bunches, green ginger, and pickled lemons and mangoes.' The mango, coincidentally, is said to be one of the main reasons why so many Muslims travelled to India from abroad, including—it is claimed—Babur who was so enamoured by Indian mangoes, that he thought it necessary to father the Mughal dynasty.

As Battuta tucked in, a curried fowl was brought out, followed by 'another species of fowl' and then even more, in an endless stream of delicacies. 'When the different kinds of fowl have been done with, there follow diverse sorts of fish and more rice with them. After the fish, they serve vegetables cooked in butter, and milk foods, also taken with rice.' Eventually, the royal repast is rounded off with buttermilk!

Feeling envy over the royal treats Battuta savoured, I feel it's time to head to Odhen's, named after renowned restaurateur Othenan whose sons nowadays run the canteen, which is counter-intuitively pronounced as 'Onden' locally. In fact, it's such a landmark that the road it is located at is known as Onden Road. Whatever one does, one is advised not to reach any later than 12.15 p.m. as the food will invariably run out quickly (they stay open only until 3.30 p.m.; Sundays closed). Latecomers end up queuing endlessly in the sweltering heat, though if one doesn't get a seat one may instead check out another nearby attraction: Room #309 at the Hotel Blue Nile. Just around the block, it's been preserved as a shrine in memory of footballer Diego Maradona's 2012 visit, with everything intact as he left it—including the prawn shells from his supper! But at twelve o'clock there are still empty tables and I quickly grab a stool. Gents and ladies sit waiting in expectant silence, facing the kitchen from where a thick fume of coconut oil bursts into the hall. The atmosphere is that of a temple moments before the theyyam dancer takes the stage.

As if on cue, the first waiter waltzes in, handing out banana leaves to one and all. In his footsteps tap-dances the rice man with a cauldron of 'boil rice', the typically plump reddish grain that is preferred in Kerala, dishing out a huge scoop on each leaf in a choreographed manner as the patrons carry on the ceremonial routine by patting the rice down into circular discs. This is followed by the meals man who, using his ladle as if it were a flamenco dancer's wooden castanet, apportions out the set lunch of sambar—a more veggie-rich Kerala variety of the southern standard curry—and dry vegetable pooriyal, plus ladles of mathi (sardine) curry, cucumber-curd pachhadi (a lightly cooked version of raita) and pickles. Finally comes the senior waiter, who performs a most seductive belly dance with his tray sumptuously weighed down by the seafoods of the day. I pick their incredibly attractive bread-crumbed aikora fillet (my darling kingfish), koonthal (squid fry), and chemmeen (prawns) shallow fried with crumbly peppery coating. As usual, the rich coconut oil lends the meal a uniquely sweetish note, reminiscent of hair oil perhaps, which may be an acquired taste but I do find it irresistible. The meal goes well together with a steel tumbler of hot kanji vellam, watery rice gruel drunk as stomach-calming soup on the side.[19] By the time I go to wash my hands, another fellow gastronome is already claiming my seat even before the banana leaf is cleared away.

IV

Tamil Tuck, Deccan Dining and Goan Grog (Circumambulations in South India)

'He is a good companion who enjoys dining with ordinary people.'

—*Purananuru*, lyrical Tamil anthology compiled between first and third centuries CE

Andhra coast

In the morning, I get off the train at Tiruppur, a nondescript town on the Tamil side of the Ghat Mountains. It's at the heart of the cotton-growing Kongu Nadu region which encompasses much of north-western Tamil Nadu. Pankaj Mishra, the only other travel writer to have written about the town (as far as I know), dismissed it as being 'to underwear what Sivakasi was to firecrackers' in a couple of hours—and as few pages—in his celebrated 1990s' travelogue *Butter Chicken in Ludhiana*, before scuttling onto a bus for Kerala.

True, it's one of those places where no tourists go, there's virtually no information online, no guidebook recommends it, my trusty TTK road guide only knows it as 'famous for hosiery products' and it never occurs to my bucket-listing friends, who go fashion hunting in New York or Paris, to stop for shopping in the original 'Banian City' where export surplus showrooms line the streets—and they have chic names like Homme & Femme or Tee Totaller—interspersed with low-budget business lodges, which I guess is Tiruppur in a nutshell.

An epic cyclone hits town in the afternoon—which is odd, since the area is known to be extremely arid, its river a mere trickle of sluggish textile factory goo. The deluge brings everything to a standstill as 47 mm of rainfall in an hour turns streets into interconnected jacuzzis, fells over 100 electricity poles and uproots 200 trees. Luckily the main street features several congenial dives that I can seek refuge in and jolly staff plies me not only with beer, but treat me to complimentary snacks too—which seems to be the hallmark of home-grown bar culture. For every bottle I order, I get fruit salad, handfuls of peanuts and a namkeen platter with puffed rice in large enough quantities to constitute a fulfilling meal.

Suddenly I feel at home, which is quite different from the vibe I got when I stepped off the train that morning. For a fraction of a second I felt almost like Mr Mishra asking myself what I could possibly expect to experience by way of excitement, perhaps I too should simply move on—the smallness of the station made me suspect this was going to be the back of the beyond of the boondocks. But before the question took on an existentialistically defeatist overtone, I spotted a restaurant, Junior Kuppanna, right behind the station, whose reputation for serving authentic Kongu food I had come across. The spacious eatery was empty but clean, a smiling and polite waiter invited me to sit, the kitchen turned out to be ready to feed me even at that early hour despite me being the only guest.

I ate a soulfully rustic mutton pallipalayam—a dry-fry item named after the tiny town Pallipalayam from whence the recipe originates—which is possibly one of the most unique Indian non-veg dishes as it's cooked without oil, instead, relying on the meat juice seeping out from chunky love-me-tender-love-me-true-mutton, seasoned with chillies, diced coconut, shallots, onions and garlic. I just love having dinner in the morning. Further thrills are caused by the simple fact that here in Kongu Nadu, unlike everywhere else, meat isn't necessarily marinated but cooked as is—preserving its meatiness—and it seems as if all ingredients have more texture, and are more natural.

Besides, India's sweetest coconuts grow in Kongu Nadu, around the town of Pollachi, and they do their usual trick of balancing the spicing. In the first minutes of my Tiruppur sojourn, I gobbled up the pallipalayam along with a stack of Erode-style dosas that are fluffy like appams from the top but crisp-fried underneath, and afterwards I just had to order the fêted egg preparation kalakki—a poached omelette with a silky smooth inner core. I decide to stay on and eat my way through town.

The original Senior Kuppanna was founded over sixty years ago in Erode, another smallish place some 50 km away, distinguished as the world's turmeric capital, the largest producer and trader of the GI-tagged spice since Vedic days. Hence nicknamed 'Yellow City'. From there, Senior Kuppanna spread its tempting tentacles by specialising in Kongu non-veg favourites to thirty-plus branches that by logic all carry the name Junior Kuppanna. But while foodaholics go gaga over Pondicherry's flamboyant Creole-cookery served up in stylish *maisons*, and scorching Chettinadian non-veg which may appear to resemble Kongunadian food but uses way more chillies, and the meaty biryanis of Dindigul and the legendary biryanis of Ambur that are said to follow the personal cookbook of the Nawab of Arcot, comparatively few hedonists are familiar with the cuisine of Kongu, despite it having deep roots in the Sangam age. By the way, Kongu Nadu isn't officially a place—not a district or a state, but it has always had its own identity as a heartland of sorts in Tamil Nadu.

Apart from Tiruppur and Erode, the region also encompasses the coffee-growing district of Salem, the ancient capital Karur, Pollachi that links Tamil Nadu across a mountain pass with Kerala's Palakkad and the heavily industrialised Coimbatore, renowned for its heavy-duty wet-grinders. Intriguingly enough, archaeologists have found traces of foodstuffs corresponding to modern eating habits during excavations—remains of rice, pulses and millets—hinting that culinary culture has remained intact since forever. The many kinds of millets that are still eaten today—like ragi, bajra and jowar—make for robust food,

Coconut is very important in Kongu Nadu.

rooted in the soil so to speak, as already in the Sangam age these were staples. So we may say that Kongu Nadu's discreet food is genuinely time-tested.

Kongu has always been arid, hence farming methods developed with mixed cultivation so as not to drain the soil of its nutrients, and the main crops are such that thrive on less water. Irrigation channels from thousands of years ago are still in use. Textual sources too list indigenous ingredients that thrive in the dry climate. These comprise, for example, sesame (*Sesamum indicum*) and its oil, known here as gingelly, sought after since Harappan days and exported to the ancient Greeks as it happens to be one of the first cooking oils produced by humans. Sesame seeds are also popular, though coconut is evidently the #1 ingredient—it stars in pretty much every meal in one avatar or the other. Also, as mentioned, plenty of pungent turmeric grows in the area without which curry would hardly look like itself. India produces and consumes almost all the turmeric in the world. Turmeric is very good for health as it can prevent infectious diseases and hence it is frequently tagged as a panacea, an all-healing super-food, and interestingly, the early Buddhists used it to colour their robes. But in Kongu Nadu, the rhizome is treated in atypical ways, such as grated fresh and then roasted, before it's ground and used in cooking.

Edible heritage apart, I spend time and money on bargain shopping in India's top garment manufacturing hub. In an average year, Tiruppur exports about Rs 275 billion worth of knitwear or half of India's total and a fair part of that ends up as surplus—which makes it the perfect shopping destination for anybody wishing to renew one's wardrobe. I mean, why fly to foreign fashion capitals to dress up, when everything is made right here anyway? At any point of time, garment importers from scores of countries are shopping about in the thousands of manufacturing units that employ half a million labourers to produce knitwear, innerwear and sportswear for the likes of Yankee brand Ralph Lauren, classic Levi's, trendy Scandinavian H&M, dowdy Marks & Spencer of the UK and youthful international fashion house Diesel. So when not eating, I browse factory outlets, export reject godowns and cut-rate fashion emporiums where couture can be bought for a pittance.

After shopping and feeling well-dressed, I get hungry again and head for Kongu Mess, a promising name that shows up on my GPS. When I get to the location, nobody's heard of any mess or Kongu specialities to be eaten so to cut a long story short, I end up at Junior Kuppanna again. With tempting options bearing names like 'naadu chicken gravy' and 'leg piece fry' and 'boneless chukka' and 'brain fry' and 'mutton kola urundal 5pcs' and 'kaadai roast' which isn't a roasted wok (like one might think) but quail...I wish I could order everything but eventually settle down to do justice to a mesmerisingly sublime atavistic mutton curry or so-called kuzhambu that has a delicately lingering tinge of freshly-ground black pepper. I eat it with veechu parathas that turn out not to be at all like the Kerala parathas I've been having lots of lately, but eggishly-egging translucent versions of rumali rotis folded like a postal letter. Except they have no stamp.

The next day I'm determined to find more unusual food and discuss my mission with people who look at me kind of strangely, as if I'm David Bowie in his *Ziggy* Stardust phase, asking me: 'You want north Indian?'

'No, no, I want Kongu.'

'Go to A2B,' someone suggests, referring to the chain which is like the McDonald's of Tam-Brahm quick meals.

Could it be that they are unaware of their culinary heritage? Or is it the usual reason: Homely isn't eaten out?

Indeed, there's much inventive cookery going on in Tiruppur and I see advertisements for 'chocolate chicken' which appears to be grilled chicken stuffed with chocolate, 'dozza' which I understand to be dosa with pizza topping, and 'disco parathas' that I presume are best inserted into a CD-player. I eventually spot the promisingly named Tiruppur Mess, which should be able to dish up a feast. It's a cavernous hall that could have seated my entire family tree, but there are only a couple of aged plastic chairs and grubby tables in view. When I ask for the menu, the chef who is dressed in sooty boxers and rubber flipflops, but with no shirt, replies, 'Fried rice.'

'Anything else?'

He stares at me as if I'm being a troublesome customer, then says, 'Fried noodles.'

I clarify: 'As this is Tiruppur Mess, I'd prefer Tiruppur food.'

He shakes his head, 'There's no Tiruppur food.'

I don't think it meaningful to argue with that since we're anyway not on the same wavelength, or ever going to be Facebook buddies and he's barely dressed. I personally like to wear clothes when I visit restaurants, especially in towns famous for their garment manufacturing, and it's a nice touch if staff wear them too.

Instead, I hunt for what supposedly is the oldest and most reliable local biryani joint, but the area I mapped it to turns out to be another endless stretch of fancy garment surplus outlets and nobody has heard of any biryani. It also pours again, so the only thing I can think of is Junior Kuppanna and when I enter the eatery this time, I'm feeling I might as well move in and apply for a job as their in-house food quality inspector. I dine on pepper-fried brains and on top of it I order the mildly coconutty chicken biryani; it's made with *al dente* muscular jungle fowl rather than softly spineless broiler. I'm quite taken by it—and not at all surprised when I learn that according to *The Times of India*, online food delivery company Swiggy's statistics show that biryani is Tamil Nadu's most popular order.

In the end, my Kongu food adventure turns out to be exclusively centred around Junior Kuppanna, where I have breakfasts, lunches and dinners. On the other hand, I don't mind it at all—the menu has so many items that I don't eat the same dish twice. For as the oft-repeated foodie saying goes: A good restaurant is a good restaurant is a good restaurant. Or was it Shakespeare who said, 'A biryani by any other name would smell as good?'

❖

Coming to Puducherry, on the Tamil Nadu coast, is like nibbling off the yummiest plates of Europe's best restaurants, but hotted up to match Asian sensibilities—think Parisian fine dining, but tastier, less inhibited spicing, more daring creativity, veritable bliss for lovers of fusion. And what fusion!

Pondicherry, as it was known back in the day, was founded by Frenchmen in 1674. The reason why they built their colonial city here and not on the west coast where all the precious spices could be found, is said to be that the fashion-conscious foreigners were more interested in trading cloth and textiles—which, as we just learnt in Tiruppur, parts of Tamil Nadu remain prominent for. Besides, it was a cosmopolitan coast which already had a Danish settlement 100 km south at Tranquebar, while the English competition was comfortably distant, 130 km north at Fort Saint George (which grew into Chennai). They were all welcomed by Tamilian kings—only the Swedes were chased out (by the French) when they tried to colonise Porto Novo in 1733, no more than 50 km away it was too close for comfort. When the French moved out almost three centuries later, in 1954, they left an occidental *esprit* behind: Street names are still prefaced with Rue, the leafy avenues are lined with plenty of mansions called 'Maison Something or the Other' and policemen wear red pillboxy caps. (I verily feel like I'm inside a Tintin comic.)[20]

Partly, this is thanks to the modern Puducherrian insight that with an economy increasingly dependent on tourism, there's a need to preserve architectural monuments—or less tourists will come—but also partly because of the culinary entrepreneurship that inhabits those preserved buildings, basically making the bar-hangers and restaurant-goers provide for their upkeep. Even new constructions are built to blend in, I notice, as I check into Palais de Mahé on 239, Rue de Bussy. It looks like it might have been there since colonial days, but is in fact, a new addition to the city scene. The sophisticated rooms have all mod cons required for a posh stay, at the same time, every detail down to the wrought-iron door keys bespeaks of tradition-mindedness.

The gourmet fare at the hotel's airy roof terrace is as flawless as it gets. Chef N. Kathir excels at Kerala cuisine, such as prawns in mango-seasoned curry or kokum-marinated fish grilled in banana leaf wraps that preserves the aromas of the juicy flesh (the way he says it's done in Mahe, yes, that other ex-enclave in the previous chapter). But even sublimer is his

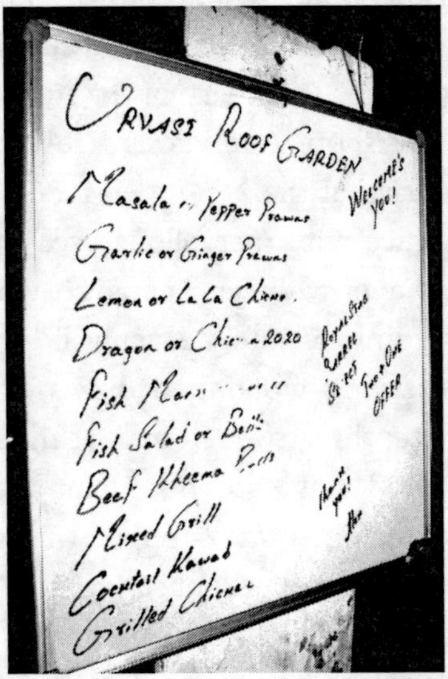

My favourite Pondicherry bar menu.

Indian *haute cuisine*, or what he calls 'progressive'. Dishes to die for include the garlic-marinated medium-rare steak in a peppery gravy served alongside taro root wedges tempered with mustard seeds and a touch of chilli; next I'm totally floored by a fennel-and-lime-crusted kingfish fillet accompanied by a Spanish-influenced roasted paprika sauce—based on the highly complex *salsa romesco* of Catalonia—and crisp-fried julienned veggies; finally I reach nirvana when I bite into grilled curry-marinated tiger prawns with traditional lemon rice (what a masterstroke!) and stir-fried buttery babycorn. Spice levels are heady without overpowering the natural flavours of other ingredients.

Between meals, the town is perfect for a Proustian stroll to build up more of an appetite. I turn the corner into the charming Rue Romain Rolland, named after a long-ago winner of the Nobel Prize for Literature. It is lined by a library, a theatre with an antiquated Pathe-Cine-movie hall sign still intact over the gate, and various other rendezvouses suitable for judicious flaneurs such as La Maison Rose, a café-cum-cocktail bar that is a sibling of Chennai's legendary bistro Amethyst, which also houses an arty bookshop. Afterwards I reward myself with a refreshing banana lassi at the 24/7-open Le Café, housed in the former harbour office with marvellous ocean views.

Puducherry is a pizza-lovers' paradise where authenticity and affordability combine into heavenly hogging. I drop into a random place serving wood-fired pizzas, which also offers cocktails in any size; three sozzled girls at the next table down a pitcher of Bacardi. I make do with a pint and since we're on the coast I order a seafood pizza—topped with generous chunks of fish, sliced black olives, chopped veggies and smothered in a rich layer of cheese. Eating, I observe a girl entering in burqa, dashing into the restroom, coming out in jeans and tank top, and ordering a drink. It's very à la Puducherry or, as Francophones might interject, *ooh là-là*.

However, one needs to pick one's eating options with circumspection, as the scene changes rapidly—yesterday's talk of the town which was top-ranked in guidebooks may be gone… or gone down the drain. For example, a charming courtyard restaurant in Rue Labourdonnais with tables set in pillared verandas attracted me on earlier visits for its grub and gets fine write-ups in all travel handbooks. Now, the owner appears dodgy when I ask for a bottle of red, which eventually arrives, decanted in a teapot. The wine is chilled, which suggests that the bottle was opened long ago and kept refrigerated. Rather than the expensive dry Shiraz I am paying for, they seem to have mixed dregs from different half-drunk flagons of cheap port. When I request to inspect the label, the Frenchman treats me like I'm some kind of second-rate Grimod de la Reynière and evades the question.[21] The meal that hits the table after an inordinate wait, despite the fact that I'm the only customer, is like what a Michelin star might appear like if it turned into a black hole. The meat is as chewy as Charlie Chaplin's shoes and the butter knife I get to carve it with doesn't cut through the leathery slab. The proprietor shrugs when I complain and mutters in a Gallic dialect something that sounds suspiciously like 'up yours', but which hopefully is just his way of wishing me *bon appétit*.

When I need a time-out to digest, I pop into the Bengali poet-guru Aurobindo's former ashram for silent meditation or explore the exhilarating museum-turned-home of poet Bharathiyar who wrote:

Poets in the Tamil land
Made a heady mixture in glee
Of wine, fire, wind and sky
And passed on that potion to me

...or I study the more action-packed Police Museum with its collection of old-worldly uniforms and weapons, and after that I end up at the Puducherry Museum housed in a colonial merchant's eighteenth-century villa. The latter displays a whimsical jumble of things left behind including rotting pianos and a *pousse-pousse* type of car powered by two people who ran behind pushing it. People like me will be most interested in the mock-up of a dining room including special wine cabinets, at the sight of which one easily conjures up the milieu in which Franco-Tamil cuisines fused into Creole, once the French bachelors married Tamil wives. Although milder than regular Tamilian cooking, here *à la Français* grub was spiced up with pepper and made golden by turmeric, with light coconut milk instead of heavy cream, and curry leaves replaced Mediterranean herbs.

After days in the European parts, I shift to the Tamil quarters and check into the pleasant Maison Perumal (58, Perumal Koil Street), a 130-year-old merchant's mansion that's often talked of as Puducherry's finest place to stay boutique style. In its courtyards, artists exhibit their work and the cheerful chef COUGARBABU, a born and bred Puducherrian who writes his name in block letters, puts together an elaborate sampling menu of house specials. Entrées consist of intriguing Tamilian 'falafels' that are called vazhapoo vada and made of mashed banana flowers served with a coconut dip, khuzipaniyaram (dhal with delicious spongy rice balls), karuvepillai varutha meen—fleshy and sweetish mahi-mahi (Hawaiian dolphin) fillets baked in leaves with a sweet-and-sour sauce of jaggery, chilli and tamarind; era podithooval (shrimp sautéed with 'gunpowder' mixture) and parlameen kuzhambu (a hot and sour bluefish curry)—altogether taking the art of cookery to celestial levels.

To make life perfect, Puducherry also happens to have an evolved drinking scene: bars are a dime a dozen and cheaper than anywhere else in the world. Rock-bottom options include a surplus of popular dives such as the friendly Poudou-Poudou (31, Rue Labourdonnais) which combines cheap booze and decent seafood, De Bussy Permit Room (81, Lal Bahadur Shastry Street) offering luxurious tandoori snacks to go with frothy mugs, and last but not least, the Amnivasam Factory Price Retail Outlet Budget Bar (corner of Montorsier and Ellaiamankol Streets) that is perhaps the most cost-efficient of all the city's drinking dens for an ice-cold beer. But my favourite roost is Dhanalakshmi Urvasi Roof Garden (59, Rangapillai Street), on the upper floor of a mansion with a balcony that overlooks the street, making it perfect for people-watching. Despite a certain seediness, it's an easy-going haunt, with uncles in loincloths sipping hard drinks, a bunch of youths chanting 'Happy birthday to Thambi', and a squirrel tries to jump into my beer mug when I'm distracted by the delectable sides such as the 'prawn-fish munch' which is exactly what it sounds like: A hearty mix of fish and prawns fried with spices and veggies.

As I board the train at Puducherry's congenially tiny station, I'm already missing everything about the town.

❖

The journey north towards Telangana goes through arid countryside, which has a rugged beauty, but the entire stretch also happens to be the home of classy non-veg and at virtually all stations one gets hygienically packed biryani-in-a-box. Being a certified glutton, I have one for lunch (a juicy chicken-leg biryani with spicy veggie gravy) and craving more, I buy another for dinner.

Moreover, the train halts at Guntur which is supposedly the true home of Andhra cuisine, and I regret not having scheduled a proper stopover. Then for an hour, the train doesn't budge and I calculate whether to risk running out to shop for more grub. As it eventually rolls again, a vendor hops on to peddle crispy bite-sized samosas served with those revered flaming-hot thin, long, deeply red chillies, so providentially I do get my mouthful of Guntur. Andhraites grow about half of the chillies in the country, with Guntur being the epicentre of chilli-farming.

Getting off the train at Hyderabad's Deccan station at the onset of the holy fasting month, topmost on my list of tourist attractions to check out is the city's GI-tagged (since 2012) ghee-soaked, hard-stirred until ultra-smooth, slow-cooked on wood-fire for twelve hours, meat-wheat paste-like porridge or potage...and which is more commonly simply known as haleem. It ranks as Hyderabad's top contribution to the world's breakfast tables. The singularly filling and nutritious dish has its roots in Central Asia or possibly Iran, but reached its zenith here where it powers the citizens during their austere month of fasting. Apparently, 3,500 goats are cooked nightly and with any luck some of them are positively destined for my tummy.

I check into a lodge where the receptionist proclaims that temperatures average 50°C and sells me an overpriced mosquito-infested so-called AC room. The museum-worthy cooling-machine burps icily and then electricity collapses. Through the night, my perspiration is distilled on my skin into greasy patches until I can't take it anymore. I have a bucket rinse and head out into the dawn. The receptionist was right, the city is suffering from an unprecedented heat wave that, according to the morning papers, is expected to kill off thousands of chickens. Is it the usual greenhouse effect or has the world turned into a tandoor? My guesstimate's as good as yours, but one thing's for sure—soon people may need to only put chicken in a pot of rice outdoors, and hey presto, there's a hot-hot biryani!

My survival chances seem bleak, but I tell myself I'm not a chicken. Instead, I slither like a sweaty beanbag down the road towards the old town where I right away spot the 1980s' Irani canteen Nayaab (Nayapul Road). As luck has it, it's open early and fully non-veg. From a courteous waiter I order the cholesterol-lover's all-time favourite bheja fry, a velvety brain pulp seasoned with a highly agreeable masala—the ideal morning meal for thinking humans. Mopping it up with soft naan, I relish every morsel like a zombie that tastes IQ for the first time.

Down the road, the Charminar circle has been pedestrianised to make it easier for tourists to appreciate the medieval monument. But most of it is covered in ugly scaffolding, because part of it has collapsed, so I can't really take selfies with it in the background. Nevertheless, Hyderabad is gracefully ramshackle with its stately buildings crumbling and bricks tumbling, from once-splendid arcades, to litter the pavements. The countrywide smoking ban doesn't seem to have taken effect either; fag butts crunch underfoot as people happily puff everywhere like it's the first morning after many Arabian nights. A helmet and gas mask might have come in handy, I ponder, as I explore Hyderabadi culture.

I've never been to Pakistan but this feels about as close as I will ever get—everywhere, merchants advertise Pakistani garments and, when I stop for lunch, I sample Pakistani curry at a hyped restaurant near Madina Circle. It's one of the swankier 1990s' joints, its AC-hall crowded with ladies in burqas surrounded by shopping bags, tucking into biryani after biryani. In case you've ever wondered what Pakistani food's like, I can tell you that according to their chef it's vividly phlegm-green and their 'Mutton Pakistani' is a mixture of salt, caramel colour, possibly nuclear waste, and microscopic pieces of something goatish, but only the health ministry of Pakistan would be capable of determining what animal protein it really is. Unable to finish the portion, I don't even consider asking for a doggy bag. Then again, the philosophy behind this book is that I sample dodgy stuff so you can avoid eating dogs, say, by mistake.

But everything else I devour in this town that is ranked as *the* culinary Mecca of India, adds up to a sheer epicurean pilgrimage. Which is why UNESCO included Hyderabad in its list of 'gastronomic metros'. One out of ten Hyderabadis earn their bread and butter from the city's 150,000 food outlets (if you include pushcarts or so-called bandis). The rest love eating—obviously—and every morning in the newspapers I come across alarmist reports devoted to the mounting obesity cataclysm, with helpful fat-burning hacks thrown in.

The oldest heritage snack stop on my tour, Munshi Naan, dates back to 1851 and is a fifteen-minute walk from the Charminar in a street known as Purani Haveli, after the one-time mansion of the Nizam. It's basically a corner shop tandoor that bakes 'char koni naan', squarish thick breads, rich and oily, soft on the inside but with a crisp outer layer. The business is run by fifth-generation descendants of the original munshi, the Nizam's letter-writer, who set it up.

Indeed, much of Hyderabad's cookbook is linked to the Nizams (who ruled the town until Indian independence) but its deeper heredity is actually found in the elitist Mughal 'high cuisine' of Delhi, further traceable to luxurious Persian, elegant Turkish, classic Afghan and rich Arab origins. Muslims from across the world migrated to the Deccan about half a millennia ago or so. But they also combine in them a curious southern accent in the form of great vegetarian dishes prepared with ingredients like coconut, eggplants, peanuts, sesame, tamarind, those extra-deadly Andhranese chillies and, sometimes, even crushed pearls. One of the veggie hits is mirchi ka salan, consisting of whole but rather mild chillies cooked in thickly nutty, gingery gravy. Thanks to its pickle-like character it keeps so well that it is a preferred traveller's lunchbox. Even the meaty biryanis are dramatically spiced up by distinctly un-Mughal ingredients (as against the classic Mughal biryani that packs in slightly gentler aromas, such as saffron). The tamarind sourness that balances out the profusion of chillies, supposedly perks up the appetite at the same time as it improves digestion. But why eat too many chillies in the first place? Well, they believe that chillies are better than air-conditioning or ice-cream, because to eat the heat is to beat the heat…

The ultimate in local fine-dining is the loaded Hyderabadi biryanis, of which more than forty varieties exist (including vegetarian) and that generally have roots in Persian *pilaus*. One of the numerous permutations is made with a complete goat and the animal becomes the vessel that the meal is served in, as it is jam-packed with dry-fruit-enriched chicken-egg pullao. But other than that radically rare dish, everybody has their preferred versions, debating differences between, say, Shah Ghouse Café's branches or the Paradise chain. Personally, I fall for the welcoming 1930s' Grand Hotel (Bank Street) which isn't particularly grand and has no rooms or branches; but their dining hall with its high ceiling appeals to me as does the

A 'bad' Andhra offer one can resist.

splendid mutton biryani. As I am eating, I think of how novelist E.M. Forster loved Hyderabadi food and wrote two books based on his Indian experiences—his greatest novel *A Passage to India* (set in the 1910s) and the lesser-known but equally engrossing non-fiction *The Hill of Devi* (about a sojourn in the 1920s). While his friend Somerset Maugham obsessed about Hinduism, Forster was drawn to Islamic culture which of course included lots of non-veg. Perhaps, I speculate, he tried the biryani cooked up here at Grand?

In *The Hill of Devi*, Forster described journeying to Hyderabad in November 1921 (and even if it was in the winter his train reminded him of 'a stewpan') to spend a month with his 'greatest Indian friend' Dr Syed Ross Masood, a founding father of the city's Osmania University and who was 'fantastically generous, incredibly hospitable…a connoisseur; he loved good books.' They had last met up in Patna ten years earlier (a town that Forster fictionalised in *A Passage to India*) but knew each other from long before; Forster had been Masood's tutor in England. And in turn, Masood tweaked the novelist's mind as Forster wrote in his essay collection *Two Cheers for Democracy*: 'Until I met him, India was a vague jumble of rajahs, sahibs, babus and elephants, and I was not interested in such a jumble; who could be? He made everything real and exciting as soon as he began to talk, and seventeen years later when I wrote *A Passage to India* I dedicated it to him out of gratitude as well as out of love, for it would never have been written without him.' Indeed, Dr Masood was immortalised in that very novel as Dr Aziz (essayed by Victor Bannerjee in the Oscar-winning movie) whose predicament is central to the narrative.

Sightseeing with Masood, Forster found Hyderabad full of 'beautiful things to look at, interesting people to talk to, delicious food,' and after *A Passage to India* became a bestseller he made a 'substantial donation' towards the building of an Urdu Hall just 2 km from the Grand Hotel where I'm swilling down my biryani. Masood passed away in 1937, ending their friendship thus, yet, Forster returned to India for a last trip in 1945, barely months after World War II had ended. He may on that final visit have seen the hall he sponsored which until today houses an archive and a library dedicated to Urdu literature. He doesn't mention it in his writings but he described that out of modern architecture in India, 'the chief example I saw was the great new university at Hyderabad' which 'attempts to blend two styles of architecture which occur in the Hyderabad state—one style being Mohammedan, and the other derived from the famous Buddhist caves of Ajanta.'

By the time I finish my biryani I'm 100 per cent sure (without a shred of evidence but feeling it both in my bones and belly) that Forster too must have eaten similar biryani. 'I have been in my life three times to Hyderabad, some of my happiest Indian days were spent there,' wrote Forster after this last visit to town, and he speaks of discovering the pleasure of buffet dinners: 'Long tables are loaded with Indian food, and sometimes one table is labelled "vegetarian" and the other "non-vegetarian". You help yourself, or are helped. I take away pleasant memories of these buffet dinners, memories of Indians moving elegantly through well-filled rooms, with well-filled plates in their hands, and miraculously conveying food to their mouths in the folds of a chapatti.'

Forster would surely have gone for the biryanis. But before I leave town I learn of a newer novelty, yet another unique biryani variety has taken the city by storm: it's the customary dish of Yemenites, *mandi*, brought by soldiers who migrated here centuries ago to work as royal bodyguards. Their former suburb of military barracks is known as Barkas and its Arab-descendants are estimated to about 100,000 in all. But their eating habits were never talked about until foodies noticed the sweetness of their version of haleem, that evolved from a primeval Arab staple by the name of *tharid*—don't be shocked but rumour has it that sugar is combined with fatty meat in this heartbreakingly rich dish! Also, thanks to the fact that many Indians have worked in the Emirates or done the Haj (and returned feeling sentimental), the Saudi *laham mandi* became a rage in the 2010s.

It may be that 'authentic *mandi*' is advertised on hoardings across town, yet it's rumoured that many spice it up with typically Indian masalas to make it inauthentic, basically turning it into normal Hyderabadi biryani. Therefore, after some excruciating bargaining, I take a rickshaw to Barkas. Passing the Taj Falaknuma Palace, I get off at the humble suburb that at first glance looks rough with smallish pukka houses and even smaller industries. Maybe it's meant to resemble a village in Yemen. People are friendly enough and across from a burial ground the tombstone engraver greets me in Arabic as I ask for directions.

He points me down Mandi Road, named after its illustrious culinary offering. I stop at one out of the thirty or so eateries, the Mataam al-Arabi which supposedly fired up the Arab food trend and sits in a, from all appearances, recently-built complex symptomatic of how once-simple canteens are upgrading thanks to their rising fame in epicurean circles. It's decorated with cannons outside to establish the owner's warrior ancestry, but the dining hall is almost unfurnished save for carpets on the floors.

After kicking off my shoes, I sit on the carpet at a low table to study the colourful menu which is a masterpiece of simplicity and tempting non-veg at rates to suit all pockets from full goat with all the trimmings (to be shared by twenty-five diners) to elementary, cheap mutton soup. I focus on the *laham mandi* that I came for. As I wait, I worry that I'll get enough to feed a joint-family, but the waiter sensibly refrains from stacking the silver platter that's about as wide as the length of my forearm, for which I'm graciously charged half the menu rate.

The elongated rice grains are beautifully separated in a master class of social distancing, scented with saffron, fried onion, and cashews, and a crusty mutton slab sits on top, breaking apart on mere touch—and it's stunningly succulent. Regarding the cooking method, it seems that lightly spiced rice is garnished with dry fruits and then topped by a wire mesh upon which the mutton pieces rest gently; an Arabic version of the classic dum-pukht (which is basically what *laham mandi* is).[22] A dish with its roots in a very old world, it's slow-cooked in a sealed vessel until the meat juices permeate the rice. As a contrast to its subtlety, it comes with chilli-enhanced fresh tomato chutney of the kind one gets complimentary helpings of in northern Africa.

Another nice touch is the desserts selection that includes Bahraini halwa, the Hyderabadi 'cult' dish qubani ka meetha of syrup-boiled apricots in thick cream, and teeth-curlingly sweet baklava sourced from a genuine Turkish pastry chef, no less, oh, so delicious with its nuttiness, honey, and piquant spices wrapped up in crisp-baked flaky-buttery filo dough. I hesitate to leave, because I could easily lie down on the carpeted floor and go on stuffing myself forever. But work beckons—with my next meal in the next town down.

❖

Somehow, Goa had been filed away at the back of my mind as the quintessential hedonist hotspot with its hippies, who still hope that the Beatles will reunite for one last gig in Anjuna with George Harrison playing the Ouija board and John Lennon as the spirit in the bottle. Culture in Goa seemed, at the most, to be about its use as a backdrop by filmmakers—as the perfect hideaway for Matt Damon in the Hollywood blockbuster thriller *Bourne Supremacy* (but the action hero's enchanting Goan bungalow was erected specially for the film and demolished immediately afterwards so there's no point trying to rent it).

Simply a place for letting loose and getting tight, eating on its beaches where shack-chefs innovate permutations of British, French, German, Iranian, Israeli, Italian, Japanese, Mexican, Russian, Swedish and Thai cuisines, and whatever else the tourists' palates crave, to the sound of pot-smoking karaoke artists crooning reggae hits long forgotten in the rest of the world.

Nowhere else in India has restaurant culture aligned itself so perfectly with what tourists need, which can be a welcome change if one has been travelling for too long and is getting tired of the predictable urban multicuisine. Many of the Goan food outlets, whether fancy or humble, rank among Asia's best.

But maybe this is how it should be, considering that Goan cuisine itself is born out of a fusion of colonial influences and local food habits, in particular that of the Saraswath community. The chillies, that are part of nearly all Indian dishes, were brought here by the colonisers (as were tomatoes and potatoes and many other good things) along with the methods for baking leavened bread—Goa's famous pav.

Even their most world-conquering dish bears witness to this, the venerated vinegary vindaloo: Hot-and-sour overnight-marinated pork curry starring a rainbow of spices such as cardamom pods, sticks of cinnamon, several cloves, ground coriander, cumin seeds, roasted fenugreek, much garlic, fresh ginger of course, mustard seeds, big onions, a spoonful of peppercorns, often also some sugar or jaggery, turmeric for sure and heavy-handed usage of those red chillies introduced by the Portuguese to India. It is derived from a Portuguese original, namely *carne de vinho e alhos* or wine and garlic-stewed meat, a name that after a few fennies too many, will sound like vindaloo.

Tourists and restaurateurs apart, in the last two decades it seems that a mysterious migratory trend has made plenty of litterateurs and other intellectuals move in—and Goa has seen literary festivals where one might spot one of my heroes, Amitav Ghosh, who bought a mansion in the picture-perfect bucolic interiors of Goa. As have many other writers that I enjoy reading like Sudhir Kakar and Sunil Khilnani, apparently…and so I was getting mental images of 1800s Berlin or *fin-de-siècle* Paris to where artists from all over the world were pulled…or the Carmel to Big Sur stretch of Californian coast that attracted Robert Heinlein, Henry Miller and even, for a bit, the perpetual hitchhiker Jack Kerouac, who wrote the documentary novel *Big Sur* (1962) about his stay—and of course Big Sur is something of a hub in 'Steinbeck Country' considering John Steinbeck even wrote a novel set in the fish-packing plants at Cannery Row. And being on California's coast, the analogy isn't too much of a stretch.

As much as Goa attracts outsiders, the Goans themselves are attracted to the world and will be found in the Indian diasporas from Africa to New York; rumour has it that there are more Goans in Europe and north America than in Goa itself. Yet few visitors are aware that one such 'expat', Abbe Faria who was born in Candolim in 1755, developed a method for *hipnotismo scientifico* way back before hypnotism was officially invented and became so famous in Paris, of all places, that

Abbe Faria's birth home in Candolim before
he became globally famous.

Alexandre Dumas based a character on him in his swashbuckling bestseller, *The Count of Monte Cristo* (1845).

The celebrated travel writer Norman Lewis, who came to Goa when it was still a colony, wrote in his book *The World The World* that descendants of Abbe Faria's disciples, 'a club of Goanese [*sic*] hypnotists held regular meetings and practised his techniques on each other.' But that apart, 'Goa offered little in the way of entertainment. Night-clubs were banned, the cinema showed Western films only when a minimum audience of fifty could be rounded up. Otherwise there was snake-charming.' Nevertheless, the who's who of travel writing passed through. Shortly after Goa's liberation, Graham Greene, then in his late fifties, partied energetically in 1963 at all-night bashes for two weeks, predicting that here 'are great beaches waiting for great hotels.' But in those days even the venerable Mandovi Hotel in Panjim town wasn't good enough for him to stay at, so he preferred to have long fenny-boosted evening conversations as a house guest of local writer Maria Couto (who subsequently authored her first book on Greene).

This reminds me of how some years ago, on a beach holiday, I was browsing at the Literati bookshop—in a century-old bungalow which has a bookcase devoted to Goan writing. There I bumped into Booker-winner Kiran Desai and her then boyfriend Nobel laureate Orhan Pamuk, who had rented a home across the road. Autograph hunters love this charming shop because Literati has over the years hosted events with everybody who is anybody and...well, myself.

At Literati, I learn that Goa has always been a literary hub. The state's multicultural traditions run deep, as is proven by the fact that Goan literature is written in Konkani, Marathi, Portuguese and English too—its most well-known English writer being memoirist Maria Couto, who during her lifetime captured, in her very personal way, the past and present of Goa as well as the 'composite identity' of Goans who she saw as Indians but deeply European at the same time. Picking up the charming anthology *Ferry Crossings*, I read some of the finest Goan writing, compiled by the renowned Goa-based poet Manohar Shetty. It includes the Jnanpith-awarded Damodar Mauzo whose Konkani novel *Karmelin* won the Sahitya Akademi award in 1983—and who happens to be one of the nicest writers I've ever met—and excerpts from Victor Rangel-Ribeiro's *Tivolem* which is one of those novels that seem to encompass an entire universe between the covers.

Dropping in at some literary event in the state's cultural complex Kala Academy, as luck would have it, I run into the afore-mentioned Amitav Ghosh who invites me home for a party. He explains that he'd been visiting Goa for decades, until he found a crumbling mansion which he bought and restored. One wing was in such a state of disrepair that it had to be almost fully rebuilt. Ghosh's study, which naturally interests me the most, impresses with its large writing desk and a luxurious range of hidebound Egyptian notebooks that apparently contain the hand-written first drafts of all his novels. For Ghosh, one of the pleasures of Goa is that it's such a literary place—he likes to entertain other writers at tremendously enjoyable dinner parties.

At the party, apart from chatting about Graham Greene's and Umberto Eco's visits with Ghosh's neighbour Maria Couto, I enjoy bar-hanging with the humour columnist Cecil Pinto, a distinguished connoisseur of caju (i.e. cashew fenny, also spelled as feni or in Portuguese fenim). He's brought the most exquisite village-distilled brews from his collection to Ghosh's party, where he takes it upon himself to teach the noble art of imbibing caju to guests ranging from the lowly yours truly to Nobel Laureates such as Orhan Pamuk whom I had celebrity-spotted already at Literati. Despite rumours that the Turkish intellectual might, too, be pondering a long-term home in Goa, he sniffed sceptically at the homemade booze which had been poured out of a recycled Smirnoff-bottle.

Being slightly tipsy, I tried to help Pamuk by pointing out that caju becomes sublime as soon as one gets drunk enough—only later did it occur to me that any Nobel laureate sticking his nose into a glass of the potent brew might worry more about potential brain-damage than its rather extreme bouquet. The fact that fenny is a GI-tagged product and the pride of Goa neither tickled his tastebuds nor his intellect. Other foreign writers have taken more interest in the eminent beverage, such as Alexander Frater who wrote (in *Chasing the Monsoon*) that in a small village, he found a country liquor shop selling 'fenny distilled from the crown of the palm, the drink of the monsoon. A single tiny room with a barred window, it contained three men who told me the strength of fenny was such that it could only be comfortably taken in cool weather. I tried some. It was very strong with a kind of curious cheesy aftertaste.'

Fenny, like vindaloo, is an outcome of the colonial

presence—the colonials planted cashews in India and when their imported wine ran out, Jesuit monks who observed how locals made booze from coconut trees found that in similar manner cashew fruits could be distilled into potent liquor. As for myself, fenny has always made me think of tequila—it can actually be drunk similarly with salt and lime—and an interesting new trend in distilling is embodied by Maya Pistola Agavepura which (due to GI-tagging rules) may not be called tequila, but is 100 per cent tequila in all other aspects except, well, that it's made in India. There's also caffeinated gin with beans from the Western Ghats, which is perfect for those who snooze from too much booze.

Goa, where you must have a Limca with your fenny (or the other way around).

When I ask Pinto what he thinks of all these literary migrants flocking to his native place, he frankly states, 'That Goa is becoming a hub for writers, is evident. But regarding your question of Goa benefiting from writers moving here, now that is a complicated matter. Writers, like people, come in different types. When a writer like Amitav Ghosh comes here, he enhances our literary environment through his interactions. There are other writers, on the other hand, who have portrayed a totally bizarre image of Goa to the world. This type we could do without.'

I make a mental note to write respectfully about Goa in this book. As if my fascination for the coastal enclave let out the genie from a bottle (of caju), I wake up with a thunderstorm in my tender and coconut-green head. Waiting for it to cure itself, I head to Old Goa, the eastern capital of Portugal founded in 1510 to manage their trade with East Asia. There the mandatory hours of basilica-beholding, cathedral-canvassing, monastery-measuring, and ruin-reconnoitring includes the stunning Sé Cathedral built in 1562 by Dominicans, the baroque Basilica de Bom Jesus which holds the miraculous body of Saint Francis Xavier (d. 1552) on display inside an ornamental circa 1690 glass coffin gifted by the sixth grand duke of Tuscany, and half a dozen other monuments. Somerset Maugham noted that in 'the cathedral they were holding a service, the organ was playing and in the organ loft there was a small choir of natives singing with a harshness in which somehow the Catholic chants acquired a mysteriously heathen, Indian character.'

Of the once bustling town with bazaars full of silk shops, porcelain sellers, goldsmiths and jewellers, taverns and brothels, nothing else remains. But I'd heard about a small hotel located within ten minutes' walk from the UNESCO World Heritage site on a quiet hillock.

Tucked away in the jungle, Hotel Champakali turns out to be the perfect base camp for me and fulfils the picture of a hidden gem. It's so secret that it wasn't until hours before I was to arrive that I was told, via an anonymous phone call, how to find my way.

'Drive towards the Church of Our Lady of the Mount,' the voice whispered.

'Is there a sign?' I asked.

'No.'

Once I eventually reach Champakali, it is totally worth the trouble. The ultra-luxury B&B feels both small and big. It consists of two whitish mansions that look like the Riviera abode of faded rock stars, encircled by trees—banyan, teak, banana, guava and as expected, flowering champak, or magnolia. Each has three bedrooms filled with antique furniture and knickknacks. I'm the only guest in my mansion; a family is renting the other one next-door.

Utterly ambrosial repasts are dished up in gazebos facing the expansive gardens and the Carambolim Lake, known for its superb fishing, is visible in the distance. For starters, I'm treated to a smoked aubergine soup, cold, probably the most unique thing I ever had—can't even find it in my *Larousse Gastronomique*. The pureed potage with fresh yoghurt is scented with herbs that coat my tongue like a minor key aromatic symphony. It's followed by a plate of fish fillet cooked in banana leaf, grilled vegetables and lemon rice. Again, it's subtle, oh, so subtle, because of which I request the waiter to give my compliments to the chef. He turns out to be a Frenchman called Mathieu and suddenly the eclectic fare makes sense.

Mathieu serves me a complimentary off-menu tasting—a clam soup which he has cooked exclusively for the neighbouring family next-door: Garlicky white wine broth with a salty sea aroma of clams. The dessert is *serradura*, a type of poor-man's pudding that has become exceedingly trendy in Portugal's former colonies, including in parts of China. I'm not a dessert person but this one I could have taken umpteen helpings of.

I spend the following days exploring my surroundings.

Wanting to approach Old Goa from the riverside, like the

visitors did in hoary yore, I stride downhill to where its gate still stands. Known as the Viceroy's Arch it has a statue of Vasco da Gama atop (erected to commemorate the centenary of his arrival in India). As I snap my snaps, I notice that the Mandovi ferry to Divar Island is about to leave from the jetty next to the arch. On an impulse, I jump aboard. Once I make landfall on Divar, instead of taking the ferry back I follow the ribbon straight road cutting across mangrove marshes, curious about where it might lead.

I spot none of the crocodiles that are supposed to live hereabouts, but see a huge snake sleeping on the road. Very easy-going Goan snake...and after a leisurely stroll, I reach a small village of extraordinarily pretty bungalows, where numerous bars greet me. I pick one that isn't haunted by rustic gamblers but might offer victuals instead, Rock Inn, which despite its name turns out not to be a trendy disco-bistro filled with holidaying fashionistas nibbling on overpriced finger foods, but obviously named thus because it lies sheltered by a strange rock. A black-and-white Hindi flick plays on the TV. The cavernous interiors resemble a warehouse, with beer boxes stacked along the walls, and when I ask the bare-chested and barefoot uncle if there are snacks, he rattles off all manner of scrambled eggs, burji and omelettes.

Since I didn't come this far to eat eggs, I ask, 'Seafood?'

'There's fresh snapper and prawns. Rawa fried.'

'Can I have snapper without rawa, just tawa?'

'No.'

'Please?'

'Maybe prawns,' he says and asks his wife, who mans the kitchen, to fry me a plate. Within minutes, heavenly smells waft through the hall and platters of amazingly juicy-crunchy seafood arrive to accompany my chilled beers. There seems to be a rule of thumb in Goa—find any village bar and no matter how unpromising it looks, it'll invariably serve up a feast. Come to think of it, I've never had as good bar snacks as during my travels in India. Authenticity is ensured by the fact that no tourist ever stumbles into a drinking den like Rock Inn. Instead, more semi-nude uncles drift in for pre-noon fenny pegs, 90 ml or 180 ml size appears the norm at this early hour, so once I've had my six-pack for the day I down a big peg, decamp before I fall asleep among the other drunks and revert to reality.

Crossing back on the ferry in a moderately inebriated state, I am in a position to better appreciate how Old Goa would have seemed to visitors arriving by the river and the churches-to-sightsee appears to have doubled in my absence. I stagger uphill through the archway where Vasco da Gama's statue now scrutinises me extra fiercely with his four eyes, arrive at the square where inquisition victims were flogged which makes me really genuinely guilty for being tipsy, and then I drop into each church to do penance, thinking that if I am ever crucified, I must remember to carry nail polish. In case the nails are rusty.

When I get hungry after seeing each cathedral twice—once with the left eye, once with the right—I make a detour into nearby Panjim, the biggest city of the state a short bus ride away, yet enchanting with winding lanes lined with bungalows that have red-tiled roofs. I gorge on nicely spicy mussels at Ritz, the seafood joint which is like a crammed tunnel of fishy love—squeeze in, squeeze down, eat-pay-go. Next, I digest in peace at Godinho's, founded in 1938 and more laidback than Ritz in case one wants to nurse a drink and read newspapers. Indeed, Godinho's is old enough for that connoisseur of seedy bars, Graham Greene, to have guzzled in it. This is pure conjecture, but in the *Sunday Times* (1964), Greene complained about the cheap 'raw Indian gins and whiskies' and their possible health hazards but seems to have missed the candy-sweet Port wines that Goans adapted from their colonisers. Since he would presumably have dined at Mandovi Hotel around the corner—one of the few proper hotels in those days—this would have been the logical place for aperitifs and nightcaps.

As a freelance journalist in Goa, it is probable that he was scouting out settings for a novel, like he usually did whenever he travelled wherever, but decided otherwise—maybe because the hard liquor was too hard or Indian culture too complex—and I can almost hear him sigh, as I sip my fenny, the way Catholics do when they think of Mary. Bloody, that is. Maria Couto later asked why he hadn't written about India to which Greene replied, 'I think India rather frightened me by its size. I have enjoyed myself very much during two weeks in Goa, but to write about India in a novel I would have had to live there over a considerable period of time and I think I was daunted by the problems.'

If one doesn't see a problem with it, there are certainly worse ways to waste weeks than bumming in Goa, over-eating and imbibing lethal levels of rustic tipple, but my marathon-length bender invariably feels unwholesome, thanks to manifold hangovers relieving and replacing one another in a succession of mitigating and palliating manoeuvres, until such a point that one is surprised every morning where one wakes up. This has as much to do with my own priorities as with Goa—about 10 per cent of my days consist of healthy tourism, 90 per cent is spent on hunting things to eat and drink excessively.

The beverage part of my diet is, as always, very straightforward: Zero in on any downmarket bar to sample unbranded beverages, such as that infamous cashew fenny, a decent vintage of which can give the costliest of artisanal tequilas a run for their money. I take it as a compliment when I order a caju with a slice of chonok—a sublime fish often cooked in seedy watering holes—and a scruffy bartender, who until then acted indifferent, stops whatever he's doing, stares at me for three seconds, before he asks: 'Sir, are you Goan?'

My tummy which (perhaps due to the plenitude of fishy bar snacks) has been producing gallons of loose motions, 'Goan gas-tricks', is much improved on the last day, most likely thanks to the underestimated medical properties of fenny that has not only killed many of my brain cells but also all the bacteria in my gut. The train is to leave from Vasco-da-Gama station at 3 p.m. and I decide to have my ultimate final marine meal in the vicinity. For those who haven't been to this town named after the eponymous coloniser, suffice it to say that the port town where the railway line ends and begins is a transport hub, with none too many tourist attractions. In fact, none. Except perhaps for a singular restaurant that has something of a pan-Goan reputation. Avoiding the quick meal joints immediately opposite the station, I peregrinate until, down a side street leading away from the municipal square, I spot Anantashram, that's neither posh nor dingy, but normal-looking and crowded with Goans. Not another tourist in sight, but their evocative slogan beckons with a language I can understand: 'Simply Good Food, Booze & Friendly Ambience.'

The menu includes the usual multicuisine to keep the timid happy, but I browse to the Goan section covering two thrilling pages. A special thali turns out to be something of a seafood encyclopaedia. From left to right my platter is filled with small bowls brimful of prawn kishmur (a fried shrimp salad), tisryo (spicy clams), kingfish curry, crab xec-xec (curried crab), fried kingfish (coated in semolina), bhangda uddamethi (mackerel curry with fenugreek seeds), and a sardine preparation the name of which I don't remember. The delicate aromas range from tomatoish to exceedingly coconutty.

On the side, I order a plate of pan-fried prawns, expecting standard shrimps. Instead I get a bunch of massive crustaceans tossed in a distinctly sweet and vinegary Goan masala. Demolishing that meal, I am reminded of the eminent Samanth Subramanian's travelogue *Following Fish*, in one chapter of which he trawls Mumbai's back lanes for the most authentic 'lunch home'. These are traditional eateries harking back to the industrial revolution of the late nineteenth century when cotton mills dotted the cityscape and workers needed homely but affordable lunches. They evolved with time into modern restaurants, mostly, but Subramanian tracks down the last one in Girgaon, curiously enough also named Anantashram. 'Anantashram aimed to be strictly dedicated to the act of feeding. Lunch ended not at a fixed time but when the kitchen ran out of food, and many customers sat on a bench facing the wall, ate without a flicker of an expression, and left within a quarter of an hour.' There, Subramanian has a fish thali with distinctly Goan aromas.

I wonder if Anantashram might be the name of a chain, a thalassic edition of the omnipresent Udupi 'vegetarian hotels'. But no, from what I gather this particular Anantashram that I am hogging at was born in 1970—making it much younger than its Mumbai counterpart—as a fish shack by a man named Anant, who cooked fish-curry-rice priced at Rs 0.75 per portion. As the shack's reputation grew, it was deemed necessary to open a 'fine dining' version.

Watching the people that I share my table with devour their food, I can't help but accost them—it turns out they're from Margao, a town 25 km away, and ride up on scooters at least once a week to eat here. According to them, it's the topmost in Goa in terms of value, quality and everything else. Unexpectedly, hence the best Goan food isn't found in big Panjim or on the beaches, but in the humdrum heart of a town that lacks other draws. What do you need tourist attractions for when you have Anantashram?

V

The Mahatma's Maharashtra

(Western India)

'Scarcely an American who comes to India goes away without seeing me.'

—Mahatma Gandhi to
The Hindu newspaper (1927)

Watson's Hotel where Mark Twain stayed on the top floor.

I wake up at Chhatrapati Shivaji station in Mumbai, a British-designed building that just has to be one of India's oddest UNESCO World Heritage monuments—I mean, a railway station?—and it's still in use, as lively as ever. If tourists could eat buildings with their selfie-cameras it would have been gobbled up long ago. However, right outside one can instead chew on the commuters' comfort bite, the city's beloved vada-pav to which the snack stalls around the station building are largely committed.

Although vada-pav is technically rather un-Indian—Portuguese-origin bread, filling of Latin American potatoes and chillies make it sound more like Hispanic tapas—the Internet considers this carb-rich energy-booster to be the soul of Mumbai and in 2023 it was ranked, by an online gourmet platform, as the #13 best sandwich of the world, way above any American cheesesteaks or lox-bagels. The snacky meal even rules the Indian skies as every self-respecting airline has vada-pav (though not at streetfood rates) on the menu.

Born in 1966 as a labourer's quick meal, the blobby chickpea batter-coated fritter of masalafied potato mash known as batata-vada, is stuffed in a Goan-style crusty but soft-hearted pav-bun, then tarted up with green coriander chutney and red-hot chillies.

As simple as it sounds the art of perfecting vada-pav takes eons to master. And hence one can only sample the real deal in the streets of Mumbai, where it rules the fast-food scene—or as that city's celebrated chronicler, Suketu Mehta, writes in *Maximum City,* it's 'the lunch of the *chawl* dwellers, the cart pullers, the street urchins; the clerks, the cops, and the gangsters'. According to newspaper articles, that may exaggerate matters, millions of vada-pav are eaten in town daily by everybody from regular workers to the greatest of Bollywood greats, which means basically anybody who doesn't go for the health-conscious option of getting their homely lunches brought by the city's ubiquitous dabbawallas.[23]

Now, the dabbawallas are another unparalleled food phenomenon. They predate modern restaurants, having gone into business in the 1880s, well before it was possible to get vada-pav or any other fast-food in town. The dabbawallas provided the fastest way to get lunch at work and until today their ingenious delivery chain process whizzes home-cooked meals (tiffin box lunches that wives prepare for their office-going husbands) from up to 70 km away without hardly ever mixing up the thousands of deliveries. The 5,000-man strong army are recognised by the *Guinness Book of World Records* for having been in operation for over a century with 99.99983 per cent accuracy.

Anyway, before the advent of vada-pav which the station area is justly famous for, the Victoria Terminus, as it used to be called, was the setting for Mulk Raj Anand's seminal 1940s working-class novel *Coolie*. As poet Adil Jussawalla, who used to be Anand's neighbour, reminisced in his essay 'The Reader as Tourist': 'With a few minor changes, the place Mulk described, the scene he drew, remains the same.' The nowadays highly offensive word 'coolie', a term used by British colonials for low-skilled day-labourers, indentured semi-slaves and porters who carried head-loads, is believed to derive from the hard-working *koli* fisherfolks. They conduct small-scale or 'artisanal' fishing, one could say, and are, I learn to my surprise, the original inhabitants of Mumbai—it is in fact after this aboriginal tribe that the upmarket Colaba is named, a corruption of the word *koliwada* or 'settlement of the *koli* caste fishermen'. Their name is also evident in the yummy prawns koliwada, that are coated in atomic-hot batter and fried village-style. From what I've read there are about half a million who live in *koli* fishing villages around Mumbai and supply daily catch to over one hundred fish markets, and another estimated half a million people are dependent on the fish trade.

Despite its glitzy bar scene, Colaba is also backpackerland and as usual I check into one of the many ex-hippie lodges, one of those that still dot the lanes in the shadow of the historic Taj Mahal Hotel, a bit like the seeker character in *The Razor's Edge* whose cruise ship docked for a few days in Bombay, and after having 'supper in a native eating-house' found that 'the coloured, noisy crowds, the smell of the East, acrid and aromatic, enchanted me' so, on an impulse, he decided to stay on and 'walked slowly back to the native quarter and looked about for a hotel. I found one after a while and took a room. I had the clothes I stood up in, some loose cash, my passport, and my letter of credit. I felt so free, I laughed out loud.'

Maugham of course didn't stay in 'the native quarter' but at the Yacht Club and narrates in *A Writer's Notebook* that while having lunch with a maharaja, he's asked if he knows the difference between the Yacht Club and the Bengal Club:

> *'No,' said I innocently.*
>
> *'In the Bengal Club at Calcutta they don't allow dogs or Indians, but in the Yacht Club at Bombay they don't mind dogs; it's only Indians they don't allow.'*

I couldn't for the life of me think of an answer to that then, and I haven't thought of one since.

The old Taj is where the spiritual Beatle, George Harrison, hard rock group Led Zeppelin and wealthier European authors on tour put up, like Graham Greene (who found inspiration for his novel *The Comedians* while staying there) and Alberto Moravia, and Italian film director Pier Paolo Pasolini who described it in *Scent of India* as 'riddled from one side to the other by corridors and high saloons (like seeing the inside of an enormous musical instrument)'. But it is way too expensive for me. Coincidentally, when E.M. Forster spent time in town in the early 1920s, he too shunned the Taj and preferred the downmarket Green's Hotel—located next-door to the Taj which it, in fact, predated. Apart from finding Green's affordable and less pompous, and not overtly sophisticated, Forster seems to have enjoyed the fact that it was louder and wilder, its clientele a mix of sailors, single ladies and gay gents, bohemian musicians, artists and writers (it was also a haunt of the afore-mentioned Mulk Raj Anand, for example).

Being notoriously mean, V.S. Naipaul too checked into the Green's and rather than spending on an airy sea-facing room picked a cheaper cockroach-infested one at the back, all the while complaining about how his travel agency-appointed guide, sent to receive him from the harbour, Apollo Bunder barely metres away, kept trying to strike a deal with him about 'cheej'. Naipaul of course knew no Hindi, so didn't understand that *chiz* means 'things' and that the 'shabby' Goan wanted to sell him bootlegged booze in lieu of the whiskey that the customs had confiscated. In his inimitable manner Naipaul heard what he wanted to—'cheese', he declared, 'was a delicacy in India. Imports were restricted, and the Indians had not yet learned how to make cheese.'

Naipaul's days were spent trying to find hygienic food and he genuinely despised his own choice of hotel: 'The bathrooms and lavatories are foul; the slimy woodwork has rotted away as a result of this daily drenching; the concrete walls are green and black with slime. You cannot complain that the hotel is dirty. No Indian will agree with you. Four sweepers are in daily attendance, and it is enough in India that the sweepers attend. They are not required to clean.'

Eventually, Green's was annexed by the Taj and, as it kept expanding, in the early 1970s, the modern high-rise extension was built in its place. Alexander Frater, who was *Chasing the Monsoon* (as the title of his book goes), had a better budget than Forster or Naipaul (or me), so he checked into the Taj to get a ringside view of the rains from the twentieth-floor bar. When it wasn't raining, the posh travel writer strolled around the Gateway of India, 'feeling the feathery touch of child beggars on my arms. I gave coins to one, who dashed off and handed them to a haggard, lank-haired crone squatting on the pavement nearby, suckling a baby. Her breast, though, was round and full and I realized she must still be in her twenties. Everything is relative, though in India relativity is geared to medieval expectations.'

Lunch box transportation is very important in Mumbai.

Heading further off than Frater did on his walks, I see fishing boats in a *koli* village, still located within walking distance from Colaba in the heart of the city. Here, ladies dry shrimp on the sidewalk between bus stops, and I instantaneously find myself in Salman Rushdie's *Midnight's Children*, 'follow Colaba Causeway to its tip—past cheap clothes shops and Irani restaurants and the second-rate flats of teachers, journalists and clerks—and you'll find them, trapped between the naval base and the sea.' Eulogising these aboriginals of Mumbai, Rushdie writes one of the most evocative sentences in his collected prose: 'They caught pomfret and crabs, and made fish-lovers of us all.'

Of interest to the literary tourist is the Sir J.J. School of Art, north of the Chhatrapati Shivaji station, as it happens to be the birthplace of Rudyard Kipling (whose father ran the school) who pipped Rabindranath Tagore by six years to become the first Indian-born Nobel laureate in 1907. The spot where the Kiplings lived is marked with a plaque, but the original shack in which he was born had been torn down by the time Kipling returned to work in India as a young man. This used to be the city's outskirts, dotted with palm groves and 'Rudy' rhymed his remembrances of the idyllic city in 'To the City of Bombay' (1896):

Mother of Cities to me
For I was born in her gate,
Between the palms and the sea,
Where the world-end steamers wait.

His two India novels *Jungle Book* and *Kim* capture how the country may have appeared at the end of the nineteenth century. The former is set in the forests of Seoni in easternmost Madhya Pradesh while the latter is a virtual travelogue tracing the Grand Trunk Road through north India.

The arts school is more or less across the street from another landmark: Mahatma Jyotiba Phule Mandai which was then called Crawford Market and where Kipling's father was in charge of decorations such as the artwork above the gates. The senior Kipling liked the town for being a 'cockney sort of place' that was very un-Indian. In his autobiography, *Something of Myself* written at the age of seventy, junior Kipling sentimentally recalled his first memory in life being 'early morning walks to the Bombay fruit market with my *ayah* and later with my sister in her perambulator, and of our returns with our purchases piled high on the bows of it.'

In his *India Impressions*, artist Walter Crane who came in the winter of 1906-7, noted how Crawford Market, 'has a rather English Gothic look, but inside the scene is entirely oriental, crowded with natives in all sorts of colours, moving among fish, fruit, grain, and provisions of all kinds, buying and selling amid a clamour of tongues—a busy scene of colour and variety, in a symphony of smells, dominated by that of the smoke of joss-sticks kept burning at some of the stalls as well as a suspicion of opium, which pervades all the native quarters in Indian cities.' But in Rohinton Mistry's novel *Such a Long Journey*, the market is depicted as charmless and nauseatingly menacing, 'a dirty, smelly, overcrowded place where the floors were slippery with animal ooze and vegetable waste, where the cavernous hall of meat was dark and forbidding, with huge, wicked-looking meat hooks hanging from the ceiling…' Sounds like he was trying to write a horror movie script, but in this oft-quoted passage Crawford Market represents the chaos of Mumbai. Unlike Mistry and his protagonist, I heroically poke my nose into stalls that sell almost everything edible from everywhere, finding imported pâté in a tin, cubes of meaty stock, and other ingredients to take home.

Crawford Market's bas-relief
decorations by Kipling Sr.

The insanely intense but colourfully cosmopolitan Mumbai of Saadat Hasan Manto lies a forty-five-minute walk north at Byculla. Spending a decade in town, before Partition drove him to Pakistan, Manto lived on Clare Road in the same building from where the weekly journal which he edited was published, and regularly ate at the semi-rundown canteen Sarvi (a prominent non-veg destination) where the house specialty is kainchi kebabs washed down with strong, milky half-glasses of 'cutting-chai'. Manto described the squalor of Byculla unflinchingly, 'an extremely dirty neighbourhood dotted with garbage heaps that served as an open toilet.' Nandita Das's 2018 film *Manto* was, on the other hand, mostly shot in the fancy and breezy Marine Lines, whereas the actual Byculla stood in for Pakistan where Manto died from cirrhosis of the liver in a mental asylum in 1955. Byculla market is described somewhat more appetisingly than Mistry's take on downtown's Crawford Market, by Kiran Nagarkar in his cult novel *Ravan & Eddie*: 'The vendors sat on raised platforms with stack upon stack of brinjals, cabbages, spinach, potatoes, onions, beans, pumpkins, melons, bananas, carrots, green beans and cucumbers on either side of them. But there was life under the platforms too, where the reserve stock was kept. Ravan was transfixed by a dwarf at eye level who was burrowing in a hole underneath. No, not a dwarf but a man on his haunches whose duck feet paddled him in and out of the dungeon. On his way out he brought forth an oversized, tumescent jackfruit in his hands.'

Another important spot is The Wayside—known in colonial days as 'A modern English Inn' when it was owned by an English lady—which became like a second home to poet Arun Kolatkar and other intellectuals. I still recall its red-and-white chequered tablecloths from my first visits in the 1990s that transported one to some time-warped utopia. In the 2000s, it lost its hipness and was reduced, last I saw it, to a hole-in-the-wall bakery counter.

Up the road, the disintegrating 1860s' cast-iron edifice of Watson's Hotel is sometimes named as the Indian film industry's birthplace; it's also where Richard Burton translated the *Kamasutra* that became notorious in English and Kipling stayed on visits to his birthplace; and Mark Twain—of *Huckleberry Finn* fame—rented a top-floor suite in the 1890s. Twain never set any fiction in India, but wrote on Mumbai in his travelogue *Following the Equator* something that I always have felt acutely about Indian cities: 'I seem to have a kaleidoscope at my eye;

and I hear the clash of the glass bits as the splendid figures change, and fall apart, and flash into new forms, figure after figure, and with the birth of each new form I feel my skin crinkle and my nerve-web tingle with a new thrill of wonder and delight.' The hotel closed in 1960 and the abandoned heritage structure is forlornly awaiting restoration.

At around the same time that Twain sat sipping tea on his balcony at Watson's, a young British-educated barrister, Mohandas Gandhi, tried to find work in Bombay where he wished to settle down. In 1891, he rented a small place in Girgaon from where he could walk to the High Court by the Maidan. The lack of job opportunities caused him to move to South Africa. Back again in 1902, Gandhi tried to set up a legal practice in Aga Khan's Buildings, near the High Court in what colloquially used to be known as the English Bazaar because of its businesses stocking foreign imports (now, it's the rather downmarket Nagindas Master Road). The cramped city affected his family's health so he shifted to a 'fine bungalow' at an unknown address in Santa Cruz from where he used to take the train to Churchgate station (built in the mid-1890s and so a spanking new building at the time), frequently being the only passenger in the commodious first-class compartment. But again Africa beckoned, where he got thrown off trains by racist conductors, and the rest is history.

In 1915, when the Mahatma-to-be landed at Apollo Bunder, at the cusp of becoming the best-known person in the world, he was interviewed by both *The Bombay Chronicle* and *The Times of India*. On return visits to town, such as 1924 after his first Pune jail stint, he recuperated in a borrowed house at Juhu Beach, walking by the ocean. After a wartime incarceration, he stayed in Juhu again in 1944; when the hosts learnt that he'd never seen a movie, they arranged a private screening of the then running B-flick *Mission to Moscow* (by the director of the classic *Casablanca*) and a mythological extravaganza called *Ram Rajiya* by Vijay Bhatt. Gandhi disliked both and didn't accept cinema with its half-clad heroines as a valid art form according to the book *Mahatma Gandhi in Cinema* by Narendra Kaushik; on his posthumously launched website www.mkgandhi.org, he goes on record—in an article titled *Gandhi on and in cinema* by Akul Tripathi—to state, 'I have never been to a cinema. But even to an outsider, the evil that it has done and is doing is patent. The good, if it has done any at all, remains to be proved.'

And it wasn't just Bollywood, but he, in fact, felt ambivalent about the whole city or as he said in 1921, 'Bombay is beautiful, not for its big buildings for most of them hide squalid poverty and dirt, not for its wealth for most of it is derived from the blood of the masses, but for its world-renowned generosity. The Parsis set the tone, and Bombay has ever lived up to her reputation. Bombay's charity has covered a multitude of her sins.'

It has also always been a city of poetry. Its gritty downtown fostered poets like Dom Moraes about whom many strange stories are told (for example, that he stepped out to buy cigarettes one day and then his wife never saw him again) and Namdeo Dhasal who lived near the Opera House, around the corner from Kamathipura, which has the reputation of being a red-light district. Writing his third book on India, *A Million Mutinies Now*, Naipaul visited the poet 'in the brothel area, among criminals and prostitutes...Namdeo's great originality was that he had written naturally, using words and expressions that Dalits and no one else used. In his first book of poems he had written, specifically, in the language of the Bombay brothel area. That had caused the sensation; he had been praised and condemned.'

Rather than reading Naipaul, I'd recommend *The Book of Chocolate Saints*—loosely based on the life of Dom Moraes—by Jeet Thayil that captures the once-vibrant poetry scene of the late 1900s, when city-based writers still remembered a scandalous 1960s visit by the American beats Allen Ginsberg and Peter Orlovsky. The foreign guests who were basically bumming around like the pre-hippie vagrants they frankly speaking were, on a round-the-globe trip from Paris to North Africa, and via India through Southeast Asia, landed like an alien invasion from a distant solar system. In 1962, the outwardly cool as a cucumber Ginsberg, who kept to vegetarian food in India, wrote to fellow author Gregory Corso about the cheap fare: 'Hardly been diarrhetic here even as much as Paris and I've really eaten the worst. Maybe I'm immune, immunised by Peru, Mexico, Tangier. But ritzy restaurants are cheaper than Tangier even. Bombay has great food all over…come here and have a ball in the greatest, weirdest nation of history.' Ginsberg also tried to convince Jack Kerouac and William Burroughs to join him, but only Gary Snyder turned up for that ball.

Back in the day, these poets habitually met up in so-called Irani joints that, despite the exotic nomenclature, rarely are run by migrants from Tehran. The first were set up around the year 1900 by Parsis, a small but influential community after whom many important streets are named and who, like Gandhi said, 'set the tone' for the city—including its eating-out-scene, it should be pointed out.

Fearing persecution for their Zoroastrian beliefs, they had originally fled from Persia when it was conquered by Muslims in the seventh century, to India's west coast where they found a safe haven. They moved to Bombay around the time it became British in the 1660s, to set up businesses and prospered thanks to their 'western' sensibilities. They ran, for example, many provision stores where the British preferred to shop. A second wave came when famine struck Persia in 1871 and the newcomers were experts at running lodging houses, refreshment rooms and tea stalls. Bombay's population of Zoroastrians peaked at 59,813 during the first half of the 1900s. They were renowned for their lavish hospitality and grand parties to celebrate all manner of occasions, so when they got into the food business, it was a win-win situation—the perhaps most notable outcome of which is the Taj Mahal Hotel that houses several iconic restaurants.

Being westernised, their cafés have a manifestly Mediterranean feel—one might be in Cairo or Istanbul if it wasn't for the food which combines Middle Eastern recipes with Indian spices. To fit in, they gave up beef but are still big on non-taboo meats like chicken and mutton, while their take on Western dishes, omelettes with chillies, pepper, garlic and onions, is notably spicier than in France whence the dish originated. This cultural adaptability, with menus that suited both Indians and foreigners alike, resulted in Parsi eateries kick-starting the restaurant industry. From having had barely any before 1900, save for the odd disreputable tavern catering to travellers, by mid-twentieth century, the city was home to hundreds of Irani cafés. While the original Parsis who have lived in India for more than a thousand years are called Zoroastrians, the later migrants are identified as Persians or Iranis. Hence the name Irani café.

However, in today's age of Punjabification of the food scene only about twenty remain, 'too inexpensively lovely to survive in modern Mumbai' to quote Suketu Mehta. Their cheap buttered buns had such thick crusts that they had to be soaked in chai, food suited for long discussions and hence an imperative part of art, music, and literature, nurturing generations of thinkers—for example I once spotted the living legend of Indian poetry, Adil Jussawalla, at the 1940s Irani café Stadium next to Churchgate Station.

These establishments are definitely worth visiting before they disappear, as they might well do with changing customer preferences in this epoch of cocktail lounges with App-based menus. One of the last to have retained its ambience largely untouched is the 1930s' vintage Cafe Military in Nagindas Master Road steps away from Flora Fountain, where Rushdie has been seen on visits to town and Arun Kolatkar, who didn't own a telephone, could be reached on Thursdays after his previous haunt, Wayside Inn, shut down—so that people knew where to find him. The airy restaurant takes one back to a time when real estate wasn't so expensive that tables had to be cramped together in boxy, low-ceilinged mini-halls. Here one could even dance between the tables, if it was permitted.

The name—Military—hints at the availability of non-veg, traditionally the diet for the warrior caste, *kshatriyas*, and the origin of 'military hotels' is believed to be found in the army messes that the Maratha forces set up across their domains. The concept of meat boosting physical strength and belligerence seems fairly universal, especially compared to how vegetarianism is such a non-violent activity. Here, one can still enjoy the unfashionable but classic atmosphere down to the spindly-legged black wooden chairs, panelled walls with big mirrors, odd notifications posted here and there, and linger for hours and write (or read), while sampling Parsi specials including breathtaking dhansak—imagine dhal boosted with juicy chicken—or freshly-cooked brain served whole, washed down with ice-cold London pilsner (despite its name a very local brew) or raspberry soda (which is only found in such olden places).[24] One cannot but love the café tables with yellow tablecloths, and the seediness lies in minor details such as the cheap plastic plates and pre-modern restroom.

Whenever I'm in Mumbai, I spend the full week at Cafe Military, reading and chatting, thinking and drinking. There I enjoy beering with Sidharth Bhatia, expert on Mumbai's cultural past with books on Bollywood noir and Indian rock to his credit. One day, he tells me all about how he showed his literary hero, the late H.R.F. Keating (1926-2011), around town—ironically in the 1980s, ages after Keating's award-winning first Bombay crime novel *A Perfect Murder* was published (in 1964). It is an interesting fact that the British detective novelist had written several novels about Inspector Ganesh V. Ghote without actually setting foot in the city that serves as an evocative tropical backdrop for his plots. He apparently picked the locale by flipping randomly through an atlas.

A Perfect Murder won both the Gold Dagger in the UK and the Edgar Allan Poe Award in the US, and was being made into a motion picture by Ismail Merchant, which is why Keating found himself in India—to do a cameo in it. The film also starred Naseeruddin Shah in the lead role.

'As I recall,' says Bhatia, 'he had a very striking beard, like George Bernard Shaw, and he appeared gentle, mournful but with a twinkle in his eye. He had this habit of blending in silently while moving about and I found him very pleasant.'

We try to reconstruct what else Keating experienced in town. Exactly how they came to meet is hard to say for Bhatia so many years later, but he suspects that somebody gave Keating his phone number because he's very much a Bombay boy, born in the mid-1950s at Hotel Astoria where his father—an avid reader of crime fiction (literature that his son went on to be deeply besotted by)—was a manager. Bhatia joined the *Free Press Journal* which had its offices in Dalal Street, so he was obviously a perfect cicerone for the foreign writer who wanted to be shown around downtown. Which is the favour that Keating asked of him.

Bhatia, being a fan, was happy to help. He's always felt that Mumbai is the perfect setting for detective novels, with its glamorous super-rich contrasting with the extremely poor, and once-sleazy areas like Colaba, with bars catering to sailors and cheap hotels full of hippies. 'This is a city made to be written about, but it has had no strong tradition of detective literature. It took Harry Keating to do it. Inspector Ghote is a superb character and in the absence of competition Keating did a fine job.'

To my question of how Keating managed to write about the city before he came here, Bhatia says, 'I understand that he studied Indian newspapers in the British Library, and I think he laid his hands on a police manual. He was also helped by a British adman who used to live here in the 1960s.'

Later, Bhatia takes me around the Kala Ghoda district where he and Keating walked all those years ago. He's knowledgeable about the buildings, the streets and which shops have been there for ages. 'I've always felt that the soul of the city is here. Kala Ghoda is a prime spot to set a murder mystery,' he says.

❖

'I have been a cook all my life. I began experimenting with my diet in my student days in London,' said Gandhi as he lectured residents at the Sevagram ashram in 1935. He had just relocated to the India of villages—a paradigm shift about which he felt strongly: 'Now we have embarked on a mission the like of which we had not undertaken before.' Then, eventually, he got to the point he wished to make that day regarding village reforms: 'Let us not, like most of them, cook anyhow, eat anyhow, live anyhow. Let us show them the ideal diet.' He proposed that his followers completely do away with spices and instead eat natural raw food, such as salad, while teaching the villagers to do the same—because boiling vegetables killed their vitamins. Exactly like the ancient Ayurvedic tradition, he believed in food's medicinal values.

Apart from the fact that uncooked food was practically unheard of in that era, it's interesting how Gandhi talked about vitamins. Their role in preventing illness and building health had been proposed by a Polish chemist only in the 1910s and it took much longer for vitamin researchers to win Nobel prizes. Already in the 1920s, Gandhi wrote, 'Vitamin means the vital essence. Chemists cannot detect it by analysis. But health experts have been able to feel its absence.'

Yet I can't envisage everybody salivating in joyful zeal as they listened to Gandhi that day. No masala in the curry? Uncooked food? I visualise jaws dropping and eyes popping. I suspect he wasn't entirely on to the medical benefits of certain seasonings like ginger, garlic, cardamom and turmeric, and so he went a bit overboard, but then a pioneer would probably need to do that.

This reminds me of how, about twenty-five years ago, on a train from Delhi to Kanyakumari, I broke journey midway. I had heard that Gandhi founded his ashram at Sevagram for the precise reason that it was located geographically in the centre of India, and so it seemed appropriate to take a break. The railway station was empty and I was the sole passenger alighting. The only things moving in the quiet heat were dry leaves rustling before a feeble breeze. Outside, stood a lone cycle rickshaw. No hotel in sight. It was an even more unassuming village in the 1930s when Gandhi moved in and he was particular about not making it any more assuming than it was, instructing his helpers that to build his hut 'as little expense as possible should be incurred'.

I approached the rickshaw-puller and not being conversant in Marathi, I showed him a banknote with Gandhi on it. He knew who I had come for and cycled me to the ashram where he directed me to enter. I was planning to look into the museum, then carry on to the nearest town, Nagpur, to spend the night, but before I could do so an elderly ashramite spotted me carrying my luggage, told me to follow and we passed Gandhi's simple hut made of eco-friendly materials like clay, a pipal tree planted by 'Bapu' as per a small sign (he preferred not to be called Mahatma) and we reached the guesthouse where political leaders like Jawaharlal Nehru used to stay when they wished to consult with him. I was shown a roomy room where I could stay for as long as I liked. The cot was of 1930s vintage, so every visiting celebrity must have slept in it back in those days, and there were no mod-cons. But the rent was extremely cheap, so I had no complaints. I was instructed to make myself comfortable and then join the others for supper. It was the strangest thing I had ever experienced as a frequent traveller—they didn't ask me who I was, how long I planned to stay: I was simply made to feel at home.

This 'village of service' turned into a laboratory for Gandhi as it attracted all manner of creative engineers and assorted experts who researched ecological living, devising everything from lanterns that burned vegetable waste oil instead of fossil fuel to potties that automatically segregated what was evacuated from the bowels into fertiliser and manure. Important people who arrived at the station were picked up by what Gandhi jokingly called his 'Oxford'—a broken Ford car pulled by oxen.

And then there was the alimentary mission. Despite his

asceticism and frequent fasting, Gandhi was by no means against food. He was merely keen on making the most of a precious resource. For example, later in that first year at Sevagram—1935—he advocated the daily consumption of soybeans which are more nutritious than meat and have marvellous health benefits. In a series of articles in his journal *Harijan*, he described them as what today would be called a 'super-food'; in fact, in the first half the twentieth century, soybeans were a fairly ignored foodstuff in the West and only rose to prominence as a 'vegan meat' quite recently, so clearly Gandhi saw something that many others missed.

He also introduced novelties to the village such as sugarcane cultivation and bee-keeping, which suggests that sweet teeth weren't frowned upon. Under his leadership, the ashram produced marmalades from seasonal fruits and peanut butter, and bread was made from home-ground, coarse, unsifted wheat in order to keep it fibre-rich. Gandhi even developed his own coffee substitute (he was against caffeine and other stimulants) from dark-roasted wheat. Generally, the fare seems to have been akin to what we'd encounter in the finest amongst urban India's new-fangled organic stores today.

After a bath, I headed for the dining hut. Meals were strictly timed (dinner at 5.30 p.m. as I recall) and the sun hung low on the horizon as I walked towards the hut. Food was had together, as Gandhi usually kept an eye on how much everyone ate—it was his belief that most don't know what's healthy for them and so ate themselves sick, or as he had written in a series of articles on health in 1913: 'All will agree that out of every 100,000 persons 99,999 eat merely to please their palate, even if they fall ill in consequence. Some take a laxative every day in order to be able to eat well, or some powder to aid digestion....some die of thoughtless overeating.'

Humans compared unfavourably to cows in this regard: 'Cattle do not eat for the satisfaction of the palate, nor do they eat like gluttons. They eat when they are hungry—and just enough to satisfy that hunger. They do not cook their food. They take their portion from that which Nature proffers to them. Then, is man born to pander to his palate?' He also pointed out, in a characteristically humoristic remark, that 'we have turned our stomach into a commode and we carry this commode with us wherever we go.'

On another occasion, he emphasised, 'Instead of using the body as a temple of God we use it as a vehicle for indulgences, and are not ashamed to run to medical men for help in our effort to increase them and abuse the earthly tabernacle.'

Therefore, it's not surprising that I wasn't asked for any preferences, but simply served chapattis, a boiled vegetable hotchpotch featuring home-grown beetroots, and a modest salad of raw, plain veggies. The only spice I could make out was salt. Basic but kind of interesting—and it reflected the Gandhian ideals of having food as if it were a medicine 'to keep the body going.' Apart from prayers before food, there was strictly no talking according to ashram rules, 'Silence is obligatory at meals. It is uncivil and a form of violence to criticize while eating any badly cooked item of the food. Such criticism should be conveyed to the manager in writing after the meal.'

Later, as I'm looking up minutes by visitors back in the day, I find that the menu has not changed significantly. During his lifetime, Gandhian cookery was considered truly spaced out as gastronomic experiences go: 'Steaming hell-brew served up in a great bucket' reads one contemporary Englishman's description of the 'ashramatic' menu, related in Ramachandra Guha's biography of Verrier Elwin, *Savaging the Civilized*. Elwin spent a month with Gandhi in 1931 and even jotted down a poem titled 'Thoughts of a Gourmet on being Confronted with an Ashram Meal': 'O food inedible, we eat thee/ O drink incredible, we greet thee./ Meal indigestible, we bless thee.'

Another foreigner wondered, after being fed the same mush of pumpkins cooked in spinach day after day, whether he might possibly look forward to trying something different for lunch.

Gandhi asked, 'You do not like vegetables?'

'It's just that I don't like the taste of the same vegetables three days in a row.'

Gandhi pondered this and suggested, 'Try adding plenty of salt and lime.'

A more articulate and rationalistic critique was framed in 1915 by Gandhi's own son Harilal, then twenty-six years of age, and who'd later go on to take a very different path from his father's. A letter of his suggests that Gandhi was not, for example, always into salty food: 'I cannot believe that a salt-free diet or abstinence from ghee or milk indicates strength of character and morality. If one decides to refrain from consuming such foods as a result of thoughtful consideration, the abstinence could be beneficial. It is seen that such abstinence and asceticism is possible only after one has attained a certain state. By insisting on salt-free diet and on specific abstinences, at the Phoenix institution [Gandhi's ashram in South Africa], you are trying to cultivate self-denial.'

The Bengal-born author Nirad Chaudhuri, in his autobiographical tome *Thy Hand, Great Anarch!*, described Gandhi's visit to Kolkata thus: 'Putting up Gandhi did not present a difficult problem; feeding him did. Mahatma Gandhi's dietary prescriptions were not only rigid and numerous, but also odd.' A list of the vegetables that Gandhi approved of 'was formidably long and representative of the ecology of Bengal. Of course, he did not eat the full range of vegetables at one meal or even on one single day, but he or his secretary in charge might demand one or other of them on a particular day or for a particular meal in order to test the resources and loyalty of his host.'

For modern holidaymakers, the ashram in Sevagram might not compare with a beach resort in Bali, but I actually considered staying on for some days, thinking that I'd shed many kilograms of excess flab and trot home nimble as a goat. Thanks to the light and early meal, I slept well, except for the occasional mosquitoes that I didn't dare to swat so as not to break any non-violence regulations. Anyway, the wake-up call was at 4 a.m. for prayers, just as when Gandhi was still around, so going early to bed turned out to be a sensible strategy. Next, I was told to spend my morning weeding a patch of grass behind the latrines. Following a simple 6 a.m. breakfast, there was mandatory spinning for two hours—a calming exercise akin to meditation.

The author as tourist at the Mahatma's ashram in Sevagram.

Today, as we're used to health pages in newspapers, and every magazine with some instinct as to what sells carries cover stories on wellness and the latest dietary fads, we may note that in this field, too, Gandhi was a forerunner, devoting much space in the journals he published to health. His biggest bestseller during his lifetime wasn't the autobiographical *The Story of My Experiments with Truth*, but a booklet called *A Guide to Health* which was full of interesting cooking instructions. It was constantly reprinted and translated into many languages in India and abroad. Other titles by him that might fascinate modern readers include *The Moral Basis for Vegetarianism* and *Diet and Diet Reform*. Gandhian nutritional principles, were I to attempt to sum them up after reading all that he wrote on the subject, are based on the notion that everybody must know how to cook their own food or even better not cook at all but eat it raw—which in turn, calls for simplicity and the avoidance of complex culinary methodology, something that's increasingly catching on nowadays and is perhaps best reflected in those mix-your-own salad bars that dot many cities in conventionally non-veg territories like California and Scandinavia.

Secondly, by wholesome eating, one eliminates the need for going to doctors and pill-popping—again, a fairly obvious idea to us, but we may recall how not so long ago everybody (including myself) happily wolfed down oily-spicy gravies without thinking of the physical consequences. Or as Gandhi put it: 'I believe that man has little need to drug himself. 999 cases out of a thousand can be brought round by means of a well-regulated diet...' Gandhi's own awakening in this regard happened, as he described it, during his English student days when he, out of financial necessity, learnt how to prepare his own food. Also, there were important social considerations as he found his first English friends among the members of the London Vegetarian Society.

Vegetarianism was a philosophical idea for this movement (in the 1800s when 'isms', whether political, spiritual or otherwise, were the in-thing) and the restaurants backed by the movement were more of public clubs where the young Gandhi found a platform for his personal ideological development—as well as plenty of literature that argued for the benefits of a meatless diet. 'I saw that the writers on vegetarianism had examined the question very minutely, attacking it in its religious, scientific, practical and medical aspects.' Prior to this, for the young Gandhi vegetarianism had been a habit more than a conscious choice—after all he came from India's most vegetarian state, Gujarat.

Boldly, he clarified to his new English friends that 'Indian vegetarians and meat-eaters are quite different from English vegetarians and meat-eaters. Indian meat-eaters, unlike English meat-eaters, do not believe that they will die without meat. So far as my knowledge goes, they (the Indian meat-eaters) do not consider meat a necessity of life but a mere luxury. If they can get their roti, as bread is generally called there, they get on very well without their meat. But look at our English meat-eater; he thinks that he *must* have his meat. Bread simply helps him to eat meat, while the Indian meat-eater thinks that meat will help him to eat his bread.'

Once he found his feet among like-minded folks, the movement proved as edifying an experience as studying law. 'Vegetarianism was then a new cult in England, and likewise for me, because, as we have seen, I had gone there a convinced meat-eater, and was intellectually converted to vegetarianism later. Full of the neophyte's zeal for vegetarianism, I decided to start a vegetarian club in my locality, Bayswater. I invited Sir Edwin Arnold, who lived there, to be Vice-President,' he notes in one of his autobiographies. Sir Arnold was, apart from a confirmed Indophile, also editor of *The Daily Telegraph* and so a useful contact. Soon, Gandhi was reporting on Indian food culture in journals such as *The Vegetarian*. 'Diet cure or hygiene is a comparatively recent discovery in England. In India we have been practising this from time out of mind,' he wrote as cockily as only a twenty-one-year-old can do.

It should be pointed out that this juvenile journalistic experience laid the foundation for his lifelong interest in print media as a tool for spreading ideas. In an article published in England in 1891, he pointed out that 'attributing the Hindu weakness to vegetarianism is simply based on a fallacy', and later, that same year, he wrote that 'it is a pity that so little should be known of the foods of India in England. We have not to go very far to seek the cause. Almost all Englishmen who go to India keep up their own way of living. They not only insist on having the things they had in England, but will also have them cooked in the same way. It is not for me here to go into the why and wherefore of all these incidents. One would have thought that they would look into the habits of the people, if only out of curiosity, but they have done nothing of the kind…'

Having encountered all manner of health theories, he would for the rest of his life go on bravely experimenting with food—diets such as fasting, vital foods, raw foods, no-starch (essentially a precursor of what was to evolve into the even more specialised gluten-free diet of today), milkless (a precursor of lactose-free), sugarless and pickle-free eating, and fruitarianism—as much as he experimented with truth. Now and then projects had to be abandoned as they caused depression, headaches, dysentery and discomfort to such a degree that he could barely stand on his feet. Chewing on hard, uncooked grains broke his teeth. He was well aware of his own folly and once even burst out, 'But what a sacrifice of time and trouble to achieve what is after all a selfish end, which falls short of the highest! Life seems too short for these things.' His son Harilal certainly doubted his fads and questioned these in letters to the Mahatma: 'If my own experience or experiment of being a fruitarian for only twenty days has any validity, I speak with experience—I have also observed this characteristic among those who were fruitarians for six months—that people eat fruits and nuts far in excess to even those who overeat roti and dhal. Therefore, indigestion is bound to happen. Under such circumstances I see no benefits in adopting a fruit diet.'

Nevertheless, despite occasional doubts and criticism from kin and acolytes, Gandhi developed over the years a plan which, according to him, would be the best for mankind. Free from external beauty perhaps, compared to the cuteness of pre-plated *nouvelle cuisine* (only the austere portion sizes do remind one of that nineties food fad), unadorned by sumptuous seasonings and maximised masalas, it was the most functional eating strategy imaginable—and it is, naturally, vegetarian fare rich in fruit. 'A comparison with other animals reveals that our body structure most closely resembles that of fruit-eating animals, that is, the apes. The diet of the apes is fresh and dry fruit. Their teeth and stomach are similar to ours.' The target, as per his calculations, was to cut down ingredients and dishes—one itemised sample menu from 1935 that he planned for village workers contained the following: Wheat flour baked into chapattis, tomatoes, red gourd, soybeans, coconuts, linseed oil, milk, tamarind and salt, and then some jaggery and wood apple combined into a 'delicious chutney'.

Already in 1929, he had described how a scientific ahimsa cuisine can 'reduce the dietetic himsa that one commits.' He pointed out: 'Dieticians are of opinion that the inclusion of a small quantity of raw vegetables like cucumber, vegetable marrow, pumpkin, gourd, etc., in one's menu is more beneficial to health than the eating of large quantities of the same cooked.

But the digestions of most people are very often so impaired through a surfeit of cooked fare that one should not be surprised if at first they fail to do justice to raw greens, though I can say from personal experience that no harmful effect need follow if a tola or two of raw greens are taken with each meal provided one masticates them thoroughly.' Gandhi's own food intake, for much of his adult life, consisted of fixed quantities of grains like sprouted wheat, grated veggies, 40 g of fat and a similar measure of sugar or honey, and fruit. In 1934, he gave instructions to supporters who wished to host him on his tours, 'Fried things and sweets must be strictly eschewed. Ghee ought to be most sparingly used. More than one green vegetable simply boiled would be regarded as unnecessary. Expensive fruit should be always avoided.'

For any gourmand this may sound off-putting, especially in a hedonistic panegyric like this book of mine, but experts will agree that a certain frugality might actually heighten the eating experience almost à la molecular gastronomy. In fact, what Gandhi advocated would nowadays—when most of us are BP-afflicted diabetics—be considered a preferable fare and, for ethical reasons, food ought anyway to be grown in the vicinity entailing a minimal carbon footprint for its transportation. This emphasis on fresh home-grown ingredients is embraced by chefs who see the ridiculous in, say, flying salmon from Norway to Goa where there's so much fish available. Above all, the way he explored the relationship between eating and health in an age when the concept of 'health food' was unknown to most, unlike today when we know that food habits can kill or cure, gave me plenty of—what else—food for thought. Or to quote Gandhi after one of his communal dietary adventures, 'The experiment is not an easy thing nor does it yield magical results. It requires patience, perseverance and caution. Each one has to find his or her own balance of the different ingredients. Almost every one of us has experienced a clearer brain power and refreshing calmness of spirit.'

❖

Under the Ellis Bridge in Ahmedabad, a man is selling half a vacuum cleaner. I'd heard that Gujaratis are shrewd businessmen and this one ought to have an interesting marketing strategy if he comes here every Sunday to sell pieces that lack either hose or engine or both.

Despite its chronic dustiness, because of which vacuum cleaners may be treasured possessions, the city has plenty that might appeal to the semi-professional tourist: Museums for textiles and antiques, assorted Islamic monuments, and not one, but two of Mahatma Gandhi's abodes. The more visited is the

Ahmedabad: Gandhi's room and belongings at Kochrab Ashram, which was his first home when he returned to India from Africa.

Gandhi Smarak Sangrahalaya by the Sabarmati riverfront which is a major sight. The older, at Kochrab, is a surprisingly neat and quiet edifice, where I'm the only tourist when I explore it.

Gandhi first came to Ahmedabad in 1887 to take the entrance test to Bombay University. In those days, there was no railway from Rajkot to Ahmedabad, so he had to go by bullock cart, and it was his first visit to a big city. Ahmedabad had over 100,000 inhabitants then—he was impressed by the grandeur of everything, but unfortunately didn't do well in the test. He came 404th and scored a mere 89 out of 200 in English.

More well-documented is Gandhi's later and longer stay at Sabarmati Ashram, which he established as his permanent base in 1917, conveniently next-door to the Sabarmati Jail, which Gandhi jokingly referred to as the ashram branch (apart from Gandhi's occasional imprisonments, the jail housed many of his sympathisers too). He would go on to spend about thirteen years at the ashram and this is also where he began writing *The Story of My Experiments with Truth*. It was from here that the Salt March marched—quite symbolically—in the month of March in 1930, to break the Salt Law (a tax that had made Indian cooking prohibitively expensive especially for the poor). Gandhi vowed not to live again in the ashram unless India became independent—after which he returned to Ahmedabad now and then, never for long. Some 200 families descended from the original ashramites still inhabited the premises until the 2020s.

Many of the whitewashed buildings date from Gandhi's days—including the frugal Hriday Kunj where he lived. He is said to have slept mostly on the veranda out in front while inside, I view his spectacles, sandals, some spinning yarn and other belongings. The main museum-cum-memorial building—that holds a massive amount of important correspondence and photographs—was designed by world-renowned Goan-origin architect Charles Correa as one of his first big projects, inaugurated by Jawaharlal Nehru in 1963. Afterwards, Correa became known as one of the greatest thinkers in the field of city-planning—he believed in organic architecture and just a few years before he passed away, I had the opportunity to chat with him.

He pointed out that cities should not have highly fixed infrastructure (like metros unfortunately and increasingly do) because they must remain dynamic enough to adapt to people's needs. I thought it was a brilliant observation that countered the idea of how we always end up adjusting to where we live, rather than the other way around, so it has stayed with me up to now and...ah, well, I'll stop rambling and return to my narrative...so after I cover the important sights, I still have a Sunday left and decide to hang out in my hotel—House of M.G.,which in itself counts as among the city's finest sights. Located at the edge of the old town near Lal Darwaza, it is a 1924 mansion with labyrinthine corridors, museum-like halls and terraces worth a meander—dotted as they are with old-style wooden swings and nooks and crannies where one can feel at peace. By the way, the initials 'M.G.' do not stand for Mahatma Gandhi, but for the erstwhile owner Mangaldas Girdhardas, a textile baron who was Gandhi's contemporary.

At its acclaimed roof terrace 'renowned as one of the best—if not the best—restaurants in Gujarat' (according to *The Penguin Food Guide to India* by Charmaine O'Brien), I sample Gujarat's priciest thali which gives visitors the state on a platter, including tons of snacky fried gram flour starters or farsan that are so fundamental to the Gujarati diet, followed by fluffy lentil-and-rice cakes called dhoklas, crunchy kachoris, spicy chaats and invigorating salads, topped by unlimited helpings of mains or shaaks that change daily. That day, these included bateka (a potato curry), kadhi (besan balls in yoghurt curry), fansi (beans preparation), turiya patra (gourd with colocasia leaves), mag nimogar dhal (dry lentil preparation), a couple of different rustic breads, ghee-laced khichdi and dhal (cooked with cane sugar giving the standard lentil stew a luxurious taste), alongside freshly-churned buttermilk, lemon-honey-ginger juice as well as several sweetmeats and homemade fig ice-cream. *Wah!* The lightly-curried and jaggery-sweetened dhal can be a bit of a culture-shock for someone sampling Gujarati food for the first time, but it is said that Gujaratis love eating, so to fit in I polish off everything served on my silver platter.

House of M.G. sits just around the corner from the old town and it would seem a pity not to explore the area with its shops that spill out merchandise into the roads and snack stalls tempting passers-by with intriguing street-foods ranging from cheesy pineapple sandwiches to massive ice-lollies in every colour of the rainbow. Although I know plenty of scary tales about 'Delhi-belly' nobody I know has complained of 'Ahmedabad-abdomen' so in the junk-food alley adjacent to the Teen Darwaza gate, I have kebabs so luscious that I order two more plates (to counterbalance the pure-veg fare at my pure-veg hotel). It was after licking clean the plates of meaty juices that I came across the weekly flea market—by following the trail of Sunday shoppers drifting towards the Sabarmati riverfront by the Ellis Bridge. They all knew something that isn't mentioned in the tourist guidebooks. On the riverbank, traders had set up makeshift counters or laid out tarpaulins for their wares almost all the way to the next bridge downriver.

There are many great flea markets in India—such as Mumbai's 'Chor Bazaar' and Anjuna beach in Goa—but the one in Ahmedabad is the largest of its kind. In fact, it's bigger than the flea markets I've seen in New York, Shanghai, Copenhagen,

Harare and Reykjavik put together and the ultimate place to procure a second-hand treadmill or vintage radio set, a broken laptop or rusty nail, padlocks without keys or keys missing locks, live animals like goats and chicks, a handmade kebab grill (obviously with rather few takers in this vegetarian state), cheap crockery and pottery, empty liquor bottles (remember, Gujarat is a dry state), books for kids and adults and ultra-low-cost garments or machine parts, all in a brutal jumble that gives the refuse of a megacity one last chance to reincarnate as the property of new owners. It's a thought-provoking contrast to the sophisticated selection of period knickknacks that decorates my hotel's corridors.

The customers, too, are an intriguing mix of teenagers and geriatrics on weekend outings, peasants and townspeople, and jhola-carrying arts students foraging for stuff to incorporate into installations of 'found art'. Once I'm done browsing, I ask the broken-vacuum-cleaner-seller who buys them.

'Nobody.'

'Then why sell?'

'Why not?'

Well, ain't that true? Instead, I buy a remote control—there are different models on sale at his stall, handheld units that have been long separated from whatever they were meant to steer. I'm not exactly sure what I can do with it except that it's definitely lighter to carry home than half a vacuum cleaner.

VI

Regal Repasts and Partaking of the Past

(Royal India)

'India is full of such wonders, but she can't give them to me.'

—E.M. Forster in a letter from 1913
(after visiting Ujjain)

Painted haveli in Churu.

A 180-m-tall colossus shimmers on the horizon. A bespoke desert mirage?

No, it's the Alila Bishangarh. Superimposed on a 230-year-old warrior fort standing on a dramatic granite hillock, the hotel appears to guard a remote valley in the Aravalli range, in the heart of Rajasthan. Architecturally, it blends the Jaipuri with Mughal and a dash of cinematic Disneyland. As the bucolic road winds closer, it suddenly turns up to my left, then I glimpse it to the right again, as if it were tracking my approach—its strategic importance becoming quite obvious in a region crisscrossed by trade routes of eternal antiquity.

In the chilled-out arrival lounge away from the desert heat there's no reception counter, no A&D register to fill out. I get a glimpse into the future of hospitality as a staffer takes a shot of my ID with his cellphone and a laptop-wielding lady hands me a printout of my leisure plan including meals, cocktails, massages and excursions. There's nothing for me to do but flip the switch into pause mode. In my three decades of reviewing hospitality ventures for travel publications, I've never ever flowed so smoothly into place—like champagne poured into a flute—and before I know it, I'm set as a curd.

The fort is a maze in which it is really easy to lose one's way.

But that's how it is with traditional structures; one can't expect too many straight corridors, one must just adjust and relax. I'm staying in a suite that's been shaped to fit within the two-and-a-half-metre-thick, towering walls—due to constructional constraints most suites have different layouts, like pieces of a jigsaw puzzle. Mine has a circular bedroom within a south-facing watchtower from where I keep an eye on green parakeets somersaulting in the breeze. The handy hotel handbook catalogues, apart from the usual in-room meal menus, policies regarding environmental efforts (waste minimisation, energy conservation, anti-global warming) and social sustainability (such as employing villagers or growing veggies with recycled water). I almost expect to find Greenpeace sailing in the tub when I prepare to have a bath.

There's an overall localised sensibility which is easy to appreciate. The rooftop restaurant serves the robust cuisine of the Bishangarh hamlet and the Shekhawati region, where the cooking is done like hunters of yore used to, with meats buried in hot sandpits, simmering in their own juices and fats (quite a practical idea in waterless deserts), the way brave heroes have always slow-roasted whatever mammal their arrows hit. Hunting may these days only be done illegally, but the shikar preparations remain in fashion for nostalgic reasons and illustrate, some believe, how dum-pukht was born. It all conspires to make one feel that one is really in a special place—and not in any run-of-the-mill luxury hotel whose chefs are cluster-bombing diners with multicuisine.[25] The first morning, for breakfast, I order genial millet parathas, tomato-chilli sabzi, and buttermilk, all of which reflects a typical farmer's morning meal cobbled together from rural staples. It is almost too good to be true, but it is true.

As for daytime activities, guests are taken to visit the village silversmith, then a lady who weaves carpets by hand, next a potter, and a farmer's wife named Daya cooks me a wholesome lunch with local vegetables and bakes ghee-enriched millet flatbreads over wood-fire in her courtyard. Much of the food has been grown in a patch behind the house. In the evening, I cool down in the castle's war room which is now a bar room with a cigar lounge in a turret. There, I am served an alluring snack menu that the barman calls 'Indian tapas': Pickle-powered watermelon *sashimi*, tofu cooked in chai, hummus of mashed green peas powdered with wasabi and flax seeds served with khakra crisps. Talk about thinking…no, eating out of the box.

It took Rahul Kapur and his two co-owners ten years of work to set it all up. Kapur tells me, over a cuppa at the airy infinity poolside Mediterranean café, 'There was no access road to the fort when we took it over, so we had to climb up to the ruin that was inhabited by a million bats. We found it very intriguing so we thought let's do something. But how do you take construction materials up a hill like that?'

I shrug. *No idea.*

'I became the proud owner of twenty-two donkeys. But once I had loaded them, I stood down here and tried to push them up there,' he says with a laugh.

Donkeys aren't cooperative animals or so I've heard, but I decide not to say, 'I could have told you so.'

'So, I had to hire four donkey drivers!'

Clearly, Kapur wanted to avoid damaging the existing structure or the cliff it rested on, so the property was handcrafted painstakingly with limited use of heavy machinery. He converted the ruined parts into common areas and added three floors of modern rooms on top. It's hard to imagine the complexities of putting in elevators within the rambling structure and incorporating knolls of bedrock into the design.

'We tried to make the new parts look like they were already there from before. To keep the ethos of the place, we used local stone rather than imported marble.'

'Must have still cost a bomb?'

'More than money, our hearts and souls went into this.'

Alila Bishangarh blends new hotel with old bastions almost seamlessly.

On my first trip into Rajasthan way back in 1991, I recall ending up in a nondescript township called Bundi, where one hundred years earlier Rudyard Kipling is believed to have got the idea for his novel *Kim*. Although he held Rajputs in high esteem in a general sense, Kipling had his doubts about Bundi which he ranked as the worst place he'd ever been to:

'There is no order to sell fishing-hooks, or to supply an Englishman with milk, or to change currency notes for him. He must only deal with the Durbar for whatever he requires; and wherever he goes he must be accompanied by at least two armed men. They will tell him nothing, for they know or affect to know nothing of the city. They will do nothing except shout at the little innocents who joyfully run after the stranger and demand *pice*, but there they are, and there they will stay till he leaves the city, accompanying him to the gate, and waiting there a little to see that he is fairly off and away. Englishmen are not encouraged in Boondi.'

I tried my best to walk in Kipling's footsteps but instead of encountering 'little innocents' a bunch of nasty children threw camel turds at me. In spite of this, I decided to linger, having chanced upon Braj Bushanjee—former prime-ministerial mansion, or haveli, now a lodge run by descendants of the minister. As I was served a lightly-spiced vegetarian thali on the rooftop, the proprietor explained that he mainly received busloads of European tour groups. I got a quirky room that hadn't been modernised much. Entering the bathroom, I smashed my head into the low doorframe. I saw stars. Each and every time.

I continued my onward journey with a potato-lumpy head full of bumps. But the stay became an eye-opener. Rajasthan has always been India's #1 inbound tourist destination, but it was only really in the post-liberalisation economy that its many grand heritage structures became hospitality hotspots. Take for example Rohetgarh—founded in 1622 and about an hour's drive from Jodhpur. It's one of the world's loveliest outback lodges. It appears that Rao Jodha, the builder of Jodhpur, had a brother, Dalpat Singh, who became the Thakur of Rohet. His clan has been, from then on, among the prominent breeders of Marwari battle horses—which are considered as important to the Rajput's self-image as the electric guitar is to a rock star's career. Those purebred Marwari horses are actually still there in a stable, waiting to take hotel guests on a safari or a picnic. For true horse-lovers, there's even one room with a panoramic window opening into the stable so that you and the horses can keep an eye on each other.

After independence, the noblemen had to look for other job options outside feudal careers and so the then Thakur of Rohet village, Manvendra Singhji Rathore, became a history teacher at Mayo College in Ajmer. In the 1980s, he met a twenty-something English writer who was desperately looking for a quiet room in which to sit and write, something that seemed not to be readily available at the time, so being hospitable, Singhji put him up for a couple of months. The writer was Bruce Chatwin and the book he wrote, *The Songlines*.

I later checked for further details in Nicholas Shakespeare's biography, in which Rohetgarh is described as a 'writer's paradise' for Chatwin who wrote long letters home praising his marvellous accommodation (and host). Towards the end of the 1980s, at the cusp of liberalisation, the pioneering Thakur decided to open up his home as a hotel and one of the first guests was William Dalrymple, who promptly checked into Chatwin's room (suite #15 if you must know) 'where, in a desperate bid for inspiration, I started the manuscript [of *City of Djinns*] at the desk where Bruce Chatwin wrote *The Songlines*.' Other writers who have worked in the same suite include Simon Winchester and Patrick French.

I can understand why, as writers are superstitious people. But as I don't particularly want this book to sound like its written by one of them, I prefer to stay in a different room. Despite the fact that the family now runs three hotels with a total of fifty-one rooms, their hallmark remains homeliness. The staff is hired mainly from the village, some have worked at the fort for decades, advancing their careers from room boys to chefs. The late Thakurani wrote two cookbooks about the family's kitchen and her daughter-in-law carries on the tradition of good food—there's even a demo kitchen for tourists who want to learn how to prepare heirloom dishes and house specials. I get to sample the robust fare favoured for centuries such as dhal-baati, essentially another hunters' dish of sand-roasted and ghee-drizzled bread balls, eaten with Rajasthani dhal and with it comes an exceedingly succulent laal-maas—literally, 'red meat' in a thick hot gravy made redder by a generous amount of chillies from the Jodhpur region.

Converting palaces and havelis into hotels has become something of a noble hobby—and is probably the best way to preserve these properties for the future. Eminent examples include the majestic fourteenth-century Neemrana fort, considered a path-breaking restoration project, and Jodhpur's super-chilled-out ultra-boutique Raas Haveli which impressed me with its organic design: The moment I floated into its oasis of calm in an otherwise manic city, I sincerely hoped that some form of discernment radiated from my puffy and desert-grime-covered face. The transition, as I passed the unobtrusive reception and entered into the yard where various antique structures serve as chic restaurant, spa block and heritage suites respectively, was absolutely stunning. The high walls dampen the outside noise and a cool Lou Reed song, later followed by Edith Piaf, played discreetly from ambient speakers spread across the 1.5-acre property. I wondered if I'd hear Nirvana next or simply hit nirvana.

I lifted my gaze and right above me, almost so close that I felt I could reach out and touch it, was the high cliff on which Rao Jodha planted the strikingly massive Mehrangarh citadel in 1459, one of Asia's genuinely iconic edifices and every guest room has a view of it. Rooms are all utterly ultramodern, again a stark contrast to the outside world. The floors and beds are all black hand-polished terrazzo, the walls are made of hand-cut rosy sandstone slabs, the balcony is equipped with an ingenious sliding sandstone jaali screen. Interestingly, the fancy furniture dotting the property isn't imported but made for the hotel from salvaged teakwood by a Jodhpur-based carpenter. But when the hotel proprietors bought this haveli, which used to be the city residence of the Thakurs of Ras village, it was a debris-covered ruin that practically had to be excavated.

It's a long, winding road to Churu town, 200 km north of Jaipur. There are an estimated 2,000 painted havelis spread across dusty Shekhawati towns like Ramgarh, Jhunjhunu, Mandawa and Nawalgarh, but most are locked up as the owners, well-heeled trading families that constructed them as proof of their worldly success, have settled in metros across the world.

Malji ka Kamra was built by an enormously prosperous merchant to entertain noble guests such as the Maharaja of Bikaner, who frequently made an overnight halt here on his way to imperial Delhi. But at the turn of the millennium, all that remained was a looted, squatted ruin, and that's when two brothers who own petrol pumps pooled together money with a friend and bought the mansion in 2004. They restored it over a period of six years.

The chambers where visitors slept then, are now enchanting guestrooms, which carry the original, albeit timeworn, frescoes from the 1920s. I check into suite #205 where the vaulted ceilings are entirely covered in curious paintings depicting VIPs and city scenes. Staying here is like living in an Indian version of the Sistine Chapel, and I highly recommend it as perhaps the most eccentric bedroom in Asia.

The mansion's exterior is an equally overwhelming sight, a humongous marzipan wedding cake painted pistachio green with ornamental details in sugar-icing-white. The three tiers are decorated with 3D-figures of Indians and colonials, turbaned soldiers and buxom madams.

The hotel luckily employs a historian, Lal Singh Shekhawat, who guides me through alleys to all the evocatively painted havelis dating from the region's heydays, 1840-1940. Only one seems to be inhabited, the Tola Ram Kothari Haveli from the 1870s; others are semi-abandoned and crumbling—soon perhaps lost for good. Another is used as a cut-rate garment shop, but we can still make out some faint artwork here and there.

The intriguing wall decorations around town depict everything from signs of progress like trains (such as on the 1850s' Lohia Haveli's wall) to hybrid-culture in the form of angels in saris (the circa 1925 Banthia Haveli), and even Bollywood stars (the 1940s' Bacchawat Haveli). Shekhawat tells me, 'The images provide a key to an understanding of the traditional pattern of social life.' He calls the fresco paintings 'gleeful'—like the crazy one, for example, which shows Jesus puffing away on a cigarillo.

Detail of Jesus smoking a cigarillo found at a painted haveli at Churu.

Narayan Balan, one of the brothers who owns Malji ka Kamra, later takes me out on a drive in the desert along with bottles of chilled white wine. A youngish chap, he wishes to put Churu on the map, saying, 'Whenever one travels outside and mentions that one is from Churu, people ask: "Where?"'

He's constantly searching for interesting desert picnic spots, so the next morning we eat millet chapattis and rustic chutneys at a caravanserai, which may perhaps have been part of the fabled Silk Road ages ago and must have hosted numerous travellers before me, but now the only company we have are hoopoes and partridges. As we eat, Balan tells me the moving story of how his grandfather, Pemaram, used to work as a gardener at the Malji ka Kamra mansion in the 1930s. When it was ready to be opened in 2012, the brothers were satisfied by the sight of the former gardener being able to enjoy a cup of tea on the grand veranda of his former workplace.

Back in the day, however, the maharaja would be entertained by dancing girls to enticing musical accompaniment in the colonnaded ballroom, where fancily-clad servants refuelled wine cups and topped up trays of spicy snacks. It is now converted into a restaurant where I sample my way through a limited but exquisite menu of homely fare. On my table, there's gatta curry with those distinctive lumps of chickpea flour in yoghurt gravy and again I get to hog on laal-maas, the state's signature dish of mutton cooked in red chillies. But what intrigues me most is something that the waiter simply introduces as 'desert beans'.

'Desert beans?' I echo.

He nods, yes, I heard it right. I've never eaten anything quite like it before. It is sourish, presumably from the raw mango powder, but has an earthy, deeply natural aroma, and ghee adds a rich touch to it. The stringy beans have been cooked in yoghurt with cashews and raisins. Checking the menu card later, I see that the name is 'kairsangri' which is described as dried beans and berries. Indeed, Churu district consists of a largely semi-desert landscape with sparse vegetation and tall sand dunes, so nothing much grows here except for millets, chickpeas, lentils, and anything that has deep roots and sustains on a minimum of water, which in turn mirrors the food eaten hereabouts.

One day, as I sit down to have tea at Vijaykumar Chaiwala, a celebrated stall in the Churu market that has served the citizenry thick buffalo-milk tea for the last sixty years, I ask around regarding the mysterious desert beans and am informed that they are called sangri and grow on a shrub known as khejri. 'In English, it is acacia.'

Wah! I knew that acacia yields a material used to make glue, but to eat acacia? Was I being fed gluey twigs? That's a new one. He patiently explains that these are actually hardy bushes related to the pea family, that bear fruit in the form of bean pods once a year, which are harvested and then dried, so that in the arid climate they can be stored for six years. This, I think, must be the ultimate foodstuff. Growing where nothing else grows, can be kept in anticipation of famines, keeps for days without refrigeration and is delicious. No wonder then that it is a household dish.

I ask if they're available in the market.

The tea vendor points out a nearby shop outside of which there are sacks of brownish, thin thingies like shrivelled seaweed. Because of the desiccation process, 5 kg of fresh beans becomes one when dehydrated, and as I step closer, the shopkeeper explains that 50 g is enough to cook a meal for a family of four. After thorough washing, they should be soaked overnight in buttermilk together with a spoonful of the equally costly, tangy desert berries, 'kair', until soft. The precious stuff is then fried in butter with the standard vegetable masala—though experts make their own esoteric blends that may include pungent asafoetida and aamchur or powdered unripe sun-dried green mangoes for tanginess and raisins or nuts for a hint of sweetness—and then yoghurt is added to create the creamy gravy. Sounds simple, so I stuff my suitcase with desert beans and berries to last me years—which makes the long trip totally worth it. I am not at all sure when I might be back again, but I suppose the answer is: When I run out of desert beans.

❖

In Ujjain, the temple town of central India, I'm reminded each night of the city's sacredness when the phone in my hotel room rings promptly at 1.30 a.m. When I complain at the reception, I'm informed that the telephone system is programmed to give an automatic wakeup call so that guests don't miss the early *puja* at the Mahakaleshwar temple. I explain to the receptionist that as a non-Hindu I don't really need to wake up before dawn. He says he'll have it fixed. But the next morning, at 1.30 a.m. sharp, the phone disturbs my sleep again. Must be God's will. And, suitably, God works like clockwork here.

Hours later, I'm yawning as I digest breakfast. Food in Ujjain tends to be invigoratingly vegetarian so I do feel both saintly and salubrious after a plate of crunchy poha—parboiled, flattened and savoury rice flakes that powers the people in these parts—available pretty much everywhere and cheaply too. At the stall I picked, I paid about Rs 10 for a satisfying morning meal of poha and chai. Burping spicily, I amble on the shoulder of a dusty road on the outskirts of Ujjain whose 2500-plus years makes it as antique as Rome. It was once the seat of Emperor Ashoka and then in the fifth century CE, the Guptas ruled Ujjain, ushering in a Golden Age of Civilisation, of theatre and arts and many other things. It's always been a centre for learning, while the town's astrologers are, even today, relied upon by Bollywood celebrities as well as political leaders.

Here I am, searching for one of the most intriguing extant constructions, a Jantar-Mantar on the bank of the sacred Shipra River. Out of the five that were built, this is the oldest and the only one that remains in use. The one in Delhi is a sightseeing attraction visited mostly by tourists—such as me on my very first day in India. I am inevitably nostalgic about that encounter, back in the early 1990s, when I was younger and more stupid. I'd landed at the Indira Gandhi airport that very morning, a greenhorn backpacker, suitably clueless, and it was hot—the summer was peaking, the monsoon, weeks away. Later, I read a scholarly paper on the stereotypical tourist experience of India, about how travellers 'experience a degree of cultural confusion when they arrive' and so I was, as far as I understand in hindsight, being a 'neophobic' shocked by the newness of everything and what would have been needed was 'intercultural adaptation' which should 'be applied to a travel-culinary scenario' or something like that. Whatever...I was about to shrug it off and forgive my younger self when I read that 'those travellers that exhibit neophylic tendencies, consider the experience of new or strange culinary fare to be exciting.' Clearly, I had a lot to learn.

Unpacking that academic argot, I basically understood that the way to deal with culture shock is to find something agreeable to eat or drink. And so it happened that I found myself drifting like a rudderless spacecraft in Connaught Place (as Rajiv Chowk used to be called back then) where everything seemed vast, regal and too imposing to get my head around. A bit like getting whacked with a 1000-page history book when one would have preferred the cartoon version—it took me a long time to appreciate that some of the vintage shops and dining halls are historically important and date back, incredibly enough, to the founding times of New Delhi. Touts chased me in circles, shoe polishers threw greenish snot globs on my sneakers, ear cleaners cleaned me out—in that defeated mood, I slunk into United Coffee House, the timeless café-cum-bar with its 1940s' faux-rococo décor. I ordered cheering beer and chased it down with their old-fashioned 'cona' of calming coffee (it comes in a type of laboratory flask that contains an uncommonly potent decoction). I then scurried down Sansad Marg, determined to sightsee myself out of the funk. There I stumbled upon something soothing—cool geometrical structures in red sandstone, sharp shapes that had clarity, focus and oozed mathematical precision. I instantly liked what I saw. It was fenced in, too, so the touts didn't chase me beyond the ticket booth. Inside the park, people lay on the lawns in a post-lunch stupor.

Jantar Mantar, Delhi.

I too lay down on the grass, full of admiration, but had no clue what I was looking at. Or how these massive structures had been built, by whom, or why. I was slightly stupefied by the flabbergasting samrat-yantra, a huge triangular thing which appeared to pierce the sky. As I recall, there was a stone panel next to it that attempted to explain everything. This, it said, was an instrument consisting of a gnomon (I was lost already there), the hypotenuse of which was aligned with the earth's axis (uh?), its quadrants were parallel to the equator...and by now, I was ready to faint only partly because of the summery heat in Delhi. This made me fathom—and correctly so—that it would take me years to digest India.

But the closer I looked, the more fascinated I became with these curves aimed at the heavens, like skateboard ramps built for a race of giants. One of the structures had the shape of a small Roman amphitheatre, with an intricate clockwork type system of stone slats inside, obviously for calculating...the exact time for the end of the world or...I wondered as I wandered in a state of hypnosis from one monument to the next for a good part of that afternoon, until the day cooled down... but where was I? Oh, yes, over the years I strengthened my intellect with plenty of Indian and Coorgi while studying the other monuments in the series of Jantar-Mantar observatories.

Finding the observatory in Ujjain after a lengthy suburban expedition, I'm greeted by a peon-cum-gardener-cum-self-appointed-guide, who offers to show me the finer points of these colossal shining marble constructions. Able to simplify so that even I can follow, he proudly enumerates the intricacies of things with tricky names such as shanku-yantra and nadi-valay-yantra, and I keep nodding, initially as clueless as on my first arrival in India. But then, at the massive samrat-yantra, which actually is, as it turns out, a gigantic sundial, I'm hit by a sense of déjà-vu followed by insight, as my guide points out how the dial's shadow creeps across the curved graded quadrants. I actually see it clocking minutes with twenty-second accuracy. The thing still works—but why not?—like clockwork.

Another instrument records the varying length of days: December has the shortest, the longest are in June. When the sun hits its noontime zenith, the shadow of the instrument magically disappears—again, this happens right as I stand watching it. It's a tropical phenomenon that has to do with the fact that Ujjain is situated on the Tropic of Cancer.

Kaliadeh Palace, where E.M. Forster went on a pilgrimage in Ujjain.

The resident observer, who turns up for duty a little later, tells me that the 'transit instrument' or bhitti-yantra (a high wall with esoteric markings on it), remains indispensable for computing the annual panchang or 'Astronomical Ephemeris of Geocentric Places of Planets', a booklet of tables forecasting the timings for celestial moves and shakes for the entire year which every scientifically minded astrologist refers to. Astonishingly, from his office one can buy mint copies of the first printed panchang—published in 1942—at the original cover price of Rs 10, making it an antiquarian treasure and a perfect carry-back souvenir. In it, I read that 'for centuries Ujjain has been enjoying the astronomical importance of being the Greenwich of India' and the zero meridian simply happens to be here, which goes to explain why this particular site was chosen for the first Jantar-Mantar.

If one considers that they were built when nobody even owned a wristwatch and before computer aided design (in an interesting turn of events, the Jantar-Mantars are now being studied with the help of 3D software), the levels of precision are doubly impressive. I contact Susmita Mohanty, an ex-NASA spaceship designer I happen to know, and she tells me, 'I find the Jantar-Mantar cluster remarkable for its modernist geometrical forms. Sawai Jai Singh-II must have been quite a renaissance man to leave behind such an avant-garde astronomical legacy.' To put things in perspective, she likens the construction of Jai Singh's five astronomical observatories across India, which may have taken altogether about thirteen years to build, to the same time it took to create the modern International Space Station (ISS). Whereas the ISS, because of the complexity and cost of a project to build a 417 tons heavy something over 400 km out there in space, required the cooperation of sixteen nations, by contrast, she says, the Jantar-Mantar 'was commissioned and built 300 years ago by a single empire that needed no one else to share the financial, construction and operational burden.'

You may at this point wonder what a culinary tourist can get to eat on the International Space Station and if it is open for visitors. The going rate, if one can get a ticket (as its crew capacity is limited) is in the range of fifty to ninety million dollars depending on the itinerary. But on the other hand, one gets to eat radiation-sterilised space-food such as steaks and freeze-dried hamburgers with fries out of vacuum-sealed pouches heated in special food-warmers. Condiments are available as pastes—primarily ketchup, mayonnaise and mustard, and even salt and pepper is served in semi-liquid form to avoid having stray grains floating about in a hazardous manner.

If the act of masticating such semi-synthetic comestibles, pabulum and victuals in space sounds dull, it's a vast improvement on the earliest spaceflights when all food was like pre-cooked baby food—viscous substances eaten cold, straight out of repurposed toothpaste-tubes—or freeze-dried bite-sized food concentrates such as bacon-and-egg squares, barbecued beef titbits, turkey morsels, strawberry lozenges, cheese cubes and cereal nibbles, some of which had to be reconstituted with water.

The instant breakfast drink Tang, an orange juice substitute available as a powder in supermarkets, wasn't (contrary to popular belief) developed for use on space trips—it was invented in 1957, before people took off into space—but came in handy when manned space flights became common in the 1960s, as fresh juice was impossible to squeeze in weightlessness. It was drunk on the moon in 1969, for example, because no champagne was allowed in space. Fizz makes astronauts bloat so they might not fit into their spacesuits. Caffeinists generally make do with freeze-dried, powder-based and recycled-urine-mixed coffee with dehydrated cream. Not satisfied with this solution, Italian astronauts got the company Lavazza to design an 'ISSpresso' machine to be used onboard the International Space Station, into which one basically inserts one's own urine (after its been purified) to be rewarded with a shot of espresso. A friend of mine, who aspired to be the first Swede in space, backed out of the space race when he learnt that he was going to, if not literally then at least figuratively, pee into his own mouth every day. Unfortunately for him, there's no way of avoiding drinking urine as the monthly water requirement of long-term stays in space is about 400 litres per person, hugely expensive to transport up there, and there are few water sources outside the earth's atmosphere. Though according to a post on NASA's website space pee is 'much cleaner than anything you'll ever get out of any tap in the United States.'

Once, visiting NASA in Houston, I picked up space food samples at their souvenir stall including a dried ice-cream bar which basically was like munching on a perfumed soap bar! I thought of peeing on it to get an authentic space experience, but couldn't bring myself to do so. Nevertheless, scientific evaluations of, for example, underwater crews have shown that ice-cream and other dairy products are #4 on the list of things that are most missed, after family, sex and creative activities. Further down the top-ten-list came booze.

As technologies develop, making it possible to expand the dietary range, culinary ethnicity nowadays plays an increasingly important role in keeping astronauts happy—which is psychologically important during longer space sojourns. There are therefore tortillas and even pullao on space menus, though for technical reasons spicing is moderated as the waste material can cause trouble, supposing that the pump-action potties fail. The largest selection is naturally Russian, considering how they basically monopolise transport to and from space, so expect goulash, jellied fish, mashed potatoes and meaty borscht.

Due to the travel restrictions on earth in the early 2020s, private space tourism got a boost with tycoons such as Richard Branson (of Virgin Atlantic fame), Jeff Bezos (of online-retailer Amazon), the ubiquitous Elon Musk launching their own designer rockets for commercial spaceflights bringing holiday-goers into the sky, and just as I was writing this three businessmen popped up to the ISS, spent a fortnight onboard, and popped back down to earth in what was termed 'a landmark mission for the commercial sector'. The only problem noticed was that during the first SpaceX flights, the suction stool malfunctioned and the passengers had to poop in their pants, euphemistically known as 'the undergarment option' and, of course, tourists cannot expect private plunge pools or hot showers in space. So I think I'll stay on earth.

But I digress again…now, all five Jantar-Mantars were built ages ago by Sawai Jai Singh-II, a governor and nobleman posted in Ujjain during the Mughal era and something of a Leonardo da Vinci one might say or, in Kipling's words, 'the Solomon of Rajputana…[who] led armies, and when fighting was over, turned to literature; he intrigued desperately and successfully, but found time to gain a deep insight into astronomy, and, by what remains above ground now, we can tell that whatsoever his eyes desired, he kept not from him.' An expert on Arabic, Greek and other astronomical traditions, Jai Singh was aware of large-scale brick and marble instruments built by Timur's grandson Ulugh Beg in Samarqand circa 1428; he apparently also sent a fact-finding team to Europe to check out the then cutting-edge technologies over there. Subsequently Jai Singh invented, or at least designed, many of these instruments.

Probably completed in 1719, when he was about thirty, this Ujjain observatory is the prototype for the four later ones. Apart from Delhi, Jantar-Mantars were erected at Jaipur and two sacred cities—Varanasi (a smaller one) and Mathura (from where it unfortunately disappeared in the 1800s). The one in Ujjain may be the oldest, but the Jaipur observatory is definitely the grandest. Its samrat-yantra sundial is a massive 75 ft high.

Construction began in 1728 and happened at the same time as Jai Singh was building his scientifically planned capital city around it—named Jaipur, after himself.

I understand now a little better how time works in India. All you need is a triangular gnomon 75 ft high, the hypotenuse of which is running parallel to the earth's axis, with its huge quadrants exactly parallel to the equator...hmm, I think as I book a cab for deeper exploration of Ujjain's past. The low-budget 'My Taxi' isn't air-conditioned, but I'm comfortable enough in the backseat, watching the landscape roll by. We're driving via the outskirts of Ujjain on a narrow road winding through villages on the west bank of the Shipra River. With little evidence for my fancy, I'd like to think that this was the very road taken by EM Forster but in a horse-pulled tonga, in the winter of 1912-13.

Forster was by then tinkering with his masterpiece, *A Passage to India*, the final scenes of which are based on his experiences in these parts. The novelist took an interest in all things Indian, so when he learnt that Kalidas had been a court poet of the Guptas, he took the train to Ujjain.

Arriving in this once so cultured city, Forster was told there were no antique structures extant—despite Ujjain, as already noted, being as old as Rome. At the time, Ujjain was under the influence of the progressive Scindia royals, who undertook much modernisation, so that today the city has quaint squares laid out in the early 1900s. The most expansive is centred on a grand clock tower which must have been brand new when Forster came to search for anything that wasn't new.

Making enquiries, he came across rumours of one palace ruin outside town, but the tongawallah tried to palm off every second dilapidated structure along the road as historical enough. Forster insisted that they go on until finally, arriving at the riverside, he caught sight of a rundown mansion on a desert island. He waded across, saw what he believed to be the Gupta court—'the palace that King Vikramaditya built, and adorned with Kalidas', noting to himself that 'ruins are ruins'. And so here I am, a century later, deciphering his travel essay as I'm searching for whatever it was that Forster found. The road takes a dip towards the river and crosses a charming stone bridge (why did Forster wade?) which conceals below it intricate channels and tunnels, inlets and outlets. Later I learn that the waterworks is a cooling system devised by some king who couldn't stand the heat. He apparently sat inside underwater chambers where the air was cold even in the peak of summer. Even air-conditioning seems to have been invented in Ujjain... well, that must be why it was the Golden Age!

On the island stands a handsome red sandstone structure known as Kaliadeh Palace, but with very Islamic-looking cupolas it is certainly less than a thousand years old. It isn't quite a ruin either—one can inspect the high-ceilinged cob-webbed halls provided one removes one's shoes at the entrance, as instructed by the watchman.

For as it turns out, this Islamic-period palace has been converted into a Hindu temple. There aren't any pilgrims, their focus is on the many temples of downtown Ujjain. This remote spot was made into a sacred space, the watchman explains, for the reason that it used to be a haunt of bandits and crooks who came here to indulge in anti-social activities, but after it was consecrated the bad men vamoosed.

The upper storeys are shut, but I do a round of the ground floor, my sweaty socks leaving a snail's trail on the grimy stone surfaces, perhaps wiping out all traces of Forster's footprints...but to paraphrase the philosophers: Art may be long, life surely isn't.

I come to Bhopal and the fasting month is on and I can't help but notice how it affects the city's rhythm—and naturally I worry that I might not get enough to eat but have to starve as the faithful do. When I go out shopping for shoes one morning (because my travel boots are falling apart) I find that few shops in the old town, where I'm staying in a basic lodge, open before noontime.

Even in the middle of the day, the bazaars are relatively empty, making it easy to stroll at leisure (in my bathroom slippers) so instead of shopping, I sightsee my way through Bhopal's mosques (also more or less empty at that hour). Anyway, the handle of my eco-friendly reusable shopping bag has also broken, making it hard to carry back new shoes if I find any. The Moti Masjid or 'Pearl Mosque' is an agreeable structure with reddish sandstone minarets and white domes. It is one of the subcontinent's five historic mosques by that name—the other four being in Agra, Delhi, Karachi and Lahore respectively. In the courtyard, I meet a bearded geriatric who tells me in refined and carefully-worded English, about how a 'lady' erected the mosque. He's speaking of a begum who used to dress as a man in the 1860s, which led Bhopal to be known for its liberated, progressive women.

After drinking buttery lassi in a stall, I spot an open tailoring shop and ask the modern begum inside if she would mind stitching my bag. She fixes it until it is as good as new, but when I dig out my wallet, she waves it away with a 'Welcome to Bhopal.' I find the Bhopalis very likeable.

In the early evening, after sorting out my shoe issue by upgrading from colourful bathroom slippers to new sneakers, I stand outside what is purportedly Asia's largest mosque—the Taj-ul-Masjid—as two cannon shots are heard echoing across town, which is the signal for breaking the fast. Light refreshments, fruits, dates and cold drinks are served from pushcarts and all of a sudden, the city comes alive. It's a completely different picture after dark with the narrow streets chock-a-block with happiness, not to mention meats stewing in pots signalling that something gourmet might be coming my way. Paradoxically, it occurs to me that the one month when food consumption peaks in Muslim quarters is the month of fasting when people feast on an endless banquet of the richest delicacies from sunset to sunrise in order to counterbalance the daytime austerities. And as usual, I have a set of definite targets, names of the hottest tables—one is an alley in the old parts, Chatori Galli and another is a suburban fine dining option in Koh-i-Fiza, where tablecloths can be expected.

I try the latter, thinking it might be easier to handle for a novice. I find the Filfora off Sultania Road, in a backstreet of a Bhopal Development Authority (BDA) suburb. Nice-looking, decidedly upper-crust, with fashionably-dressed kids at one table celebrating a birthday. Strangely, a poster advertises South Indian meals as the waiter emphatically claims that they serve no Bhopali cuisine whatsoever. When I draw his attention to the menu's 'Filfora specials' he argues that the cook is on leave due to his fasting, so no biryani is available. I'm feeling like E.M. Forster when his attempts at sampling non-veg in Madhya Pradesh were thwarted because his aristocratic dining companions generally were strict vegetarians.

I decide to go for Plan B or Chatori Galli. Food-bloggers rave about one particular eatery, Jameel Hotel, which supposedly is *the* place for Bhopali grub. Google maps places Jameel near the bus stand in Hamidia Road, which seems handy as my hotel is around the corner, but it turns out to be completely wrong.

The only way to find it is to ask in every other shop and get pointed deeper and deeper into the glittering night bazaars, jam-packed with burqa-clad ladies, past a trumpet seller and a hat shop for prayer caps that has one shiny red fez for sale, past a Burqa Palace, a handful of Jalebiwallas, more than a few Biscuit Corners, quite a lot of Silk Stores, a couple of Chikan Centres, and then there are shops that sell the glitzy, bead-decked purses that Bhopali artisans are known for, until I reach the very opposite side of town from where I started out, in Ibrahimganj where looming buildings timewarp me back to the Mughal highlife when begums were in charge.

But as the saying goes: Sheekh and ye shall find kebabs. Not far from the Jama Masjid (comparatively smallish mosque in the centre of a roundabout bazaar) I come to a street with lots of bakers who sell sheermal breads and buttery rusk, which is the fabled Chatori Galli.

Jameel Hotel is on the right, with Jameel Chicken Corner to the left. The reddest meat this side of the Red Sea is being grilled right there in the street so I head right. Inside, a waiter plump as a laddu slaps down the menu, which is itself thoroughly smeared in animal fat. Rather than touching it, I naturally order everything mentioned on it. Soon steel bowls of rich mutton korma appear, as does biryani up there among the best in the world, served with the garlicky yoghurt sauce known as burani. The crispy-fried sheekh kebabs on simple wooden sticks arrive by the cartload, along with hot rotis. Hungry families, who must have been fasting all day, keep coming, quickly filling the place to capacity.

My tummy has found a second home. But what about my brain? To feed it, the next morning I take a 45-km ride south of Bhopal in a taxi, to a set of sprawling rock art galleries once occupied by nameless artists who adorned the walls with paintings. The question I suddenly mull is: There's modern art and there's this art, and is there really such a big difference?

Some of the Bhimbetaka Caves' drawings of stick figures make me think of Giacometti's sculptures, other more abstract sketches bring to mind works by Picasso. There are strange mystical geometrical patterns that could be naïvist art. It feels as if I've come to the origins of world art, maybe even of culture, of civilisation, here.

Bhimbetaka is vast. Out of an estimated 750 rock shelters, 400 to 500 are adorned with paintings and fifteen of the best have been made accessible for tourists via walkways and signposting. It is splendid, a Stone Age version of the National Gallery of Modern Art. It is very peaceful too on the weekday I visit. Apart from myself, only a busload of tourists has come to see the UNESCO World Heritage monument and they spend their visit mostly in the car park, complaining about the crappy toilet facilities and looking for Coca-Cola and snack vendors who are thankfully conspicuous by their absence.

Passing under a dramatic cliff I reach the famous 'Zoo Rock' which has over 200 animals painted on it, presenting to us a pre-historic menu of sorts: Deer with stately antlers, bulky buffaloes, colossal elephants, an even more gigantic tandoori chicken, and some dozen other species as if this was a cookbook detailing what our ancestors liked to eat. They all appear to be running helter-skelter across the rock wall, a bit like the mixed grill I often order at Koshy's restaurant in Bengaluru.

After checking out this and that, further down the hillside I come to Rock Shelter #8, shaped like a pocket that I crawl into, almost like a baby returning to the womb in a reversal of the hard labour that was involved when I was born. Squatting in a semi-foetal position I'm able to study several paintings from up-close. Again, here are humans and animals in various poses and I presume I am watching non-vegetarians and their favourite diet. At the next rock, I find a crazy hunting scene depicted—arrows and spears are flying as a gang of hunters chase horned animals, an entire herd done in blood red as if the culinary preference may be labelled 'red meat', reminding me of yesterday's grill in the galli. Other artworks are painted in white, but some artists also used ochre and green. Yet another rock features rows of people dancing and a man beating a drum so huge that I can almost hear the beat 6,000 years later. Is this a successful hunt being celebrated?

I bump into some boys on holiday. One of them shouts to the other in Hindi, 'This surely isn't worth wasting time on. Let's go.' I suppose the caves can seem unimpressive in this age of multiplexes and 3D action movies, but then again, we need to see them for what they are. After the boys leave, the quiet helps me concentrate as I sit in the company of jolly black-faced langur monkeys and strangely colourful lizards. Were these caves a luxury dwelling for some tribal headman? The menu card at cavemen banquets? A religious spot? Some of the cliffs soar like temple spires. Or was it an art school—my favourite theory—because here and there newer paintings have been done on top of older ones, suggesting either recycling or imitation?

Any which way you look at it, it's a great cultural space. The mountain is part of the 1.6 billion-years-old Vindhya Hills, offering charming vistas of a thickly forested, gently undulating countryside. I'm constantly struck by the sounds of nature—birds, animals, wind rustling in the trees, an ambient jungle soundtrack that perfectly accompanies the cave paintings.

As one signboard puts it, this is 'one of the earliest cradles of cognitive human evolution', which probably means that the relics here are the first signs of creatively thinking humans on the planet—showing us the moment when our ancestors stopped being hybrid life forms of worms and lichen, and decided to become people like us instead. It's a thought that humbles me. Although most of the art dates back between 9,000 and 6,000 years, archaeologists think that the site was in use as early as 100,000 BCE, well before the art of painting evolved. The latest artwork is dated to 400 years ago—kings and sword-wielding soldiers—and subsequently the caves were forgotten for centuries, until everything was rediscovered by Indian archaeologists ten years after independence.

I continue further down the face of the hill to a monkey-infested rock that has a huge, red painting of a boar or bison or bull (experts differ), attacking some infinitesimal stick people. If it wasn't for the irony of seeing this after the previous wild hunt scenes, and the post-hunt parties, I'd almost be sorry for those long-ago hunters who suddenly became the hunted!

Well, what comes around, goes around—apparently that's the eternal karmic truth. These rocks tell lots of stories through their paintings, stories from a time long before written language existed. Maybe they're the equivalent of a Stone Age cartoon strip? The sporadic party scenes and dances interpolated into all the action remind me of Bollywood movies. Entertainment, art, religion or a bit of everything? Who can tell?

Heading back towards Bhopal in the late afternoon, I decide to have a look at the eccentric Bharat Bhavan Art Gallery, designed to adorn Bhopal's lakeside by the great architect Charles Correa in 1978. There's modern art in a cavernous hall in various levels, which immediately makes me recall my walk through the Bhimbetaka Caves, and then I find the more tucked-away tribal art gallery, with canvases painted in the traditional manner by Adivasi artists.

And I recognise motifs, artistic expressions, and ideas from the caves. Stick figures are dancing and celebrating...surely, not a coincidence? I realise that the art practised at Bhimbetaka never died out, it merely moved on to being decorations on the walls of village huts, and now, with the recognition being given to Madhya Pradesh's tribal artists, the same school of art has found its way here, to a modern gallery. The passage of art through the ages seems to have come full circle.

VII

Northern Kitchens, Northern Chickens
(The Gangetic Plains)

'Having kept nearly all the English breeds of the fowl alive, having bred and crossed them, and examined their skeletons, it appears to me almost certain that all are the descendants of the wild Indian fowl...'

—*On the Origin of Species*, Charles Darwin

M.G. Marg, Allahabad where Kipling strolled in the evenings.

It's early, but the date merchants are already in position with their pushcarts. Men are offloading bulging jute sacks from small trucks. The spice traders are only beginning to roll up shutters and dust their pickle jars. Counters are being stocked with trays of turmeric roots, nutmeg and dried chillies, and sacks of peppercorn are opened by the roadside. Strangely, the air appears quite smoggy despite the morning hour's freshness, but it takes a bit of time before I realise that my eyes are watering from the dense haze of chilli powder.

This is Khari Baoli, claimed to be Asia's largest spice market, 'the mother of all markets' and the optimal opening to a Delhi snack track. One has got to love how places like this, where one first inhales the spices by way of sampling—like the asafoetida (hing) that catapults its odour to the seventh heaven telling you that it is the A1 quality that is sold here—and then buys them loose at kilogram rates, thrive in an era of malls and online home-delivery services.

Cycle rickshaws are dragged past me, laden with cartons of dry fruits such as exclusive chilgoza pine nuts from Afghanistan or stacks of papadams and fryums going from wholesalers to retailers. Hawkers peddling on the pavements yell, it's like stepping into a medieval saga and after ransacking the condiment shops, I take a turn into Chandni Chowk where, adjacent to the seventeenth-century Fatehpur Mosque's gateway, sits Chainaram's—a sweetmeat maker's outlet founded back in 1901 in Lahore. Like so many others, they shifted shop to this side of the border to cook up their sinful Sindhi sweets in Delhi when the British cashed out and partitioned away parts of India. People tell me their main claim to fame remains the Karachi halwa that some call 'Indian chewing gum', others have dubbed it Bombay halwa due to Pakistaniphobia. Anyhow, a potent vapour of aromas draws me in. Aunties in burqas are stuffing themselves silly on puris with veggie gravy that smells like spice heaven. The hot, ballooning breads look divine and the shop is *the* breakfast joint in the area. But such an oily morning meal would totally fill me up and I need to preserve my appetite as Delhi is world-famous for its snack culture—snacking happens at all times, from morning to evening. Instead I nibble on what I'm told is syrup-glazed wheat, another of the shop's claims to fame, that tastes like boiled candyfloss: Balūshahi.

The centuries-old 'silver square' or 'moonlit market'—okay, since I don't really know how to translate properly from Hindi, let us simply call it Chandni Chowk—extends 1.5 km from here up to the Red Fort, the Lal Qila of the Mughal emperors. It was Asia's premier luxury shopping centre ages before Singapore was invented, lined with smoky Persian-influenced coffee houses where travellers rested by puffing on hookahs (today replaced by sugary chaiwallas). Shopaholics rode on camels from the Far East and the Mediterranean to lay their hands on spices, jewellery and cloth. During the pandemic, the street got a makeover to restore its former glory and is lined with 75,000 businesses (I'm told but can barely believe it) that include bargain garment stores, cheap electronic markets and, most importantly, India's best chaat. Delhi is said to have 300,000 chaatwallas (but judging by the love for snacking I wouldn't be surprised if the actual number is twice as many) and most chaats that are eaten across India, especially those based on boiled chole (chickpeas) were born, according to folklore, at Delhi's court as health food! Others debunk this as myth and maintain that chole was introduced to the diet of Delhi by Partition refugees.

Be that as it may, in the past germs were mysterious beings and harder to fight, and the waters of the Yamuna River weren't considered as pure as the Ganges—hence the royal physician prescribed a diet rich in certain spices, to nuke any germs that may enter the emperor's gut. This actually makes one think of how some modern people dismiss panipuri as 'liquid cholera' but obviously the right spice mix is a germicide. So to avoid unduly irritating the imperial bowel syndrome, the classic chaat masala was born which, I'm told, is a balanced blend of asafoetida, chilli, cumin, mango powder, pepper, rock salt and a pinch of sugar. Soon everybody was munching chaat at all times and feeling too good. Emboldened by these thoughts, I continue 350 m to Tewari Brothers, where I'm offered piping hot kachoris stuffed with pretty much anything that will make your head explode. Actually, the yummy, flaky, tan-coloured pockets of dough are filled with a piquant lentil mixture and served alongside sweet-and-sour tamarind chutney. This well-orchestrated but cacophonous riot of flavours simply has to be the ultimate killer breakfast for chilli champions. And yeah, any germ within me surely kicked the bucket, too!

The old town used to be where tourists went to see the sights but otherwise it was generally not seen as hot enough by urbanites and other moderns. However, since getting themselves a bunch of Metro stations, the bazaars have suddenly turned hot again and guides bring tour groups to enjoy the seventeenth-century ambience. I notice this when I go further down Chandni Chowk to the city's original outlet of the hundred-year-old Haldiram's and meet a Delhi lady who exclaims, 'It's a fully different life we're living! We just had some errands to do around town, me, my daughter and mum, but because the Metro makes travel so easy, we decided to go to Parathewali Galli and eat super-greasy parathas!'

She's in bliss, clearly.

At Haldiram's they're having fresh kulfi ice-cream to digest the parathas with and pick up big bags of those globally beloved, hygienically packaged snacks for a cocktail party on the weekend. Since I've just had a fiery bite, I sample over-sweet confections that balance out the kachoris.

Passing the Town Hall built in 1863 after the colonising Brits had deposed the last Mughal and many other buildings even older than it, I turn right into that much talked about twisting 'alley of paratha-makers' which is a 100 per cent vegetarian party zone dating back to the 1800s, but whether dishes are exactly the same as then, I can't tell. Parathewali Galli is mentioned in most handbooks so flocking to the first grubby paratha shop are a bunch of white tourists in cowboy hats on a food tour—it is a very different scene from a century ago, in colonial India, when freedom fighters like Bhagat Singh (who was executed in 1931, aged twenty-three) allegedly got together at these hole-in-the-wall-joints where, those days, Englishmen would not be seen dead. Or alive, even—allegedly, that is. These parathas fuelled the fight for Indian independence back in the day and it is quite expected that history would have been written here, as already then the paratha alley was a century old—dating back to Mughal times.

The next is crowded with students who have taken the Metro from the university area. The third is empty and feels cleaner, so I sit down at Gaya Prasad Shivcharan's which appears to be the oldest extant, founded in 1872. Their parathas are thin, crispy and freshly fried with twenty-five different fillings from cauliflower to bananas, but I choose the customary peas paratha that is served with five scrumptious vegetable sides including lip-smacking carrot pickles. It's not your usual flaky paratha, but a massive oil-cooked rock-hard biscuit—like biting into a 78 rpm record so it doesn't feel too wholesome considering my already troublesome cholesterol levels, but at least it is freshly cooked.

Ace lifestyle blogger Mayank Austen Soofi of www.thedelhiwalla.com fame told me once, when I asked about the must-eats in town, 'Try not to miss Old & Famous Jalebiwala.' On his food blog he elaborates: 'Thick and juicy, its food porn at its best. Jalebis, the golden-coloured rings of deep-fried maida batter, soaked in sugar syrup, fill the mouth with a warm liquid of such excessive sweetness that modesty blushes in shame. The diabetic may find joy in just looking at its preparation.'

So after a lassi—a genuinely ancient Indian health beverage and with rock salt it is said to be good for digestion—from a corner kiosk, I carry on towards the Old & Famous Jalebiwala. I've been told that one can buy confectionery of a thousand varieties along the chowk, but the topmost have always been the Persian-origin spiral-shaped jalebis that are cooked in pure ghee over smoky charcoal. This sweet arrived in India, according to sugary mythology, in the baggage of Ibn Battuta in the 1330s—he travelled with a confectioner from Yemen—and after further tweaking in India it may then have gone back with Battuta to the Mediterranean where, in Italy, it gave birth to the signature candy of Naples, the *strufoli*. Whether the Moroccan glutton actually was involved in its globalisation or not, we cannot tell. Many years later this Old & Famous Jalebiwala was opened in 1884 in its honour by Mr Nemchand and today his direct descendant sits behind the counter, unsettlingly looking exactly like a younger edition of Hollywood superstar Vin Diesel. He insists, 'Eating jalebis is the perfect antidote to the heat, so buy at least one hundred grams.'

Having boosted my energy levels with the sugar shock that the jalebis produce, I ponder should I carry on yonder or which way to go next—the tiny shop has one other item on its two-dish-menu, namely samosas. These too are a Middle Eastern import, but one that was well established on menus already before Battuta came to India—and perhaps it should be added that the migratory Moroccan didn't set foot in Old Delhi as it was only built later. In those days they also had no potatoes to stuff them with, so he hogged potato-less samosas in what is now the southern suburbs around Begumpur mosque, nearby which he stayed. Hence, to try his favourite samosas one must look for snack stalls outside the Qutb Minar Metro stop and request them to remove any potatoes from them. So I skip Jalebiwala's samosas as I still have other potentially gut-wrenching and stroke-inducing meals to digest.

To rest one's tummy, one may head a little further up the street to sightsee Delhi's divine buildings: A sanctuary of Jainism where sick birds find refugee; a prominent Sikh gurdwara; a church erected in 1814 when the English settled here; and the emblematic Red Fort that ranks as one of the main tourist attractions in the country. But since I am more of a food pilgrim with a restless tummy, I opt to head south on Dariba Kalan from the corner of the jalebi shop. It has traditionally been the street of jewellers and one still finds glimmering ornaments along the winding bazaar, but above all it is fun to observe what short eats patrons pick from the pushcarts that stand here and there. It's evidently true by now that Delhi people are snacking everywhere and always.

These bustling parts may appear a trifle tricky to find one's bearings in, yet Old Delhi has a clearly planned nature. The palatial fort of the Mughals symbolises its brain, Chandni Chowk its spine, its side streets are the ribs, the spice market its tummy (or primary gastric malaise depending on one's tolerance levels) and the main mosque is the city's beating heart that has a capacity to hold an astonishing 25,000 devotees. On his last visit to India, in the 1940s, E.M. Forster made it a point to come here after landing in town and 'stood on the high platform of the Great Mosque, one of the noblest buildings in India and the world. Profound thankfulness filled me. The sky was now intensely blue, the kites circled round and round the pearl-gray domes and the red frontispiece of sandstone, sounds drifted up from Delhi city, the pavement struck warm through the soles of my socks; I was back in the country I loved, after an absence of twenty-five years.' The jewellers' bazaar which I follow leads me straight to that great mosque.

Dhabas at Main Bazaar, Delhi, offer both veg and non-veg options.

As much as Chandni Chowk is a vegetarian street, bearing the stamp of the strict Marwari trading community, by the mosque one has transited into the carnivore club, to feast on the cheapest kebabs in the city.

Tourists flock to Karim's which grew from a pushcart kitchen outside the mosque into a destination listed in all guidebooks for its meats swimming in grease and their dining halls, surrounding a grimy courtyard, that have a distinctly oriental charm. The foundational dish on their menu, dating back to those pushcart days, was the meaty potato stew known as aloo gosht.

To tell the truth, I prefer the more low-key neighbour Yaseen Hotel (on the corner immediately south of the mosque) where they don't charge tourist rates and the gravies with fresh flatbreads are less likely to cause cardiac arrests. Their signboard—'good taste, cheap and best, hygienic environment'—says all that needs to be said. Coincidentally, the area features prominently in Booker-winner Arundhati Roy's *The Ministry of Utmost Happiness*, the sequel to her two decades older global bestseller *The God of Small Things*. When I met her for coffee in Delhi, I asked about how come so much of the novel is set in Old Delhi.

'I actually have a place there.'

'Near the big mosque?'

'Yes, a rented small room, so I've been there for many years. You sometimes feel under siege. It was not that I went there because I was going to write about it, but because I went there it became very much part it. I go there, wander around late at night.'

'All those rabid street dogs, they don't chase you?'

'Not at all. Humans are rabid, dogs are okay.' She has adopted two of them. At one point as we're chatting away, one of her dogs climbs all over me. I'm more accustomed to dogs barking the moment they see me but, puzzlingly, this one wants to lick my face.

Arundhati Roy with her adopted dog at home in Delhi.

Arundhati laughs. 'She's flirting with you. They are both street dogs. She was born outside a drain. Then her mother was hit by a car. That other one I found tied to a lamppost, cruelly.'

'Do your dogs have names?'

'Yeah, her name is Begum Filthy Jaan and this one is Maati K. Lal. That means "beloved of the earth". Both Lal and Jaan mean beloved.'

'So they make up your family?'

'Yes.'

'They're very well behaved to be street dogs.'

'Street dogs are more civilised than other dogs. They're the best. I'm also a bit of a street dog.' A little later, she tells me something I can relate to very much, about life in India as a writer, 'It is a very anarchic, unformatted world that I live in. To me, if anything, it is an overload of every kind of stimulus.

I suppose I'm not closed off in some family thing. There's a porous border between me and the world and lots of things come and go. That's the way I live. There are so many *brilliant* people doing things around me *all* the time, like even just in the process of making this book—if I want someone who's an *insane*...who's actually not a human being, but a printing machine, I lean this way. If I want someone who is skulking around the city taking pictures, I lean that way. One is just surrounded by unorthodox brilliance all the time. And that's my real inspiration. If I want really *badly* behaved dogs I have them too.' She laughs and hugs one of her dogs that is barking, presumably impatient with our talking.

I'm reminded of her words as I dogtrot in the winding bazaars, building up appetite for my umpteenth breakfast, or perhaps I should call it a light brunch by now, that awaits behind the mosque in Chawri Bazaar. This is another artery of the vintage town, where hardware wholesalers have been running shops since the nineteenth century. But hardware is not all there is to Chawri Bazaar, there's also interesting 'software' at the famed Shyam Sweets. It is more of a big kiosk with stainless steel tables abutting the street, making it the perfect place to hang and people-watch (until other foodaholics come and claim one's table). The jolly proprietor, Anil Aggarwal, proudly informs me, 'My grandfather's grandpa's grandfather started this business in 1910.'

Their bedmi aloo, oily hard-puffed lentil-filled breads like edible gold bars served with rich chilli-red and piquant potato curry and veggies pickled Delhi-style, go perfectly with a cooling lassi that has a mild scent of roses. Potato and roses, spicy and sweet, deadly and lively, male and female, yin and yang, East and West, Hollywood and Bollywood, happy go lucky—it's all there in a quick meal.

Next I drag my tummy up Ballimaran, a meandering alley which eventually leads to a memorial in honour of the poet Mirza Ghalib—in fact, this was once his house but now all that is left of his haveli is a portion of its courtyard, the rest having been encroached upon by anybody and everybody. As William Dalrymple laments in *City of Djinns*, 'The *haveli* was a world within a world, self-contained and totally hidden from the view of the casual passer-by. Now, however, while many of the great gatehouses survive, they are hollow fanfares announcing nothing.' There's a collection of objects that give an idea what life in Delhi may have looked like two centuries ago, when Ghalib skulked about popping kachoris and kebabs into his lyrical mouth in these streets. After having snapped my mandatory selfies, I carry on down the ever-narrower alley until I suddenly emerge right next to my final stop for the day: ninety-year-old, barely one-square-metre small Ashok Chaat Corner. Their yogurt-based snacks, such as dahi-vada of savoury, spongy balls (or 'bhalle' that are of course deep-fried) smothered with spiced-up yoghurt, are the best way imaginable to offset a daylong junk-food orgy.

As I bolt down the last cooling vada, it occurs to me that while chaat may be the Indian equivalent to Mediterranean *meze*, there's a great difference. The short-eats of southern Europe are something you dig into over a leisurely evening of nice wines or cold beers, over hours and hours, but chaat can only be eaten methodically and in moderation, in short bursts. Typically cooked in plenitudes of oil and exceedingly spicy, chaat might have killed Mughal germs but it also takes its own toll on the gastric system as well as causing superfluous cardiovascular problems, which differentiates it from the Mediterranean snacks that can be enjoyed to one's heart's delight.

But the occasional encounter with Old Delhi's junk-food is

great for the mind, stomach and wallet. And happily, when I feel the time has come to purge my belly, Ashok Chaat Corner is within walking distance of my lodge—a choice haunt among backpacker flophouses, around the corner from the Main Bazaar. The art deco hotel used to be called Airlines back in the day, but despite its name it primarily catered to passengers from the New Delhi Railway Station diagonally across the road. It's still a great place to stay and drifting into town again decades after first landing in India, I feel a comforting nostalgia as I, for old time's sake, book a room there. The basic lodge I stayed at in 1991 on my first visits (and where the manager memorably plied me with pegs of Bagpiper after all my valuables had been stolen on a trainride) is long gone and the bazaar's lodges have become fancier overall so I end up shelling out more than expected at the renovated Airlines where ACs have replaced fans, but unlike the good old days of shared baths and squat potties, I get a clean attached bathroom with modern commode, bum-shower, shampoo on the house, the works.

By and large the Main Bazaar, or Paharganj as it is also called, has remained more or less the same—a travellers' hub where all manner of neo-hippie firangis converge: Spanish punks with tattooed foreheads, Danish druggies with colourless eyes, Israelis whose hands and fingers seem to clutch invisible Kalashnikovs, American preachers with pierced nipples and tank-sized Russian ladies shopping in bulk, to smuggle and sell garments and trinkets back home, thereby earning their airfare.

Small bookshops like Jacksons sweep up the literature left behind by tourists, so it's a great spot to pick up foreign editions at bargain rates. As a film buff I enjoy spotting locations where *Holy Smoke!* (starring Kate Winslet) as well as the award-winning surprise hit *Dev D.* (starring Kalki Koechlin) were shot—the latter was incidentally filmed in Arakashan Road, a couple of blocks north of the Main Bazaar. In the more recent *Paharganj*, a Spanish tourist is trying to find a dead lover in the bazaar area's underground universe of sleaze, drugs, sex and many other things that I personally haven't encountered here in real life.

The bazaar was born as a royal grain market situated outside the city's south-western gate—where customs duties were collected by the rulers. When the New Delhi Station was built in the 1920s, the area was slowly overtaken by cheap lodging and boarding houses, and the old produce market expanded to encompass garment stalls and cloth merchants. The advent of foreign tourism (with the hippies of the 1960s) also means that Main Bazaar has turned into an international hippie bubble and it is your best bet in Delhi to grab some affordable, cosmopolitan grub: German bakes, Israeli hummus, Japanese or Korean delicacies, Nepalese or Thai curries, Uzbek uh—whatever they eat in Uzbekistan. Food and beer come cheaper than anywhere else in town.

At last count, the bazaar and its alleys had some 400-500 small hotels and an even larger number of food outlets. I used to eat at the classier yet budget-level Metropolis Tourist Home (1634, Main Bazaar), which began as an unassuming travellers' dhaba two years after the station had been inaugurated in 1928. Over time, it grew into the bazaar's first proper hotel, until recently run by the founder's grandson—though on my latest visit in 2023 it was shuttered down, hopefully just awaiting a much-needed renovation. It featured one of the cosiest imaginable rooftop bars with a mixture of retro-food, such as the only known Soviet gourmet dish Chicken à la Kiev, that somehow found its way to India (from Tashkent, they say) not to mention terrific wood-fired pizzas that helped one dream oneself away to Italy for an evening without having to fly all the way there. And to tell you the truth, the pizzas in Rome weren't half as good as the ones served here.

I must admit that I always have trouble convincing my writerly Delhi friends to join me for a night of fun in the bazaar, as their wives presume that they're going to end up indulging in immoral illegalities. Only goes to show that Delhi wives don't trust their husbands too much. And it is true that intellectuals generally don't want to set foot in the area: V.S. Naipaul who toured Delhi chaperoned by Khushwant Singh enjoyed the ruins of older Delhis like Tughlakabad, where they picnicked on bacon-and-egg sandwiches, and he stayed as a paying guest in the newer parts—far from the bazaars. But perhaps they're not to be blamed as even the handbook *Rough Guide* warns of 'police raids on budget hotels' in the bazaar. *Lonely Planet* states that 'Paharganj—with its seedy reputation for drugs and dodgy characters—isn't everyone's cup of chai' and all tourist websites and every travel expert online issue dire admonitions such as 'tourists are advised to avoid the area' because it is 'noisy, filthy, and full of touts' not to mention 'high amount of crime, poverty, drugs, sexual assaults and scams.' The 'lodgings are popular with some Western tourists seeking easy access to cheap and widely-available drugs, and the large number of sex parlours and brothels involved in the sex trade' with links to 'gambling and other illicit activity, resulting in death of tourists.' I may be myopic, but the only parts of all this that I notice are the shops that sell paraphernalia for pot smokers, chillums designed in Italy and rolling paper with exotic Latin American scents. Of the eating options, the above guidebooks dismiss all those catering to international backpackers because 'it's a shame to dine in Paharganj, even if that's where your hotel is. Most of the restaurants on the Main Bazaar are geared to unadventurous foreign tastebuds, offering poor imitations of Western, Israeli, Japanese, and even Thai dishes, or sloppy, insipid versions of Indian curries for foreigners who can't handle chilli.'

Survival is an understandable concern and it is true that many end up at least with 'Delhi-belly', the city's trademark sickness caused by over-exposure to spices and the richness of ghee. Strictly speaking, let me tell you that Delhi-belly wasn't invented in the Main Bazaar, but down the road in tony Connaught Place where, during World War II, foreign soldiers kept boozing until their bellies gave away and they ended up spending much of the war topping up the latrines.

According to studies, 60 per cent of international travellers who visit developing countries experience stomach upsets, so one should perhaps not be shocked if shit happens. Sometimes it isn't even a bug that causes it, but the fact that their tummies are unused to extreme spice levels and the rich ghee content that oils the intestine into a waterchute amusement park for amoebae, thereby switching off the basic digestive functionality of one's intestines. Luckily, in case one develops an urgent need to see a latrine, one can take the Metro from the Ashram Marg station (at the western end of the bazaar) to the Sulabh International Museum of Toilets, which lends perspective to toilet-related matters.

Over my years of travel, I've seen many illustrious restrooms—the one where the Beatles peed after beer-binging in Liverpool, another at a bar in New York in which poet Dylan Thomas' bladder exploded (leading to his premature demise later that same night), a protected monument in Texas on which hard-rocker Ozzy Osbourne urinated and for which he was arrested, and other similarly famous or infamous celebrity privies. But I've never before laid eyes on such a potty collection documenting 4,500 years of scatological technology, a feat that earned this museum a listing in *Time* magazine as one of the world's ten weirdest museums, alongside another darling of mine, Boston's Museum of Bad Art.

At the museum one can see the throne of the French king Louis XVI to whom Tipu Sultan sent an ambassador and which has an inbuilt bed pan so that he could defecate and host courtly dinners at the same time, study Indus Valley civilisation sewerage systems (yes, India invented the first WCs in the world), Roman emperors' golden chamber pots and other exhibits including samples of toilet humour as well as poopy poetry. Established in 1992 by

Dr Bindeshwar Pathak, a social activist and founder of the Sulabh Sanitation and Social Reform Movement, the museum is the perfect sightseeing site when one's gastric system is up to dirty tricks.

❖

Returning to Chandigarh after many decades, I have a really simple plan. I'm looking for Mr Singh *and* for a tandoori chicken. You'd think it ought to have been easy—isn't every second person in town named Singh and doesn't he eat tandoori chicken for breakfast, lunch, tiffin and dinner? But I'm in search of a particular Mr Singh.

In my nostalgic mood, I roam the Rock Garden—a misnomer as it is only partly made of rocks—and where I remember last having seen Mr Singh. The forty-acre surreal artwork is made of broken bangles, empty bottles, oil drums, plates and teacups, tubelights and other recycled debris of modernity, shaped into fantastic birds, monkeys, humans, houses, bridges, winding cobbled paths, waterfalls powered by rainwater harvesting, palaces of discarded rubble...like a caricature of the well-planned city of Chandigarh outside, but I see no gilt-edged roasted chicken flapping its wings. There's great junk food in the vicinity, enticing chaat sold from almost hygienic pushcarts by the entrance gate, but it's veg throughout—not even a masala omelette to raise my cholesterol levels.

Chandigarh Rock Garden built of broken teacups, saucers, etc.

The creator of the Rock Garden, Nek Chand Saini, initiated his art project in the early 1960s when he was turning forty and it was still a work in progress when I visited—probably making it one of the world's grandest works of art. Compare those six decades to the four years that Michelangelo took to paint the celebrated ceiling of the Sistine Chapel! But there's no sign of that specific Mr Singh in the garden as far as I can tell.

By and large, Chandigarh feels much the same as when I visited it first in 1991. In the three decades that have passed, it hasn't, unlike most other cities, become more congested—like the arteries of cholesterol junkies like me. The wide roads that back then used to be empty save for the sporadic squeaky-creaky cycle rickshaw, a scattering of rattling Ambassadors and as I recall an overcrowded scooter with father, mother, granny and kids riding pillion, still easily accommodate traffic. It was once a futuristic city, but now that we live in that future, it has turned into the probably most liveable metro in South Asia. My friends in Delhi keep moving to Chandigarh to improve their health—mental as well as physical.

I chatted once with an Indian architect who complained about Chandigarh. He was a traditionalist and felt that cities of yore were built to match the climate, the culture and above all the lifestyles. Winding, narrow, shady streets work better than wide avenues drenched in sunshine. Open courtyards that facilitated natural air circulation were better than modern airtight glass-façade office complexes that drain precious energy to run their air-conditioning systems.

When I first came here I too found Chandigarh's design puzzling—until I met that particular Mr Singh. I was in my twenties and changing buses in town, on the way from Dharamsala to Delhi, which necessitated an overnight stay since the monsoon had rained on my backpack on the roof of the bus and everything was soaked. As I dried myself in the station canteen an elderly, bespectacled, turban-clad Sikh sat down at my table. 'I'm Mr Singh,' he said. I suspected he might be a tout, but he was a tad too polite and didn't want to sell me a handmade oriental carpet or a houseboat in Kashmir.

It transpired that post-retirement, Mr Singh had taken it upon himself to be the unofficial tourist ambassador of Chandigarh and so he offered me a map and showed me, on it, how the city had been built to reflect the human body—not unlike the Walled City of Delhi, in fact, but this was a much more futuristic take, an ambitious post-independence project to invent a new kind of Indian city. And by the look of it, it was quite obviously designed by a European architect influenced by cubism. The government buildings to the north, in Sector 1, were obviously the brain, the commercial centre where we sat in the Sector 17 bus station encircled by restaurants was the gastric system, the central parks with their flower gardens were the lungs and the roads its arteries. A city as a living organism? *Where was its soul then?*

'Let me take you to the Rock Garden,' said Mr Singh with a gentle smile, and after suggesting a homely guesthouse, he showed me the way to that marvellous tourist attraction.

Leaving town, I forgot all about Singh until years later, when I met another senior tourist and as we shared a tandoori chicken—reputed to be the original recipe—at the anachronistic Moti Mahal in Delhi, we compared notes on places we had gone to. When I mentioned the innovative layout of Chandigarh, he told me of one of the trippiest experiences of India—and I interrupted, 'Yeah, I've been to the Rock Garden.'

But he protested, 'No, the man who collects tourists.' His encounter with Mr Singh, way back in the 1980s, led to them spending days together and eating so much tandoori chicken that he could only cackle at the memory now. Singh wasn't merely an unlicensed tourist guide, my friend explained, but a 'bona fide tourist collector' whose ambition was to meet and greet every single foreigner passing through town, welcome them heartily and make them feel at home according the Sikh tradition of hospitality and cultural tolerance.

So this time, when I land up in Chandigarh again after decades, I want to thank Singh for that map that opened up the city for me. I hope to find him and then ask where to get a perfect tandoori chicken, partly to make up for that chicken I once ate in Patna—as described in the beginning of this book—that caused me ignoble tummy troubles years ago. So I spend an afternoon stalking about the bus station which has grown and is jam-packed with Singhs, but none of them is the right Mr Singh. Hence, I turn to Anthony Bourdain's immortal words, 'Checking off my list of things to do in the Punjab, I gotta score some animal protein. It's time. I've been going all Morrissey for like two days now, and frankly, that's enough. I need chicken. When we're talking [Punjab] must-haves, tandoori chicken is just that.'

It looks like I have to procure my own chicken and so to make it as genuine as possible I try to figure out which might be the oldest kitchen in this modern town—or at least one that was already in existence in the times of Mr Singh. There turns out to be one obvious choice, the somewhat forlorn Ghazal

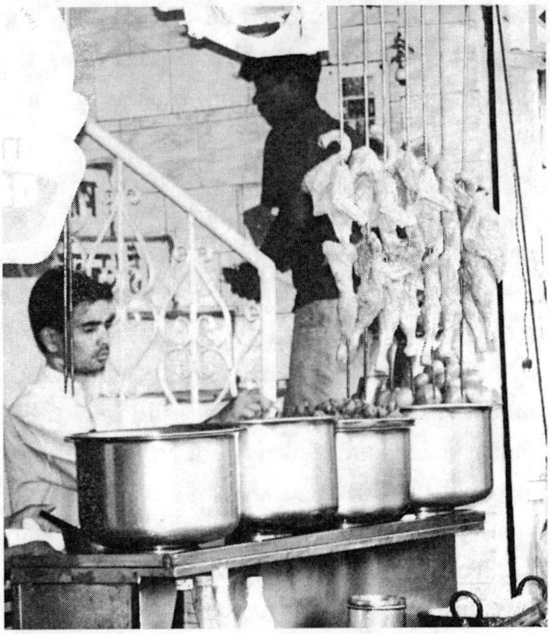

Punjab's national bird, tandoori chicken.

in the Sector 17-C market. In those days, I recall the entire market square was totally un-happening—not a soul used to be seen—but today, it beats the most cosmopolitan plazas with all the bright fast-food joints of the world at your greasy fingertips and bars where mixologists pour genteel cocktails down your throat. When I find it, Ghazal is a refreshing return to the past with its gloomy lighting, clunky tables and old-fashioned deep sofas that scream: 'Let's go back to pre-1991, pre-liberalisation!'

When the 'murgh' joins me at the table, it thankfully isn't one of those modern deep-red food-colour-spray-painted ones, but crispy turmeric and Kashmiri chilli orangish. Don't misunderstand me—it's a normal, traditional tandoori chicken and one can probably sample a similar fiery fowl in many places, including at Old Delhi's hallowed Moti Mahal. But in this world of escalating complexity, when everything must be fashionably fusion and gastronomically molecular, it is increasingly rare to come across classic honest-to-goodness simplicity. Munching on that hapless hen, it occurs to me how its species of poltroonish pea-brains conquered the world not once, but twice.

Its first ancestor on our planet was a wild jungli murgh (wild fowl) living millennia ago in what is now West Bengal and Bangladesh. After a couple of aeons, these were domesticated by the Harappans 4,300 years ago if not earlier, approximately in the area that is now Punjab, which might explain the Punjabi obsession with chicken. Offbeat scholars claim it happened millennia earlier in China or southeastern Asia, but even then their chickens were likely to have been imported from India—probably via Southeast Asia where Vietnamese archaeologists have found a bronze statue of a chicken dating back to 1,000 BCE. This implies chicken were domesticated around the same time in many parts of Asia.

The Harappans are however credited with building the first tandoor, or at least prototypes for top-loaded clay ovens four-five millennia back in which bread could be baked and meat roasted, though thousands of years before that Mesopotamians supposedly preceded them by using pit ovens known in Babylonian as *timuru* (which we now pronounce as tandoor). Anyway, without going too deep into who invented what and when, it is clear that the Harappans were the first to eat something similar to what's on my plate at Ghazal because once you have a chicken in one hand, and a tandoor in the other, combining the two in the correct manner is just a matter of practice. At least one thing is for sure that the tandoor is emblematic of Punjabi cuisine and since Indian restaurants across the world have their roots in the Punjabi dhabas, tandoori cooking is therefore perceived as virtually synonymous with Indian food. And this is how it happened.

From India, the flightless birds somehow spread westwards, most likely via Persian intermediaries, reaching southern Europe on a happy day in the seventh century BCE (which we know because chickens appear on Greek vases and feature as a delicacy at symposiums) and then onwards to northern Europe in order to become rather common among the Celts and Germans, ruling the non-veg roost about the year 0 when the Roman Empire invaded territories further and further north, which coincidentally is the date from when Europeans count years—but maybe not exactly for that specific reason. To the Americas, chicken migrated as late as five centuries ago, brought across the Atlantic Sea by none other than Columbus himself in 1493, and for all that I know it may well be how the state of Kentucky got its name, from the eponymous fried chicken. About one in every three chickens living on our planet ends up 'Kentucky-fried' while another third is either curried or tandooried.

During the previous century, this prehistoric invasion was followed by a modern conquest when actual tandoori cooking as we know it was developed back in pre-Partition Peshawar, now across the border in Pakistan and some 800 km from the Ghazal in Chandigarh. It conquered New Delhi through the Moti Mahal, owned by a Partition refugee whose food-stall had gained so much fame for its chicken dishes that he upgraded, became the post-Partition foodie rage in the 1950s, the place to be seen at, and it is still a great trip into the past. Curiously, prior to this momentous development there apparently weren't any tandoors in Delhi. In fact, there were hardly any grillable chickens either, only hardy hens, as the soft-fleshed broiler—bred for grilling purposes in the USA since the 1920s—only became available at dhabas after independent India's Second Five Year Plan highlighted the need for industrial-scale poultry production (according to an article in *The Economic Times*).

I'm reliably informed that no radical changes have been made to the Moti Mahal menu card since about 1947 except for adding butter chicken to it—invented in the 1950s, it's essentially a way to use up chicken leftovers by cooking them in creamy tomatoish gravy (the cornerstone of a true Delhiwallah's diet). So even if the tandoori chicken may have Harappan pedigree, it received its modern form at that particular outlet. Moti Mahal was also, in fact, the only proper restaurant in the old parts of Delhi thereby creating something of a template for the archetypal evolved dhaba (and it gained international fame because the then prime minister, Jawaharlal Nehru, took important foreign guests there).

The first tandoor oven outside Asia was installed at Veeraswamy's, which coincidentally is the oldest surviving London-based Indian restaurant (from 1926), and according to food columnist and gastronome extraordinaire Vir Sanghvi the tandoori chicken only showed up on US menus in the 1960s. The original Moti Mahal of today is a somewhat bedraggled shadow of its former self, but it has plenty of branches and wherever one goes—whether San Francisco or Melbourne or anywhere in between—there'll be a piping hot tandoori chicken not far out of reach, connecting us moderns to the Harappan past.

Burping my way out of Sector 17, I think that even if the Rock Garden is still under construction, growing more incredible by the year, and I failed to locate Mr Singh, at least Chandigarh—in other respects—appears to retain its soul in a place like Ghazal, and its heart still belongs to Punjab's beloved national bird: Tandoori chicken.

❖

During a week in Allahabad (now Prayagraj), I do what everyone else goes there to do and visit the Sangam, where the Ganges and Yamuna meet, for holy boating. Then I roam the old town's knotted-up bazaars to shop for snacks and sweets. But the place I am constantly gravitating back to is the Civil Lines. More specifically, its main street, M.G. Marg. It is hard to put one's finger on what's so special, but, on some level, it gives me the odd sensation of having a walk-on part in an E.M. Forster television adaptation, except that M.G. Marg was called Canning Road in those days.

It's a set waiting for the costume drama to begin. Many a paan stall is named Sophiya Laurence Beetle Shop after the bustily bosomy European cine-star of the 1950s, Sophia Loren, who must have been all the rage in the looming cinema buildings that line the street, adding a touch of cosmopolitan elegance. Unlike so many other towns that are busy turning themselves into Singapore-replicas, Allahabad helps tourists imagine the past—as if time left it behind and forgot about coming back to wind its clock up.

Oodles of charisma ooze out of the Indian Coffee House (founded in 1957), where I reboot with a stack of keema omelettes washed down with roohafza, that early 1900s sweet beverage of pre-Coca-colonised India. The café sports sprightly waiters in antediluvian uniforms, uncles crowd tables, hunch over chipped cups, debating in paan-scented Hindi. This would have been where the stalwarts of modern Indian literature sat and made literary history. Allahabad was then known as the

Indian Coffee House, founded in 1957, where stalwarts of modern Indian literature used to meet.

Oxford of India whose Civil Lines was a hub of bookishness, embellished by bards like Firaq Gorakhpuri, who lectured at the university; his bungalow on 8/4 Bank Road was a gathering place for poetry-loving students (such as my late father-in-law) and novelists such as Premchand.

And not to forget Rudyard Kipling, who in the late 1800s, found his first high-profile job at the then principal newspaper of colonial India, *The Pioneer*—'India's greatest and most important paper'. It was in India that he honed his writing craft. For example, the newspaper started a special weekly edition which would print fiction, amongst other things. 'Would I edit it, additional to ordinary work? Would I not?' In *Something of Myself*, he described how he churned out 'soldier tales, Indian tales, and tales of the opposite sex.' Thus he made his 'own experiments in the weights, colours, perfumes, and attributes of words in relation to other words, either as read aloud so that they may hold the ear, or, scattered over the page, draw the eye. There is no line of my verse or prose which has not been mouthed till the tongue has made all smooth, and memory, after many recitals, has mechanically skipped the grosser superfluities.'

The Wheeler's chain of railway bookstalls was founded in Allahabad and they introduced the novel idea of paperbacks with their cheap editions of, well, what else but Kipling, long before the rest of the world bought paperbacks en masse (in the 1940s post-war era when cheaper printing became a necessity). Basically, Kipling popularised the format by upgrading what used to be known as 'dime novels' to encompass good fiction. The main Wheeler's Bookshop (of 1966 vintage) is still found on 19, M.G. Marg and they published many of Kipling's earliest books, both story collections and travelogues of India, including *Plain Tales from the Hills* that lampooned the imperial high-society of Shimla. It is believed that it was Kipling's idea to have stalls at all Indian stations to peddle his books.

An entire galli devoted to snacks in the bazaars of Allahabad.

After a few days, I find the house in which Kipling lived just before moving away from India, and where he—in a handful of frenzied months—penned his celebrated Indian stories. The English family who lived there provided Kipling with 'the Blue Room for his study and the guest room with the big four-poster bed, bath and east veranda'. Today, due to karmic interference its houses a printing press known as the Belvedere Printing Works (56A/13, Moti Lal Nehru Road). The proprietor tells me that he focuses on spiritual pamphlets and what were Kipling's rooms then are now part of an adjacent orphanage where nobody seems to know that a world-renowned children's writer, author of *The Jungle Book* and a Nobel winner, stayed in it. Every morning young 'Ruddy' ate his breakfast on its veranda and I picture him planning, plotting his stories there, in the throes of manic inspiration, before sailing off to embark on his international literary career.

In his travel collection *From Sea to Sea*, Kipling describes the scene as he is about to leave Allahabad for good: 'The Copper-smith sang in the garden and the early wasp hummed low down by the door-handle, and they prophesied of the hot weather to come.' And he wasn't the only literary star around, because the poet Harivansh Rai Bachchan also lived in the same compound at the time when his son Amitabh was a toddler (before he grew up to be the shiniest and biggest Bollywood star ever). Another city poet is Arvind Krishna Mehrotra who, although he lives in a different part of town, in an ode about childhood games reminisces, 'Our tomahawks are butter knives, our crow/ Feathers are real, and riding out from behind/ Plaza Talkies we ambush the cowboys of Civil Lines.'

Which brings me back to the main streets of the former English cantonment. Mofussil charm reveals itself as I loiter about in town. Splendid art deco structures, odd bungalows and equally antique upper-class uncles and aunties dressed in dated fashions hog daintily in fine-diners that haven't changed since the mid-1900s. The chicest, El Chico from 1964, has a completely retro menu of delicacies forgotten by the rest of the world but still au courant here: Russian salad drenched in rich mayo dressing (a memory of those Cold War-decades when India was one of the few non-communist lands with a reach behind the Iron Curtain), soul-stirring 'cottage cheese cutlets' (never has paneer melted in my mouth like this) that I follow up with a hillock of mutton roast plated with butter-sautéed beans and cauliflower. Tea is served in a reassuring pewter pot set. The other guests consist of a geriatric Anglo-Indian taking his greying spinster daughter out for their habitual lunch, a bunch of paunchy men in white kurtas—contractors closing a shady deal—and two families out-bragging each other about their most recent European holidays.

'Was Amsterdam in Germany or in Switzerland?'

'No, sweaty, you're mixing it up with Brussels, where they have the tulips.'

To experience prehistoric grocery shopping, I drop in at Beni Prasad Laxmi Narayan, a congested store in a graceful mercantile arcade from 1934 (which Arvind Krishna Mehrotra told me is a must-see). For my next meal, I step into a servery that advertises itself as over-six-decades-old and my initial reaction is to gasp at its stuccoed ceilings, plaster-of-Paris medallions on all-white walls, and wooden furnishings with red upholstery. It's all classy classic. A certain romantic Frenchness is added by how couples rent the upstairs family compartment, spend fifteen minutes perhaps doing some family planning activities, and hurriedly climb down the steps zipping flies and buttoning up gowns and covering their faces. However, it turns out there's nothing edible available except for mixed-veg curry made with rotten veggies, mouldy papadam and undercooked, doughy chapattis—I usually digest anything, but this is a mortally deadly funerary feast for suicidal omnivores with no sense of what's good for them.

For once, I cannot finish my meal and instead, after sufficient recovery time spent in one of M.G. Marg's characteristic dive bars disinfecting my bowels with vodka, I splurge at the smart Tepso's Jade Garden where muzak wails softly.

It gets crowded with aunties who order Chicken Tikka Masala, that most British version of Indian dishes—a humbug makhani murgh or butter chicken imitation created by Bangladeshi migrant chefs trying their hand at Punjabi cookery, tweaking it to suit palates in London (or Glasgow, if you listen to a Scotsman). The story goes that they made it from leftover chicken kebabs boiled in sweetish canned tomato soup. Whatever the case, 'CTM' recipes in their quintessential Britishness invariably include tins of chopped tomatoes, spoonfuls of cream, glow-in-the-dark radioactive food colouring, yoghurt-marinated chicken, moderate spicing and sugar. It is estimated that Britons devour twenty-three million portions of CTM per year at the approximately 15,000 outlets that have it on their menu.

At Tepso's I rather prefer the cheese-baked fish in white sauce, a sinful dish if there ever was one, made not with frozen fish but freshly-caught North Indian river sole from the Ganges, assures the waiter, and the cheesy crust is honest-to-goodness Amul, finely shredded.[26]

M.G. Marg isn't really built for serious pubbing, but whenever I crave a sunset double-pint along with pre-dinner snacks, I head for the tourist bungalow next to the noisy bus station. For pub grub, the food is decent as evidenced by retired uncles whiling away afternoons sipping beer and nibbling on chicken cutlets. And if I'm still peckish late at night, there are gourmet chefs with pushcarts everywhere, attracting custom for their litti-chokha, whole-wheat dumplings stuffed with mustard oil-and cumin-seasoned roasted chickpea or lentil flour, then baked in cow dung ash which imparts a unique flavoursomeness, rinsed in a cup of melted butter before eaten piping hot with chokha, charred eggplant-cum-boiled potato puree. It is a dish that has quite likely been prevalent in these parts since two or three millennia by now and it tastes as great today as when perhaps Buddha himself—who once toured in the area—would have eaten it.

It is perhaps appropriate that Civil Lines has retained its nomenclature instead of being renamed, because civil is what it is, and if you read between the lines you'll get food of the sort that's hardly imaginable anymore in this epoch of global sameness: Allahabad's flavours of pre-liberalised India remind one of a young country that had just gained independence under a prime minister who—naturally—was born in Allahabad. M.G. Marg remains a living museum of food sophistication from a hallowed history before global junk food machine-gunned its way into our tummies.

VIII

Where Teatime is Anytime
(The East)

'Come, oh come, ye tea-thirsty restless ones—the kettle boils, bubbles and sings, musically.'

—Rabindranath Tagore,
winner of the Nobel Prize for Literature in 1913

Friendly bartendresses running a bar in Bhutan.

'Welcome to Bihar,' says the student who wants to shake my hand as soon as the train rolls into Patna Junction, the modern incarnation of Pataliputra, the once-upon-a-time headquarters of Mauryan civilisation. 'I hope you'll come back again.'

I wouldn't know. Bihar seems nice but people persistently warned me before this trip: 'Don't expect to come back alive from Bihar,' they said. Don't expect any roads, they went on gleefully adding, 'Don't expect electricity.' So, despite the warm welcome by the student on his way to his 'native place' by the Nepalese border, I am wondering how unwise it might turn out to be a vagabond hereabouts. I can't help but notice how the platform behind the student resembles a freshly-ploughed potato-field.

Nevertheless, I've always had a soft corner in my heart, and a rough spot in my tummy, for Patna, perhaps more for its literary importance than its occasionally deadly foods. Patna is, in a manner, where this book, started with *that* tandoori chicken which I can never forget, but it holds more stories than that. To the north of town, in Motihari, a house is identified by a concrete sign on the roadside as George Orwell's birthplace. His father was an opium-tax collector in the Opium Department, a strange British-run government-owned industry devoted to peddling narcotics (which would have landed Orwell's dad in jail had he been alive today). And so young Orwell spent his first years around here. In adulthood, he worked as a colonial police officer in another remote area—erstwhile Burma, which falls outside the scope of this book. His novel *Nineteen Eighty-Four* coined the expression 'Big Brother is watching you' and perhaps it was inspired by the Soviet Union, but apparently it can also be read (alongside his *Animal Farm*) as a fictive history of Myanmar.

Patna is furthermore the model for E.M. Forster's fictional Chandrapore—a city on the Ganges where the 'very wood seems made of mud, the inhabitants of mud moving. So abased, so monotonous is everything that meets the eye, that when the Ganges comes down it might be expected to wash the excrescence back into the soil. Houses do fall, people are drowned and left rotting, but the general outline of the town persists, swelling here, shrinking there, like some low but indestructible form of life' he wrote—after touristing in town for some two weeks—and it is here, where much of the action in *A Passage to India* (written 1912-24) ostensibly takes place.

Except for those pivotal picnic passages in the spooky Barabar caves about 100 km to the south, which he visited in January 1913 and fictionalised as the Marabar Caves, and that literary scholars have been speculating over for nearly a century.[27] Forster was frequently enough quoted as saying, 'When asked what happened there, I don't know.' He visited the caves in a disturbed state of mind and spent much time sobbing in Patna, where his friend Dr Masood (the novel's Dr Aziz) at the time was teaching, which is reflected—or perhaps repressed—in the fictional scene. And which prompted him to write the novel *Maurice*, upon his return to England, although it was only to be published posthumously.[28]

The director of the sumptuous silverscreen spectacle, David Lean, rejected the real caves as not mystical enough. He worked on the screenplay in New Delhi using elements of Karnataka-born writer Santha Rama Rau's stage adaptation and set the film in Karnataka instead of North India, shooting mostly in and around Bengaluru's surrounding rocky landscapes and enigmatic crags. There, a decade before, the wild west-style Hindi blockbuster *Sholay* had been filmed and, at the time when it was still called Bangalore, the town had a fair amount of milieus suitable for a colonial period cinematic extravaganza—some of the recognisable shooting locations include the city's palace and the old Bangalore Club.

The table of fare of the novel's over-the-top picnic remains another mystery save for one man tippling and another smoking a fag, apart from which there is just a fleetingly referenced porridge dish (khichdi?). One may only speculate what Forster's characters ate during their last meal before the culture clash—one colonial-era Indian menu devised for English people I study for reference, in a musty autobiography, mentions hilariously named fusion fare such as cutlets, that are not meat slices as Britons might expect, but potato patties. To further befuddle the English, such veg cutlets are also called chops which as per the dictionary means 'small piece of meat on a bone, usually cut from a sheep or pig'. Or take *hotche-potche* soup. I've no idea what that might be but hazard a guess it is rasam which, after an unknown 'Madrasi cook' added chicken and rice to make it soupy, came to be better known as the colonial Mulligatawny Soup. Then they were served *cotholathe mouthong* (presumably genuine mutton cutlets this time) with *poulay* (most likely a chicken pullao) and *cocks turky* (roasted chicken legs?), and *maccaroning* (hmm...curried pasta?). However, what really takes my cake is a menu of Rice Dumplings with Doll Curry and

Cock-Nut Sauce—it took me a while to decipher it as your standard idli-sambar with coconut chutney!

Of what he encountered on Indian menus, Forster was (as already noted in Hyderabad) into biryani which may have resembled aforesaid *poulay*. And jackfruits were 'extraordinary' according to him. But although the picnic in the novel was hosted by Aziz, the friendly Muslim, vegetarian fare was obviously served as a Brahmin cook is mentioned and one of the characters, Professor Godbole would only eat 'vegetables and rice if cooked by a Brahman; but not meat, not cakes lest they contained eggs, and he would not allow anyone else to eat beef: a slice of beef upon a distant plate would wreck his happiness.' And I'm reminded of how, when Forster lived in Madhya Pradesh, he got tired of the vegetarian spreads—this picnic perhaps mirrors that frustration?

Patna also inspired the city of Brahmpur in *A Suitable Boy*, the 1990s' hit novel by Vikram Seth, but Mira Nair's TV-series based on it shunned Patna just like Lean's movie did decades earlier, and it was primarily canned in Lucknow which was deemed a more suitable backdrop. Despite how it has inspired great novels, Patna isn't a glossy town like Paris, or Rome. Clouds of dust hover over the streets. Hogs dig into piles of garbage—this simply isn't the hottest destination you will read about in award-winning travelogues. Most people, in fact, tell you that it would have been a better option to come here in the days of the Buddha, who wasn't born in Bihar (his birthplace is believed to be Lumbini in Nepal) and didn't die here (he died in Uttar Pradesh). But he did spend much of his life here, roaming around an area covering 180,000 square kilometres or twice the size of present-day Bihar.

It seems to have been an interesting time, but no trains in India run that slow that they can arrive late by 2,500 years. Yet trying to forget the present, I check out the chief attraction at the museum, apparently nicknamed Jadu Ghar ('magic castle'), on Buddha Road which is a life-sized statue of a well-developed woman known as the Didarganj Yakshi, dating from those times. The museum collection also has statues of Buddha. He was so respected in Pataliputra—filled with good people who were 'the most distinguished in all India' according to the ancient Greek geographer Strabo—that one of the sixty-four gates in the city wall was named after him. Perhaps he even strode down Buddha Road, maybe he met and preached to the voluptuous model, I muse in the garden outside the museum. Maybe she ran a tavern in town?

As a matter of fact, Buddhist jataka tales contain India's earliest food-writing—if one may term it so—giving a fair idea of what foodstuffs were on offer to travellers. Bihar itself is named for the many viharas (monasteries) that once existed in the state, both centres of learning as well as safe accommodation where one might break journey for the night and be provided a wholesome dinner. Many monasteries were virtual food plants with sugar mills and oil presses. K.T. Achaya, who studied the matter of Buddhist cuisine, mentions chickpeas and various other pulses, condiments such as black mustard seeds and asafoetida, fruits (bananas and grapes), and also sugarcane which remains a major crop in Bihar. Dishes in Buddhist texts that sound tempting include barley-honey balls—laddus?—and staples such as wild rice khichdi and honey-flavoured kanji. A monk who sailed from China to the Nalanda monastery described a menu of rice with peas and boiled barley—the latter being eaten already since Vedic times. Many kinds of flatbreads were part of the diet, salad and fruit, and—hold your breath—non-veg.

Pigeon meat was familiar fare, fish was also considered

permitted food, perhaps braised in fruit juice like some Asiatic Buddhists still cook them. At one modern monastery inhabited by monks from Cambodia, the chatty disciples I met were cooking what looked like pigeon, squeezing some esoteric fruit juice onto it, but it turned out to be a chicken curry. Some monks, during the Buddha's lifetime, brewed a potent beverage known as Pigeon's Liquor (not made out of pigeon's poop, as you might think, but it was a fortified palm wine thus named due to its somewhat murky greyish colour). This practice stopped in 520 BCE when the Buddha found an old monk lying drunk outside a monastery. Non-veg was also flavoured with lime juice—limes were special fruits for Buddhists and are even depicted in the cave paintings of Ajantha, and it was Indian monks who introduced limes to China in the fourth century CE.

Before achieving enlightenment and after having starved for weeks, the Buddha is said to have eaten a traditional Bihari rice pudding which opened his eyes to the futility of extreme asceticism. And thereafter his diet was quite typical of any Indian—rice and dhal, occasionally non-veg items such as fish and eggs, as well as sweet items. He is even quoted as describing what to him counted as soulfood, 'I recommend food made out of rice, barley, wheat, all kinds of beans, ghee, oil of sesame, honey, sugarcane, sugar, and other seasonal foods which are full of soul qualities...' Such foods were considered rich in merits, virtue, wisdom and they warded off evils. He urged people to embrace moderation and self-control, not to lust too much after delicacies that were bad for karma, as all craving was back in those days before consumerism became our modern religion. Statistical experts have concluded, after studying the meals described in Buddhist literature, that he was 40 per cent vegan, 54 per cent vegetarian and only every twentieth meal he had was non-veg. In fact, the menu consisted of whatever the monks were given in their alms bowls, whether veg or non-veg, and to this day one sees monks in Southeast Asia walking from door to door, between restaurants in the mornings, to collect their daily meal.

Most intriguingly, the Buddha is believed to have spent time in the company of cannibals as he, in the *Lankavatara Sutra*, discussed the problems of cannibalism faced by a king whose 'excessive fondness for meat, his greed to be served with it, stimulated his taste for it to the highest degree so that he ate human flesh.' This of course alienated a ruler from his kinsmen if they suspected that he might cook them. 'In consequence he had to renounce his throne and dominion and to suffer great calamities because of his passion for meat,' said the Buddha as he advocated the benefits of vegetarianism. Though this was of little use as the monarch's rebelling subjects killed him in the end.

If the Buddha has living descendants, it is reasonable to assume that they can be encountered in present-day Patna's restaurants.

❖

On the train east, at most stations, they sell the sinful luchi-sabzi of starchy cholesterol-rich puffed breads dunked in greasy gravy that Bengalis love so much, which tells me that the train is entering West Bengal. Hawkers come on-board to peddle milky mishti-doi, date palm jaggery-sweetened curd in clay pots that are perfect to cool one's intellectual turmoil.

As far as I have counted, there are in all 7,325 stations in India, each of which is likely to be a theatrical display of energising sweets and quick bites often with some regional specialities up their sleeve. I've only visited about 500 of those, so I'm left with this nagging feeling that there's lots left for me to explore in terms of railway food. And it's an absolute fact that food, for some reason, tastes better on tours—like the unexpectedly delicious fish curry I once had in the canteen at Jamshedpur station, the robust Tamil biryani sold on the platform at Khatpadi Junction, Kerala's banana fritters, the chikki peanut candy at Lonavla, the unbelievably smooth dhoklas at Gujarati stations, the aloo tikkis of Uttar Pradesh and choles of Punjab...and not to forget the crunchy Maddur-vada at the eponymous train stop between Bengaluru and Mysuru, which coincidentally was invented by a man peddling snacks on the platform one day when the train wasn't as delayed as it usually was. He suddenly had to cook up a quicker fast-food than his normal offerings (hence he made the vada flatter to fry it faster). Basically, while other tourists take the train to see the world, I do it to eat the world. Or its most intriguing bits.

Finally, I stretch my legs in Kolkata's railway station where India is camping out on the floor, a human tsunami trying to flood the right train in the poorly signposted, cavernous halls that are full of traffic-jammed porters struggling with overloaded carts. I decide to break journey for a week or two.

Eventually every travelling booklover reaches Kolkata where there's so much culture—and where East and West cohabited as Britons built their great eastern metropolis of which Kipling rhymed:

Me the Sea-captain loved, the River built,
Wealth sought and Kings adventured life to hold.
Hail, England! I am Asia—Power on silt,
Death in my hands, but Gold!

Although the Nobel-awardee-to-be was quite dismissive of the 'city of dreadful night' as he liked to call it, Bengali literary sentiment spawned distinguished authors such as Bibhutibhushan Bandhopadhyay who wrote *Song of the Road* that was filmed by Satyajit Ray, Bankimchandra Chatterjee whose 'Vande Mataram' is the poem of the nation, Rabindranath Tagore who bagged that coveted Nobel Prize, besides so many others. The city houses the National Library that stores copies of everything published in India—it's apt that such an institution is here, since publishing in this country in the modern sense really started in the city, with journals first in English such as the scandalous *Hickey's Gazette*, but soon enough they were also printed in Bengali. The earliest printers were in the Chitpur neighbourhood where I still hear the churning of presses that use movable types as I poke along Chitpur Road.

The one condition that always afflicts me in Kolkata, is a profound regret over the fact that I wasn't born a Bengali. Numerous novels, short stories and poems have been translated, but the bulk of Bengali literature is and will remain appreciable only to those who can read the language properly—its nuances, its rhythms and its Aeolian cadences. Hence, being a non-Bengali-speaker in Kolkata is like being a vegetarian in a seafood hotel. My vocabulary consists of about three Bengali words, adda, bhetki, and, uh, vodka. With that, I could only write a really short haiku in the language.

While writing his *The City of Dreadful Night*, Kipling stayed at the Great Eastern Hotel (which later housed prominent communists such as Ho Chi Minh and Nikita Khrushchev) and although he loved the hotel—'Fancy sitting down seventy strong to *tâble d'hôte* and with a deafening clatter of knives and forks! Fancy finding a real bar whence drinks may be obtained!'—for some private reason he was never quite able to digest the city, but rather loved to hate 'Calcutta, which, I was to see, still persisted in being a city…I had formally cursed it one year ago.' His top tip for fellow travellers went: 'One must begin to smoke at five in the morning—which is neither night nor day—on coming across the Howrah Bridge, for it is better to get a headache from honest nicotine than to be poisoned by evil smells.'[29] For whatever reason and ever since, foreigners like to portray the city unfavourably, such as its poverty that shapes the narrative in *The City of Joy* by Dominique Lapierre. As I am trying to get my head around this, I come across the following lines by a local author: 'But to deny the undisputed rule of filth and astounding tardiness in Kolkata is to be in denial about what's unpleasant but real,' writes Inderjit Hazra as he does seem to grant the city's critics a point. 'Despite its colonial architectures, Kolkata everywhere, in all its wetness and rust and ooze, seems like a city built, or in the process of being built, on the remains of another city that someone left behind.'

Rather than ponder such bleakness, it is far better to get oneself invited to an adda, the impromptu ideating salons or vociferous tea party discussions among close friends, that blend gossip and jokes with artistic, political or scientific debates, and that take place at homes or in cafés so beloved among the talkative Bengalis, and that always include tea or coffee, and some gorgeous savouries, sweets and perhaps even fried fish. An adda can happen in any corner if the right quantity of patrons can be gathered. If there's no adda, one can always head to the university area's Coffee House in Bankim Chatterjee Street and launch one's own. The café founded in the 1940s is a Kolkata institution and is in fact housed in the historic Albert Hall (from 1876) which has been the venue of many important talks, including by Mahatma Gandhi. It was at one of these tables that Satyajit Ray scripted his *Pather Panchali*, based on Bandhopadhyay's aforementioned novel *Song of the Road*, that gave him worldwide fame, but he wasn't the only filmy regular—they all hung out here: Ritwik Ghatak, Mrinal Sen, Utpal Dutt and Aparna Sen. Towards the end of his life, Allen Ginsberg spoke passionately about 1960s' Calcutta, 'We poets—Sunil Ganguly, Shakti Chatterjee, and others—met a lot in the coffee houses. Peter [Orlovsky] and I were excited by the idea of there being a whole gang of poets like there were in New York and San Francisco, who were friends, and that we could communicate across the Pacific Ocean, and that East could meet West...' Indeed, West did meet East and so when Ginsberg flew to Bangkok in May 1963, his travel companion Orlovsky stayed behind as he had fallen in love with a Bengali musician.

In the more genteel Park Street, on the other hand, I spot litterateur Amit Chaudhuri having his solitary adda, sipping daintily on a cup of what looks like Earl Grey with low-calorie sweeteners and low-fat milk at Flury's, the 1920s' Park Street tearoom fashionable for its scones and parfaits. This is apparently where Chaudhuri goes when he is slumming according to his book *Calcutta: Two Years in the City*. Although the poet's preferred haunts are the city's exclusive clubs and fully air-conditioned five-star-hotels, he does ask himself 'thinking about this book which I had taken upon myself to write: How would it start?' So after a cuppa at Flury's, he crossed the road and ventured into the somewhat less posh Free School Street: 'Earlier, I would have denied this place its existence, would have seen it but shut it out, would have looked at it as a stubborn aberration...' But on that afternoon he studied it for as long as it took to walk the 650 metres to Sudder Street and back to Flury's, while observing the poor wash their pots and pans in gutter mud, homeless people 'bored, doing nothing' and handed out Rs 50 to an ailing child labourer. This is perhaps the best description I've read of the city's elite viewing their less fortunate fellow city-dwellers.

Whereas streetsy chai-drinking is an all-day affair, high tea in orthodox circumstances is served at 4 p.m. in the finer salons of the Taj Bengal or Great Eastern where éclairs and croissants adorn the spreads, and trendy newer places like Karma Kettle celebrates colonial nostalgia with their 'Gora Sahib High Tea' of chicken roulades, tea-cakes and scones, yet in Kolkata's streets, teatime is anytime if one patronises the chaiwallas who pour milky brew into earthen cups.

There's a lot to be said about tea, the beverage that mankind associates with India. It is one of the two main British contributions to Indian food culture, the other being sliced white sandwich bread which can be stuffed with spiced up veggies, dipped in batter and deep-fried into something that no Englishman would recognise as a sandwich, just like chai is remote from the sedate English Breakfast teas. Technically speaking, tea-drinking was 'invented' according to calculations in the 2730s BCE in China's south-westerly mountains bordering North-east India. And although China remains the #1 producer, a huge share of what the planet consumes comes from Assam's thousands of tea gardens while the most exclusive varieties grow in northern Bengal's hilly Darjeeling district, with Kolkata being the industry's primary trading hub. One Assamese tea estate is movie star Julie Christie's birthplace.

Before the plantation industry commenced circa 1840, the beverage was nigh on unknown here—except by some medievals who traded with China and Assamese tribals in the remotest North-east who plucked wild-growing tea off certain trees (*Camellia sinensis var. Assamica*) which must have spread across the mountains and taken root here by themselves. This slow growth of tea culture is astonishing, considering that there were overland trade routes from China to Assam operational already by the second century BCE—well before the Silk Road opened for traffic. Incredibly enough, only in the years after independence did tea gradually metamorphose from a symbol of colonial snootiness to a national drink when the Tea Board started promoting it as an important Made in India product. Nowadays, all tourist guidebooks and travel documentaries feature, as a characteristic character, the ubiquitous chaiwallah who is boiling (rather than brewing) his maximum spicy and high-punch sweetish concoction, encountered on railway platforms, in bus stations, street-corners, yes, everywhere.[30]

Connoisseurs say good tea is like champagne, to which no Old Monk rum needs to be added, making tea-sipping every bit as exciting as wining-dining-shining in Bordeaux. At least I suppose the Hollywood actress Vivien Leigh may have thought so—as she was born in Darjeeling in the winter of 1913, she

Potential adda in Kolkata.

must have smelled the spring flush as a toddler before her cavalry officer father was transferred to Bengaluru. She then went to school in another tea-planting district, in the southern Nilgiri Hills where she acted in amateur theatre productions. Even after her cinematic career took off in the 1930s, with *Gone with the Wind* turning into an award-winning box-office hit, she went on reminiscing about a masala dosa that she had eaten with her chai in India.

When I'm not busy swilling tea and exploring intellectual life, I drink in the headiness of age-old 'Calcutta' at the 1950s' eastern-European style Broadway beer hall (27A, Ganesh Chandra Avenue) where one might expect Karl Marx to make a meteoric entrance at any moment to snap one's tankard away. Auxiliary peckishness is cured by the mutton kathi rolls that are something of a heritage dish, having been invented at Nizam's near the market a century ago, in about 1930. Also, there are any number of kachoris, puchkas, bhelpuris and jhaalmuris and other dubious but dependably tempting street snacks that I obviously can't resist, with each street vendor (the city has about 130,000 of them) adding his own twist to the mixes that usually contain some cooked but cooled veggies, chillies and onions, puffed rice and crunchy-fried noodles ('sev'), various reddish and greenish spicy chutneys and suchlike tasting both cool, hot, sour and sweet at the same time, then perhaps coriander that gives a soapy tinge, black salt which adds a somewhat farty scent and the chaat masala without which nothing would be anything. Kolkata is like a peckish poem...or at least, I get uncommonly verbose when I try to briefly outline my eating experiences.

Across the road from the hippies' beloved lassi stall in Sudder Street, Tagore composed 'The Awakening of the Waterfall' that inaugurated his poetic career, standing on a balcony (in his brother's house) which was still there thirty years ago. This time, I find that the balcony is walled in and the building turned into a hotel called Plaza. So much for literary heritage buildings in the city of literature. Soon enough it'll all be gone, like the Sudder Street relic Fairlawn Hotel, in which it was possible to be transported back to the Raj and imagine oneself as an extra in some period TV serial. Fairlawn was purchased by a luxury hospitality group recently and will probably be reopened as a boutique inn with a flashy bistro.

Uptown, Tagore's birthplace Jorasanko (Dwarkanath Tagore Lane), where he also breathed his last, has been preserved as a museum, and his deathbed stands in the room where, before dying, he wrote somewhat morbidly, 'O my day-break sparrow/In my last moments of sleepiness/While there is still some darkness/Here you are tapping on my window-slats/Asking for news/And then dancing and twittering.'

As a food tourist in his house, I am frankly speaking most touched by the kitchen where one can see a rather—from a modern point of view—primitive stove, upon which I imagine that the womenfolk prepared his sugary jasmine tea and his meals. He usually wanted Bengali food for lunch (mutton curry without chillies but tinged with sugar), followed by Western for dinner with soupy starters, meaty or fishy mains, and pudding for dessert. But he was against fusing the two—and all was eaten with imported cutlery, according to a story I heard from another museum visitor who seemed to know a lot about Bengali food culture. Coincidentally, Tagore's niece Prajñasundari Devi wrote one of the earliest Bengali cookbooks in 1902 and not many know that the bard coined a slogan to market tea—apart from inventing several desserts such as modified jalebis to tantalise the Bengalis' collective sweet tooth.

This obviously makes me hungry for Bengali specialities so

I head off, rather impatiently and not too far, to Siddeshwari Ashram in Mirza Ghalib Street (near Janbazaar) to have lunch at the no-frills and very business-like 'pice hotel'—one of the last such remaining, and known by that name because once upon a time food items could be bought for one paisa. The idea was that instead of ordering a full meal, money-minded customers could pick as many items as they could afford. Today, of course there aren't any paisa coins in circulation and dishes are pricier at Rs 100-200, but well worth it as their chingri is the biggest, freshest, juiciest estuary prawn I've ever sank my teeth into, virtually lobster-sized, and fried in a creamy gravy tempered with the typical five-spice blend 'paanch phoron'.

Earlier, the town was full of similar canteens to feed labourers who migrated here in search of work. Even this one existed in Tagore's days so he, being a foodie, may have ordered home-delivery or, perhaps, even sat at one of the marble-topped tables to sample its fare along with his culinary clubbers.

Another, about half-as-historic place but one that I love, is the all-women-run Suruchi (89 Elliot Road) where the divine bhetki tastes truly motherly. The perch-like fish is robed in a banana leaf that traps the aroma of the yellowish mustard paste and other spices during the cooking process. The one pungent note peculiar to Bengal's fishy dishes is 'shorshey tel', I think that may be how it is to be spelled, the local mustard oil that is a must and adds an unusual sharpness like a winding guitar solo in a 1970s' heavy metal tune. Apparently, it is because they view fish to be a vegetable of sorts, albeit one that swims and thinks, that the Bengalis have such evolved intellects and always were pioneers of modern literature. It is said that only every seventeenth Bengali is a vegetarian, the other sixteen love fish—including heads, brains and all.

One more experience of literary interest is the Park Street

cemetery. There's something about its decay that makes it utterly realistic. No plasticky Disney makeup covers its scars, everything is the real deal. The caretakers nap inside the cool crypts of towering tombs that constantly remind of exotic ways to die—the descriptions range from monsoon melancholia to choking on pineapples. It's hard to find anything comparable outside New Orleans's voodoo walks that take one to horror-movie spooky cemeteries, or Paris where everybody who is anybody, from Jim Morrison to Chopin, take final rest at Père-Lachaise, or London's supposedly occult graveyard at Highgate which has an interestingly swinging party crowd (provided that there's an afterlife) including Karl Marx whose tomb has been bombed several times, one alleged vampire who is said not to rest peacefully, not to forget *The Hitchhiker's Guide to the Galaxy* author Douglas Adams, plus music industry phenomena such as Malcolm McLaren (of Sex Pistols fame) and George Michael (of Wham!).

The Park Street cemetery's fame with film buffs has grown after the 2010 Bengali movie *Gorosthaney Sabdhan* based on Ray's story (translated into English as 'The Secret of the Cemetery') turned out to be a box-office success. And the literati are keen on exploring the necropolis of which Rudyard Kipling wrote in one of the more hallucinatory chapters of *City of Dreadful Night*: 'The eye is ready to swear that it is as old as Herculaneum and Pompeii. The tombs are small houses. It is as though we walked down the streets of a town, so tall are they and so closely do they stand—a town shrivelled by fire, and scarred by frost and siege. Men must have been afraid of their friends rising up before the due time that they weighted them with such cruel mounds of masonry.'

As for myself, I bite into a clove of garlic as I enter the cemetery, well aware of the rumours of haunting, how visitors experience spells of breathlessness and dizziness due to weird shapes peeking over their shoulders in their selfies. One tomb is claimed to occasionally bleed, sadly not when I'm visiting. I'm mesmerised instead by the eloquently inscribed tombstones,

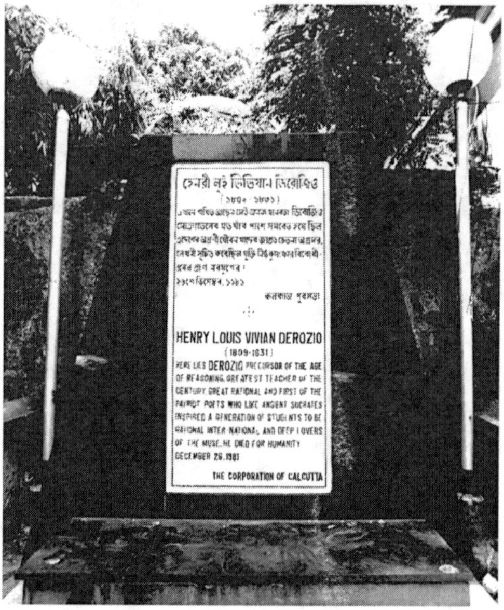

A poet lies buried at the Park Street cemetery entrance.

which read like poetry about British times. Already at the entrance, visitors are greeted by the plaque commemorating Henry Louis Vivian Derozio (1809-1831), who according to Kipling was the 'poet of the race' and who influenced a generation of Bengali writers with his passion for everything Indian:

My native land hath heavenliest bowers
Where Houris ruby-cheeked might dwell,
And they are gemmed with buds and flowers
Sweeter than lip or lute may tell.

The most monumental grave belongs to philologist William Jones (1746-1794), a scholar who proposed a world-shattering theory about the relationship between the tongues of India and Europe. This developed into the idea of Indo-European languages, meaning that whether one is a Bengali-speaker or Englishman, what you say has a common source.

Overall, there are more than 1,600 graves, a phantasmagorical assemblage of towering obelisks and pyramids, cryptic cenotaphs and vaults, sarcophagus and catafalques, urns and cairns, occasionally bearing elements of Indo-Saracen architecture's distinct domes amidst Gothic and Greco-Roman designs. It correctly says on an enthusiastic notice board at the entrance that there is 'perhaps no other (non-church) exclusive colonial cemetery of this variety and dimension anywhere else in the world!'

Kipling was particularly drawn to the tomb of one Lucia Palk, 'hot-blooded young writers did duel with smallswords in the Fort ditch for the honour of piloting her through a minuet at the Calcutta theatre or the Punch House.' Unfortunately, 'Lucia fell sick, and the doctor—he who went home after seven years with five lakhs and a half, and a corner of this vast graveyard to his account—said that it was a *pukka* or putrid fever, and the system required strengthening. So they fed Lucia on hot curries, and mulled wine worked up with spirits and fortified with spices, for nearly a week; at the end of which time she closed her eyes,' he jotted in *City of Dreadful Night*. Subsequently, Paul Theroux exploited the boneyard in his Orientalist detective pulp *A Dead Hand*, while William Dalrymple's *White Mughals* drew on characters buried here such as 'Hindoo Stuart', an Irishman who tried to convince memsahibs to don saris ('the most alluring dress in the world') and who rests eternally in a mock Hindu temple.

Maybe the saddest grave is that of Rose Aylmer (1780-1800), who came to India as a teenaged beauty queen and died from enjoying those aforementioned pineapples—in excess. One of her admirers was the cavalier litterateur Walter Savage Landor, a close friend of Charles Dickens whose son Walter is also buried in Calcutta. Dickens junior wanted to become a writer too, but Dickens senior insisted junior take up a military career in India where he promptly died. Landor is best remembered for an elegy to his great love:

Rose Aylmer, whom these wakeful eyes
May weep, but never see,
A night of memories and of sighs
I consecrate to thee.

Booklovers will recall how Amit and Lata, the lovebirds of Vikram Seth's bombastic bestseller *A Suitable Boy*, initiate their infatuation in the graveyard, quoting to each other lines from Landor: 'Amit paused, "Ah, lovely poem, lovely poem," he said, looking delightedly at Lata.' I spend a good hour reading inscriptions about many other prematurely dead Britons who'd be long forgotten but for the memorials preserved here. I've heard it said that two monsoons used to be the lifetime of any foreigner in Kolkata—and the same went for Mumbai and Shillong too—and if not killed by malarial illness, men often succumbed to addictions. The death of one Englishman, for instance, was brought about through 'an inordinate use of the hokkah' though most others simply ate and drank themselves to death.

A chatty Anglo-Indian aunty stops to tell me of how her own ancestors 'came out' back in the day and tore up their British passports when India gained independence. According to her, Anglo-Indians are the finest race that spawned the likes of

Bombay-born 1950s' popstar Tony Brent (who used his music business fortune to open a chain of tiffin joints in Australia), Madras-born Engelbert Humperdinck who had Indian blood (through his mother) topped UK charts in 1967 with nostalgic singles like 'The Last Waltz' as memories of the Raj were fading fast, and Lucknow-born super idol Cliff Richard. The latter's dad was a caterer for the Indian Railways and did his bit to popularise the Anglo-Indian traveller's favourite 'railway mutton curry'.

'Have you heard of him? We used to get his singles before anybody else. He grew up in Howrah because his dad worked for the railways.'

So many stars were born within the community, but 'our race has degenerated through intermarriage'. The constantly scornful Naipaul, in town when the community was at its most vibrant, looked down his nose at Anglo-Indian culture—'those sad bands, those sad Anglo-Indian girls at the microphone, and the air full of dated slang. "Oh, just bung your coat down there."'

At first the expression 'Anglo-Indian' used to refer to Brits residing in India, while those today known as Anglo-Indians would've been labelled Eurasians then. So for example in the 1800s Kipling proudly called himself Anglo-Indian as he thumped his chest—'we who were Anglo-Indians separated ourselves a little from the crowd'—but in the 1900s, the longer colonials stayed on, they became all too happy to mingle and hence the generation of Anglo-Indians that followed had an Indian parent, almost always on the mothers side. This spawned badmouthing to such a malicious degree that even Kipling, fluent in Hindustani as he was, was rumoured to be 'eight annas to the rupee' or what Kipling himself termed 'hyphenated white male' or half-caste. There were a variety of levels to this—

country-bred (educated in India but not born in the country) being slightly less pejorative than country-born (born in India) and so that gradually, as the aunty explained to me, people had less and less of English blood and manners in them. Yet, from an Indian point of view, they were seen as not Indian enough, leaving them in an escalating limbo after 1947. And everybody who was anybody migrated to other former colonies such as Australia fifty years ago anyway. 'Few today have blue eyes and pale skin, and most don't know proper English but make a livelihood begging outside churches,' she laments. After the lady takes my leave, I wonder for a second if she was real or if I had encountered a spectre.

Here then dwell the ghosts of what was Britain in India, in the gloomy necropolis that remains a calming counterpoint to the glitzy tap-dancing highlife of jolly Park Street outside its looming walls, where shady men proposition me—'anything?'—that I gently refuse. They remind me of that bawdy passage in *Calcutta Chromosome*, when Amitav Ghosh's protagonist found such offers 'irresistible. All I had was five rupees but that was enough. He led me down one of those tiny alleys around Free School Street, just around the corner from the Armenian school, where William Thackeray was born. We went up a dark, stinking staircase that looked like it led to the anus of the earth. But then we got to the top and suddenly there was this great sunburst of light and noise and voices and music: it was like walking into a fairground—a huge room, with little curtained cubicles all around it, and vendors selling paan and tea, and all these women sitting on chairs lined up against the wall, with flowers around their wrists. I never looked back; I was hooked. I loved them; I loved everything about them, even the way they laughed behind my back when I was running down the stairs, afterwards, my pants half-unbuttoned.'

That fictional character got syphilis, so as I'm writing non-fiction I studiously avoid such offers. After giving the well-dressed and courteous Anglo-Indian beggars what coins I have in my pocket, I head to Mocambo's, the heavy doors of which preserve an almost sepia-tinted universe within, coincidentally on the same side of the road as the house in which eighteenth-century novelist Thackeray was born (watch out for a plaque on the wall). His dad was a bureaucrat in the East India Company and he was shipped back to England at a tender age. Barely a toddler, Thackeray grew up on Indian food because his aunties in England were addicted to curry—he even published a poem on cooking curry (in *Punch* magazine in 1846 at a time when he was already a celebrated author, so he used a pen name) rhyming:

> *...beef, mutton, rabbit, if you wish*
> *Lobsters, or prawns, or any kind of fish*
> *Are fit to make A CURRY.*

Two years later, a funny wordplay of chillies versus chilling comprise the comical highpoint in his most famous novel *Vanity Fair*, in which Becky falls for a curry-lover and in order to impress the wealthy Anglo-Indian, ladles in curry by the spoonful—only to suffer from its heat. 'She thought a chili was something cool, as its name imported, and was served with some. "How fresh and green they look," she said, and put one into her mouth. It was hotter than the curry; flesh and blood could bear it no longer. She laid down her fork. "Water, for Heaven's sake, water!" she cried.' She might have fared better if she had sampled Mocambo's interpretations of Continental cuisine. Luckily, the fine-diner has remained much the same for seven decades and even if the food they serve isn't the same that Thackeray loved, many of the dishes on offer are pure Anglo-

Indian heritage of the type sometimes labelled 'club food', that go on attracting tummy-tourists like me and puts it firmly on all must-eat lists.

As I relax in the company of my seventh beer, I imagine how in classical Calcutta, the city of too many joys, Anglo-Indians enjoyed a jovial fare of 'pale ale and hot curries, heavy tiffin, and numerous cheroots,' as mentioned by diarists of the time. Dishes in their cookbooks bore intriguingly rhyming names such as ding-ding, dol-dol and pish-pash. The latter is described in one dictionary as 'slop of rice-soup with small pieces of meat in it, much used in the Anglo-Indian nursery' and the name is variously attributed to Persian, Old English, or simply babytalk. All this would presumably be washed down with heady punch cocktails, another Anglo-Indian invention that enriched the world's party scene. 'A bowl of punch was the planter's most companionable drink' it was said and its nomenclature is linked to Hindi 'paanch' due to the five ingredients that went into it—originally half a pint of coconut arrack but nowadays more typically rum (preferably distilled from Indian sugarcane) mixed with cane sugar, lime juice or some other souring agent, and two other ingredients that may vary but generally spice up the mix. A proper punch would contain a choice of cardamom, cinnamon or cloves, or nutmeg. Others added rose water, milk, egg yolks, beer or even tea to soften the blow.

Instances of being punch-drunk were first recorded in 1630s' India, but the classic rum punch was concocted in 1654 after rum production began in the West Indies, and it became a common cocktail in London's harbour areas in the 1670s, even if the word 'cocktail' hadn't yet been coined—making punch the grandmother of all cocktails. It was considered healthier than getting drunk on hard liquor and its ingredients protected sailors against scurvy, and before long it invaded the coffeehouses of

London, too. Today any fruity booze mix is termed punch, but in the 'punch houses' that were set up across India's more westernised parts, from Goa to Bombay and Madras to Calcutta, the Indianised version, sometimes referred to as khimad, was a hot concoction based on orange juice and country liquor served in shot glasses.

Speaking of mixology's Indian roots, Kolkata cuisine is a veritable kedgeree of foreign influences—from those aforementioned Anglo-Indians to exotic Armenians, to enterprising Jews and Parsis, and last but not least the Chinese, who all came here dreaming of making themselves fortunes but in the process joined hands to turn Kolkata into the world's premium food city.

During my sojourn, I go to New Market several times to eat the addictive vanilla fudge from Nahoum's, their pizza puffs and fishy short eats, rum balls and cheese straws. Founded in 1902, the bakery is the last vestige of the Jewish community that once lived hereabouts, but there are so few Jews left today that Nahoum's doesn't cater especially to that community anymore. They've stopped preparing their own salty Jewish plaited cheese, even if people still enjoy their cheese pastries. Luckily, around the corner, two shops still sell a particular kind of Portuguese cheese named after the colonial settlement of Bandel, a short distance upriver. As it is smoked and dried it keeps long enough without refrigeration for me to stuff my bags with it as a souvenir.

Eventually, as I prepare to take off again, I'm quietly wondering what might constitute a final memorable meal and get a brainwave: Kolkata supposedly has the only Chinatown in India and I vaguely know where it is. I haven't really breakfasted yet, so why not go Chinese for a change? Maybe pick up a pair of handmade boots, too, because rumour has it that there

New Market—and Nahoum's, the last Jewish bakery in Kolkata.

are excellent shoemakers in Chinatown and with the amount of walking I've been doing, I use up shoes at a mad pace as I write this book.

I hop into a cab. Half an hour later I'm in Christopher Road, the main street in Tangra. Not much of a street, more of a meandering lane lined with tanneries and eating-houses. Many are shut this early as it turns out—a bunch of students tell me so—that their primary fame is as dirt-cheap bars mostly open at night, after six o'clock. Some showcase crooners, but don't expect Shanghai jazz here, the musical fare is more Tollywood. Until about 1950, the area was infamous for its opium dens. Post-independence they all shut down and boozing took over.

As I walk, I see a Chinese cemetery dating back to 1900, a Formosa Inn for those who wish to stay overnight, and a Kali temple which is getting its gates painted red ahead of some Chinese festival. Next to it, I chance upon one of the few early riser eateries—aptly named Sunshine—where the morning menu consists of wonton and shingara chow. Chinese samosas? Stuffed with instant noodles, perhaps? (A dish that I think impossible to imagine until I learn that it is rather trendy in parts of India! Culinary experimenting knows no limits. Just the other day, I read that enterprising persons had cooked up Maggi-noodle-milkshakes and Fanta-Maggi-floats). I pick the wonton and get a huge plate of meaty dumplings very similar to Tibetan momos, served with fiery sauce and the main difference is the accompanying steamy egg drop broth. Stomach satisfyingly full, I continue my exploration and find a seller of paper lanterns—oddly enough a young Bengali lad—and a soy sauce factory founded in 1954, apparently using traditional slow fermentation methods. According to my GPS, there's a Lao-tzu temple in one of the winding alleys, but I don't find it. One can furthermore buy economy-size bags of MSG—that essential cornerstone of Chinese cookery, which is why eating Chinese can be so addictive and nauseating at the same time—but there's unfortunately not a single shoe shop in sight.

Labourers from the Canton area started migrating to Bengal in the late eighteenth century and a first settlement came up in Kolkata around Tiretta Bazaar (in the centre of town). However, Chinese Buddhists had been travelling to Bengal for at least 1,500 years before that, so Bengalis and Chinese weren't exactly strangers to one another. Until modern times, the Chinese population was large enough to warrant a printed Mandarin newspaper and Chinatown was a lively place with authentic eateries catering to the community. But one chap I speak with estimates that after the 1990s, that saw a lot of migration, only 200 families remain—doing a rapid headcount I figure here must be more outlets selling noodles in Kolkata than there are Chinese descendants. Many relocated to Canada and I only spot about a dozen elderly Chinese during my walk. Two aunties who look like they might belong to the T'ang dynasty or thereabouts, purely agewise if not otherwise, are charmingly clad in flowery silk pyjamas of the kind that must have been very fashionable in mainland China before the 1949 revolution. It is because of that revolution and the fact that today's China isn't the China of their ancestors, that few of them consider moving there an option.

Getting ready for lunch, after a morning's peregrination, I pass a mom-and-pop-style eatery simply called Chung (47, South Tangra), where ladies sit stuffing crab claws. I try to get some, but am told that the crabs are being cooked on order specially for a get-together. Instead, I'm given a generous plate of fried noodles with shrimp, a chowmein variety that in its Tangra translation of the Cantonese *cháau-mihn* uses Indian standard ingredients like chillies and garlic. Canton, as Guangzhou used to be called, is considered the food capital of China and there's even an ancient proverb that goes: The Cantonese eat everything with legs except a table, and everything with wings except an airplane. So when food at Tangra is labelled as 'Can' it obviously doesn't stand for Canada, the new homeland of Indian-born Chinese, but implies Indianised avatars of this celebrated cuisine. Much like in the US where Chinese eateries avoid idiosyncratic delicacies like duck's feet and stir-fried dogs. Americans prefer Americanised Cantonese—like 'American chopsuey'. In China itself, I only found it at restaurants near foreign embassies and its closest relative is the Toisanese *tsap-seui*, which means 'miscellaneous leftovers' or what poor farmers cooked for themselves out of whatever no buyer wanted to purchase from them.

A radio plays distorted Chinese pop. Soon the clan arrives to feast, filling two banquet tables loaded with off-menu specials. Some are indeed visiting from Canada, as if to prove what I've just been told, bringing fancy gifts like iPhones. The MSG-overdosed Canadian-Chinese kids horse about doing cartwheels as they simultaneously update their Facebook pages with fresh selfies, while their Indo-Chinese cousins are silent in wide-eyed wonderment.

Others worth trying are Kimfa (9, South Tangra), considered a pioneering legend and well-liked by the Chinese themselves for genial fare, and Beijing (77/1, Christopher Road), whose fine dining is all the rage with Bengalis (even the author Amitav Ghosh was spotted there when he was working on his big novel trilogy that was partly set in China). Beijing is at the forefront of what is labelled as 'Tangra Chinese' which makes it a point to cater to Bengali tastebuds in particular with extra-spicy, extra-oily, manchurianised starchy gravies, with extra food colouring to make dishes such as chilly chicken vividly neon-red, and an unusually extensive vegetarian selection in which veggies are cooked way softer than their lightly stir-fried Chinese counterparts would be. To just pick one anomaly off the menu there's a highly Tangrafied take on Peking duck: 'Pieces, medium spicy in gravy' the waiter enlightens me. Either they take radical shortcuts or he's unaware of the original's complexity: How the alluring duck first is force-fattened for six weeks, then pumped full of air and dry-roasted on a hook until its fatty skin achieves perfect crispness, before it is served thinly sliced without ever setting a duck's foot in any gravy, so it is rather bland but goes well with palm-sized wheat pancakes and a piquant fermented hoisin-style dip-sauce on the side.[31]

In fact, many of India's commonly eaten off-mainland staples are not really available in mainland China itself, such as gobi manchurian, as cauliflower isn't eaten much in China—in the 1600s, when an independent tribal state called Manchuria actually existed (and whose cuisine is known as Manchu), the European vegetable had only travelled as far east as to India, hence the dish is not only a geographical malapropism but an anachronism too. Or for that matter, take Bengaluru's beloved instant-noodle cheese-paneer dosa—truth is, the Chinese aren't that much into dairy products so the closest to paneer one tastes in China is the nutritious but non-dairy tofu. Unsurprisingly, the chilli-garlicky manchurian cooking was invented by a Kolkata-born Chinese chef (naturally)—Nelson Wang who used it to popularise his restaurant in Mumbai in the 1970s. It has been enthusiastically welcomed everywhere in India as a domesticated form of Chinese food. For example my cosmopolitan hometown Bengaluru's unofficial national vegetable among barflies is the Andhra-style extra-spicy gobi manchurian. So who am I to complain, because after MSG-modified food and too many beers to rinse the MSG-taste out of my mouth, Tangra with its oozing black gutters looks decidedly less grimy and I summon the courage to knock on the gates of a fortress-like tannery where hides are still tanned the traditional way in soaking pits.

A polite lady informs me in Chenglish that they make no shoes. 'You must go to Pen Ching Stli. All sooo-sops are there.'

It sounds like she's telling me to cross the border to China itself, so I get her to spell it out: 'Bentinck Street.'

Aha! That's the street east of Dalhousie Square (BBD Bagh) where those who arrived in the wake of the British sea trade with the port-city of Canton (when opium was shipped from here to pay for tea bought there) set up shops in the 1800s. The area even has an Old China Bazaar said to date back a century further, to 1757, where chinaware was sold.

Worried that I'll find no shoes there either, I stop the taxi just before Bentinck Street, outside Chung Wah on 13A, BCR Avenue, which is a sight to behold for anybody interested in Indo-Chinese fusion food history. In fact, foodies kept mentioning it as *the* landmark when they heard of my plan to go to Kolkata and luckily I remember now that I had made a mental note to check it out. As I step in, I am bowled over by how it retains an effortlessly retro vibe with its all-red interiors, and its private booths popular with secret lovers having tiffs over tumblers of Old Monk. The man at the next table doesn't even remove his motorcycle helmet to down his quota of seven pegs before he shoots off into Kolkata's traffic jams.

Allegedly inaugurated by Mr Wah some 140 years ago when this was a bustling Chinese neighbourhood, I'm told by the bartender who is probably making this up to keep me happy, it's no longer Chinese-run. The menu, DTP printouts in plastic pockets in case one's Daredevil beer spills, offers hybrid delicacies such as chicken tandoori chilly, Chung's special fish-manchurian masala and I half expect to be offered tandooried noodles—but it doesn't get that radical.

Fortified thus, I find that Bentinck Street indeed has about a dozen shoe shops. Some are run by dignified Chinese gentlemen and I buy nice boots—at about one third of what similar footwear might cost in branded chain stores. A little later, at dinnertime, I reach Tiretta Bazaar (famous for its Chinese breakfasts sold from pushcarts at sunrise) and take a right turn into Sun Yat Sen Street, named in honour of the father of the modern Chinese nation, where I ferret out more grub. To begin with, Tangra's Sing Cheung sauce factory turns out to have an outlet on the parallel road which is known as Lu Shun Sarani (named after writer Lu Hsün who is considered the greatest socialist realist by the Chinese communists). The secret of cooking Chinese—apart from MSG which adds killer thrills to eating—is the right sauce. The selection is magnificent, ranging from stir-fry and momo sauces to Schezwan hot sauce in anything from 210 ml bottles to 2.5 kg jerry cans. I go silly and fill my jhola with oyster sauce, wasabi paste and dried shitake mushrooms at highly affordable rates.

Next to it, I spot a picturesque Chinese church, the Sea Ip, which dates from 1905 and I continue eating in Tung Nam (24, Chattawala Galli), at whose eight tables local Chinese are dining and the menu seems totally authentic, as does the pork in hamei sauce. It's quite similar to the simple canteens I've been to in China and Taiwan, with tiny low stools so that many can squeeze in at a table. It even has the mandatory screen to ward off evil at the entrance.

Other gems include D'Lay, Pou Hing, and Eau Chew—the latter opened in the 1920s and is the oldest Chinese family-run eatery in India—and according to tradition its owner invented the Schezwan sauce, and it remains a truly authentic place to sample the times when Kolkata was a melting pot of cultures, by which I end the day. Somehow I manage to pig-out there too—a second round of dinner—call me a monstrous glutton if you will.

❖

Next day, my train trudges northeast. Outside, dreamy sun-bleached landscapes of almost black-and-white paddy fields and lotus ponds look straight out of the Satyajit Ray's *Pather Panchali*. Early afternoon, a eunuch startles me by fondling my behind and I wake up from my slumber to the song of a wandering baul minstrel who provides musical teatime entertainment—as in Kolkata teatime is anytime on regional trains—while vendors peddle nimbu cha, lime tea with a hint of chaat masala. The route through north Bengal that crosses to the North-eastern states has always been great for shopping, as lots of goods are smuggled in from neighbouring China. A man sells colourful shoulder-bags and I buy a few more jholas to organise my gastronomic souvenirs.

A freshly-cooked dinner proves that the best timepass on trains is eating, as it has always been, but there are differences between now and the previous millennium—nobody's smoking after dinner and the pantry crew isn't accommodating enough to supply optional quarts of cheap booze from pocket-stashes any longer. Everything has become wholesome, including the quantity-conscious meals of 'Rice (150 gms), Chapatti (04 nos.), Dhal (150 gms) and Mix Veg. (100 gms)'.

Because the train is late by too many hours, the next morning I take it easy and order breakfast in bed from the efficient waiters in bright orange uniforms, double-egg omelette with bread slices and the ubiquitous sauce that pretends to be ketchup, and liberal quantities of the Assamese national beverage of laal sah, sugary red tea without milk but served with lime.

Later the waiters tempt passengers with piping hot biryani as the lunch hour approaches. I crawl down from my upper berth to grab a window seat. A cloying scent of the Brahmaputra River, mixed with the zesty burps of passengers who stuffed themselves silly with egg biryani, lingers until the final station, Guwahati. I round off the trip with a rickshaw ride to Hotel Bellevue where, while relishing a grand view over the river, I reward myself suitably—namely with chilled beer aplenty plus their world-famous Club Sandwich, that was probably introduced to these parts during World War II to soothe battle-fatigued American soldiers.

❖

'Is it original or duplicate?' asks a tourist in Hindi. We're both staring at a lonesome rhinoceros in Guwahati's Zoo and Botanical Gardens. I glance briefly at the young man and roll my head sideways. He may have a valid point. The rhino doesn't look authentic. It is brooding, walking in rectangles, grunting like a German philosopher or caricatured cartoon character—one of those shape-shifters stuck in mid-transformation, somewhere between a big pig and an amphibious army tank.

The zoo is a mysterious place. Half the animals roam outside the cages: I bump into monkeys, antelopes, deer and pelicans that stake claim to the walking paths. Luckily the zoo's tiger, lion and leopard all remain safely incarcerated. How safely? The other day, says my taxi driver casually, a reporter tried to photograph the tigers and stuck his camera inside the bars, whereupon one hungry tiger ate up the camera as well as the hand holding it. I make a mental note not to repeat the same mistake.

Earlier, the only option for Assamese food was Paradise, an old place showcasing fishy thalis but things have changed. After the zoo, I head to the Upper Assam specialty restaurant Khorikaa in G.S. Road, a short taxi ride away. The main differences between Upper (or eastern) and Lower (western) Assamese cuisine appears to be that the Upper has a hint of Southeast Asian influences, the Lower shares certain Bengali elements (such as the love for mustard-flavoured fish curries that I found on every single menu I sampled in Goalpara, about 157 km downriver, west of Guwahati).

There's no rhino, antelope, monkey, snake or pelican on the menu, no Wuhan-influenced bat soups or barbecued pangolins (even if the northeast is one of the near extinct creature's rare habitats), or other endangered species on the menu. But they do cook plenty of other unusual non-veg items such as duck and pigeon, not to forget fish in many sizes and shapes including preparations with medicinal herbs, something of an Assamese hallmark. Moreover, there's a range of original—not duplicate—vegetarian options: banana flower fry; leafy slightly bitter stir-fries known as xaak (which appears to be how they pronounce saag here); lip-smacking pitikas of mushy vegetable mashes, of potatoes, eggplants or fermented bamboo shoot, redolent with mustard oil and the heady juice of raw onions. Oil is very sparingly used, mostly only for the sake of the exquisite aroma that the mustard oil imbues. The menu card also contains health advice: 'The food you eat can be either the safest and most powerful form of medicine or the slowest form of poison.'

Waiting for my lunch, I explore the pickle platter that includes something called kharoli, a thick paste of fermented mustard seeds mixed with (again) that heavenly mustard oil and a very unique ingredient, namely water treated with khar or banana tree ashes! (This is actually, as one tribal lady explained to me when I visited her kitchen, made by burning the trunk of a banana tree to ashes which are then mixed with water that is strained through a special filter made of cane. The resulting liquid is stored in bottles and used while cooking to give dishes an alkaline flavour—hence it is never added to recipes with sour ingredients such as tomatoes, as the two would be in conflict with one another and might cause a minor culinary war.) A quintessential Assamese side, kharoli turns out to be utterly delicious—the very opposite of overdone and over-the-top. The name of the restaurant itself refers to the wooden skewer or the khorikaa on which dishes are barbequed, such as the smoked pork that melts in the mouth. I also sample a specialty of lightly lemony ginger-garlic marinated pork chunks that are slow-cooked in a hollow tube of bamboo, sunga, which tenderises the meat beautifully. And then I get some petite mowa fish roasted in a banana leaf called patotdiya, eaten with bones, eyes and all. Besides, I cannot resist ordering a plate of lightly fried lean duck which I'm told is special festive food in the Upper Assam district of Lakhimpur where everybody apparently rears their own ducks for this purpose.

To go with this, I have a platter that comes with vegetarian items such as the leafy green xaak and delicately sweetish mashed pumpkin with dhal. The Assamese don't eat roti, except once or twice a year I'm told, but rice is eaten thrice a day.

'Let me guess: Breakfast, lunch and dinner?'

'Yes, you guessed correctly,' says the waiter proudly.

Rice overdose apart, it's a feast to die for. The piggy lard content gives me at least one extra spare tyre circumambulating my waist as if my tummy was a sacred temple, but on the whole the grub isn't as unhealthy as one might assume. Much of it is steamed, boiled or grilled, low on oil and not over-spiced, yet ambrosial.

Another establishment, which like Khorikaa is frequently mentioned when the discussion is about where to have the best food, is Mising Kitchen on Hengrabari Road. It's the most specialised mess in town, serving the rare cuisine of the half-a-million-strong Mising tribe. Like other eateries in town it is a bright cafeteria-style mess and as I step in at lunchtime, full of young tribals having a good time.

The Mising being a largely riverside tribe of possibly northern Chinese riverine origin, their menu tempts with a full page of fishy delicacies. Confused about what to order, especially as I see others tuck into soulful mutton and pork thalis with gusto, kneading the rice and rich gravies into tight mouthfuls before stuffing themselves, I go for the all-inclusive Mising fish thali. Apart from many kinds of dhal and vegetables, it comes with three types of Brahmaputra fish—a mashed fish dish which is another pitika-variety, a delicate fish roasted in a banana leaf, and a catfish ari cooked as a sour fish tenga, i.e.

a thin tart curry. Although tomatoes, lemons and mangosteen are more common souring agents, in this case they've used wild elephant apple!

After lunch, I inspect the comprehensively traffic-jammed G.S. Road that sports several elegant hotels and connects Guwahati with Assam's modern capital Dispur (7 km away). This primary thoroughfare is something of a high street featuring shopping malls, glamorously trendy bistros, even discos and one cool rock club. I spend a weekend drifting up and down the street that is also crammed with momo stalls and snack carts at any of which one may sample a fresh catch of fish and prawns from the Brahmaputra.

I peek into its many side streets—in one, Panjabari Road, I find a barn with a large farmers' market, Bhipanan Khetra, of the kind that is all the rage the world over but is rarer in India. Counters stock fresh produce such as organic vegetables and interesting varieties of rice, there's also a food court and a supermarket that sells exotic ingredients. I load up.

Late that night, I fall for the rock club Café Hendrix. I can almost imagine myself being on the Lower East Side, except that the band showcased isn't some fledgling New York underground newcomer, but an Assamese hard rock outfit that plays an intriguing heavy metal version of The Beatles' 'Come Together'. It goes well with the pork roast and the latest fad beer Simba which, with its slogan 'Roar for More', has invaded all bars along the street, giving the older brands a run for the fun. But it doesn't win me over. I feel too conservative to embrace their lager which is potable if a bit fruity and not nearly bitter enough for me, while its stronger sibling is like gunk that's already been drunk and puked up by somebody else. This may explain why so many gents openly irrigate walls, bushes and lampposts along G.S. Road in full public view.

Nevertheless, the G.S. Road bars are civilised and welcoming. Even the seediest, the name of which I initially mistook as Slime of Lice (seeing the board the next morning in broad daylight, I reread it as Slice of Lime), has friendly staff and serves sublime smoked pork. It's the best pork in the world—to have with beer—even if its fattiness makes me not want to calculate the cardiac hazards.

Returning to the initial question, about duplicate or original, I think Guwahati is peerless when it comes to thrilling eating.

❖

Halfway between Guwahati and Shillong, as the taxi stops for a tea break at Nongpoh, stalls peddling atom-bomb-hot bamboo shoot pickles herald the pleasures ahead. The golden stuff is sold in recycled jars that leak spiced-up oil into my luggage, so that for the rest of my trip I walk around smelling of fermented bamboo.

It's raining in Shillong—these are the legendary rains of the Khasi Hills that pushed colonialists to borderline insanity: A wall of cement-grey cosmic piddle rattles gutters; bullet-sized raindrops ricochet off the pavement and up my legs. Months of this, day after day of wearing mouldy socks that never dried, drove the Britons to deadly alcoholism. Nails rusted and furniture fell apart. Books rotted. Suicide was their only quick fix. While he was *Chasing the Monsoon* all the way to Meghalaya, Alexander Frater stayed at the colonial era Hotel Pinewood and visited the 'old British graveyard. A number of tombstones bore the faint, weathered legend, "Died by His Own Hand".' In the hilly landscape south of Shillong, he finally chased down his monsoon: 'A fountain of dense black cloud came spiralling over the hills, then rose steeply into the sky. It formed a kind of tent, apex high overhead, sides unrolling right to the ground. It was very dark inside but I could just discern, trooping towards us, an armada of shadowy, galleon-like vessels with undersides festooned with writhing cables of water.' But like so often it is with us travel writers, he realises then that the end of a journey never matches the way you took to reach it: 'I felt little of the excitement I had known when the burst arrived in the south. Those had been occasions for public jubilation. This was a routine matiné performance at Cherrapunji, awesome certainly but exhilarating only to earnest collectors of meteorological records; such specialists would now be watching, incredulous, as their gauges foamed like champagne glasses.'

On the other hand, according to his 'Shillonger Chithi', poet laureate Rabindranath Tagore always 'rushed to the cool heights of the hills called Shillong' whenever it got too hot down in Kolkata. This was where he got plenty of time to write and rest from his globetrotting. 'The mountain ranges with their mantle of clouds seemed to beckon weary travellers to take refuge in the deep shade of woods on their hill sides.'

When I'm not roaming in the intense maze of the women-dominated Iewduh market with its banana brokers, fresh fishmongers, honey hawkers, pickle peddlers, swine slaughterers, and tea traders, my sightseeing happens at tables laden with mysterious dishes mildly tinged with ginger, garlic, onions and pinches of chilli without ever being overspiced. I figure that warm food assuages the bone-chilling rains and luckily the town is dotted with numerous intriguing eateries. Each seems to be named 'Ja & Sha' which sounds like the name of a rap band, but I soon learn that 'ja' simply means rice—the red rice of Meghalaya particularly appreciated amongst gourmets and which is uncannily healthy. The side dishes are assumed, but include—generally—at least one pork item. And 'sha' means tea—often had just like in Assam as red tea without milk. By and large, these places have no menus, but the 'national dish' is jadoh, translating roughly as 'pork sparepart pullao of short-grain red rice cooked in pig's blood' and it is usually flavoured with ginger—as almost everything is—and turmeric. It is best eaten with a helping of the paranormally pungent tungryumbai (fermented soybeans stewed with pork) and some dohneiong (a pork curry with black sesame seed paste). These canteens are characteristically dark, cavernous and crammed with low bench seating arranged as if one is sitting inside a bus, with long narrow tables in-between benches and if one by mistake looks up from one's meal the unappetising view is of the next customer's dandruff, which certainly helps to retain focus on that which matters. As I search for mouthfuls of what is traditional, people inevitably direct me to such workers' canteens, always adding disclaimers to dissuade me: 'It will not be comfortable.'

Yet, even if the eateries are sheds patched together from flattened mustard oil tins, they're efficiently run by dignified Khasi ladies identified as 'Kongs' who ensure homely quality and reasonable hygiene. These places go on existing, anachronistically, despite how tribal cuisine has taken centerfield in posher places—its time-tested simplicity and wholesomeness is what attracts customers, perhaps combined with nostalgia for the olden days.

Earlier, as I recall from my first visit in the 1990s, all fancy places in Shillong focused on Chinese but with a pinch of turmeric stirred into almost everything to make it taste less alien, and back in those days, eating out meant pseudo-Chinese instant noodles with ketchup. One of the town's restaurants offered an incongruous 'Chinese thali' consisting of what to outsiders may sound weird pairings but that are locally immensely popular, namely 'veg fried rice, veg noodles, veg manchurian, chilli potato' that somehow was wedged in between your regular full meals and small eats. The only remotely restaurant-like place for Khasi meals, in those days, was the enthusiastically christened Trattoria Dukan Jadoh (now, simply the Trattoria) in Police Bazaar, the main drag. It isn't as classy as the Italianised moniker suggests, but brighter than average jadoh stalls, with polished stone tables and photographic depictions of dishes pasted on the walls. The ebullient proprietor, seeing that I'm a tourist in need of guidance, plates me a gustatory pork thali sampler of all the available dishes—including dohshain or pork meatballs (very yummy), the pretty spectacular semi-veg dohkhleh or boiled and finely-chopped pig's brain salad (mildly-wildly delicate as is the veggie base seasoned with a drop of mustard oil), pork chutney (spicy-dicey) and curried pork—which is a lot of pork for one man. But then I do love pigging out.

Walking about during the next one week, I notice that things have changed and I see many more eating-places advertising ethnic Khasi dishes while shops sell tribal specialities of dried pork and smoked beef—patriotic citizens rave about new eateries such as You & I Arts Café (in VIP Road) that serves back-to-basics meals consisting of native potatoes that customers peel themselves to eat with raw jungle greens, or they drive an hour out of town to the roadside servery Wah Kynshi Khasi Food, run by young ladies who prepare homely lunches for famished travellers. Certain restaurants also offer the foods of the Jaintias, Nagas, Mizos and Manipuris—to pick a few other North-easterly tribes off the magiristic map—so clearly regional pride is reflected in this new-fangled interest in rustic cookery, as in the rest of the world where global is giving way to local. Besides, the tribal foods of the North-east all share a reputation for being fresh, natural, nutritious, organic, unadulterated, well-balanced, and hence essentially the best diet imaginable. Its seems North-easterners as a rule use more herbs than the rest of India's chefs put together but avoid artificial tastemakers, and dishes are typically smoked or cooked with a minimum of oil and salt. The recipes rely a lot on fermentation; they ferment fish that are made into pungent chutneys that set my brain and intestines on fire. Despite overdosing on pork my BP is happy and I love every bite.

Pork is an important ingredient of tribal food in Shillong.

The full extent of North-eastern gastronomic glory is revealed at Phunga, spread across three cosy rooms in a charming bungalow in Laitumkrah Main Road, a bubbly student area a short walk from the town's cathedral. The restaurant is smartly decorated with cane handicrafts and indigenous objets d'art, rough-hewn woodwork and bamboo furniture, and has a stage for showcasing rock bands in the main dining hall. The word phunga apparently means 'kitchen hearth', which is where locals get together after a hard day's work not only to eat, but also to sing and tell stories. Their eclectic recipes encompass all of the North-east—from Khasi staples to Assamese samples (herby and fishy), Arunachali (with treats such as fermented bamboo shoots), Mizo (very healthy stews made out of natural roots and shoots, leaves and stems, low on salt and oil), Naga (famous for the world's hottest chillies known as bhoot jholokia raja mirchi) and Tripuri (that mysteriously merges tribal simplicity with a touch of Bengali-influenced masala sophistication), but there's a special emphasis on the foods of Manipur.

With such a vast menu, all dishes aren't readily available daily and everything I ask for takes a good long time to prepare. I wonder if they might serve that famous Naga delicacy, roast dog, but as I don't find it on the menu I don't dare to ask but go for smoked fish instead.[32] The unhurried *maître d'hôtel* returns half an hour after having taken my order only to let me know that the smoked fish is not on the menu today, suggesting I order something else. Traditional 'slow food' as a reaction against the fast-food chains in town, has apparently been trending in Shillong and this particular kitchen takes that slowness to its very extremes and beyond.

I go with the flow and let him talk me into trying a shitake mushroom dish with sprouted peas and their special off-the-menu caviar gravy, which sounds like it could be terribly pricey. I obviously must have their thali as well—the jungle chicken and wild duck combos tempt me, but in the end I go for a fish thali. A good three-quarters of an hour later, the food is ready and it's so worth the wait. The thali, for example, contains many exquisite preparations—curried, fried, fermented, dried, and mashed fish, all in all twelve bowls on one plate, and the caviar gravy is...well, not possible to describe but has to be experienced. And it must have been my cheapest gourmet experience ever.

Due to an unfortunate combination of circumstances, Meghalaya, where booze once flowed freely and seedy bars was the name of the game, has become restrictive. It is hard to get a beer in the city except at the luxury hotels where a bottle costs more than a budget room. The only proper dive to survive is the quaintly named Sweety, which has a family cafeteria downstairs and a quite lovely boozer upstairs where gents converge from 1 p.m. onwards (which is the permitted hour for having one's first drink in Meghalaya). Friendly service, functioning loos and Sino-Tibetan snacks makes it the perfect watering hole before the daily archery games in the adjacent Polo Grounds.

However, duty calls me on my mobile phone, as is its wont, just like nature does now and then in order to disrupt every enjoyable beer binge, so I say goodbye to the Sweety Cafeteria, hog the last of the porky momos and ask for the bill. There will be momos in Bhutan, too, or as Anthony Bourdain reported from his trip to Thimphu: 'If I'm not on camera, chances are I'm somewhere eating these bad boys: momos. Plump, flavourful, often quite spicy dumplings, filled with meat, cheese, or veg.'

One curious thought after eating my way across much of India, and considering how all this spice is crammed into one's gastrics to perform their gas tricks, is that 500 years ago there was not a single chilli in the Old World, not until after explorers sailed across to America and subsequently spread the plant across Asia—where the chilli found the climate as agreeable as Asians found its Scoville index. Very soon, it grew everywhere and these days it is hard to imagine Indian or even Asian food without this essential ingredient.

❖

The Drukair plane deftly skirts an assortment of mountains before it slides down a narrow valley in the Himalayas and hits the bull's-eye: Bhutan's microscopic international airport. The only thing I can remember from that intensely scary moment is how fortunate it felt that the national carrier of Bhutan isn't misspelled as Drunkair on my ticket. For your information, I double-checked. No 'n'. Waiting to disembark from the plane that is packed with authors going to a litfest in Thimphu, some of my colleagues spot a red carpet on the airfield. I do a spontaneous high-five with myself, only to see it being rolled up as soon as the VIPs in first class have stepped out.

Everything is surreal. Bhutan is one of the eco-friendliest countries on earth and merely opening one's mouth to breathe is said to be nutritious. It helps that cigarettes have been banned since 2010. I've heard that the fines for smoking on the sly equal some two months' salary. Therefore, I left my party pack at home, but those who can't live without their poison pay a hefty 200 per cent customs surcharge and must apply for smoking permits to get their stashes back.

Penalties settled, we're en route to the festival's opening ceremony at the India House in Thimphu, which was built in the 1960s and represents the first permanent diplomatic connection between Bhutan and the outside world. That was also when the country's first road was built—from Thimphu to India. Prior to that, the capital was a cluster of houses surrounding a monastery, peasants bartered between villages, transporting goods on yaks along mountain paths, which suggests a certain leisurely manner that didn't involve bitcoins and mobile wallets and scanning potentially phishing-afflicted barcodes.

From then on, Bhutan underwent what may seem like a contradiction in terms, but it actually was a consciously abrupt yet gentle progress—the first foreign tourists came in the

1970s about the same time when the concept of GNH (Gross National Happiness) was established as an unconventional gauge of sustainable growth, the adrenaline-heightening airport was inaugurated in the 1980s, TV came in 1999, democracy in 2008, iPhone7 in 2016 and rather expectedly, in 2021 during the peaking COVID-19 pandemic, it was one of the first countries in the world to provide the vaccine to virtually all eligible citizens...but there are still no traffic lights and barely any vehicular traffic to speak of. This litfest that I've come to speak at is another sign of the opening up of Bhutan. The queen mother Ashi Dorji Wangmo Wangchuck, its founder-patron, emphasises in her inaugural speech how much the meetings with inspiring authors have enriched life for the Bhutanese people including herself.

I later learn that Her Majesty grew up in a village without books. She says, 'After dinner we gathered around the hearth and my grandparents told stories. I try to keep the same oral history-telling alive by telling my grandchildren the stories that my grandparents told me. It wasn't until I went to India to study that I saw a book for the first time in my life.' Now she's writing her third book, chronicling her grandson who is an intelligent toddler. At almost every session, I see her seated on a throne right in front of the stage, listening keenly—so when I do my talkshow it makes me extremely nervous because at first she frowns when I wisecrack. As I do it again and again, and the hundreds of citizen in the auditorium get the joke and merriment spreads, she looks confused, then hesitant as she hears them guffaw unanimously and finally, when Her Majesty too giggles, I feel a certain triumph at having added a spot of laughter to the happiest country on earth. It's like they say, the hardest jobs on earth are being an ice-cream vendor among Eskimos or opening a refrigerator shop in Alaska...or having to prove that one is funny in Bhutan, where everybody is happy sixteen hours per day.

Made in Bhutan, happiest chips in the world.

Occasionally, I suspect that people here worship writers. One of the first things I did was to visit the National Library, a gorgeous building modelled on monasteries. Apparently, people circle it clockwise due to the fact that its enormous collection of religious books—by the likes of Guru Rimpoche (a.k.a. Padmasambhava) and other Buddhist prophets—bestows one with top-class karma. At the entrance, it says that a previous queen of Bhutan founded the library in 1967, and I discern a pattern: The queens here take books seriously.

Mita Kapur, an old friend and literary personality who founded the Crime Writers Festival in New Delhi and is my literary agent for this book, also manages the festival in Bhutan. She says to me, 'I am nuts about this festival, I love it, I love Bhutan, I love its people. The festival reflects shared cultural threads between Bhutan and India, and since we've kept it small, it lends itself to a lot of interaction between readers and writers.'

Small is a relative word as the festival saw 10,000 footfalls every year before the pandemic. Considering that Thimphu's entire population is no more than 91,000, it is a respectable figure. 'There has also been a fivefold increase in the number of books being published in Bhutan and now writers experiment with new genres as well. Book sales have gone up, there are book clubs in schools—it's just so satisfying to see many more people reading and writing,' points out Kapur.

She mentions that authors usually spend their evenings at the Druk Hotel's bar, so that's where I head as my literary duties at the festival are over. Dating back to the 1970s as the first 'international' hotel, it's endowed with the city's nicest drinking den. Moreover, as Kapur predicted, I do spend the night in the company of jolly colleagues—a chicklit novelist, a webzine editor and a children's writer, along with reporters looking for either scoops, scandals or bottles of Druk beer which they—as so many of us—misread as 'Drunk beer'.

A high for me as a travel writer is bumping into Pico Iyer who is a living legend that I used to read as a young vagabond in Nepal, where his *Video Night in Kathmandu* (1988) was a must-read at the time. After his lecture on *The Art of Stillness* at the festival, he confesses to me, 'I felt really embarrassed to be talking about stillness here in Bhutan, because Bhutan is really the model of sanity, quiet and health that the rest of us aspire to. Landing here, the first thing I saw was a sign that said, "Faster, spells disaster."' Bhutan, he points out, could be the paradigm for the rest of the world where everything is going faster and faster and social media has replaced social interactions. He doesn't own a mobile phone, which has—or so he feels—made his days longer and given him more time to read.

Despite his rosy nostalgia, which I envy, Iyer observes that Bhutan is changing. 'Physically, Thimphu is unrecognisable to me, coming back after decades. When I went to the Druk Hotel and back to the Swiss Bakery, what I principally remember from 1988, I lost all sense of orientation—I didn't know where I was. I thought, well, it is less idyllic seeming for me than it was, but development probably means a richer and happier life for people here. We visitors have to be careful about the wishes we project—the fact that we want places to remain beautiful for our camera lenses. But when I talk to people, they sound very similar to the people I was talking to back then.'

I ask him what else he has been up to in Thimphu. 'I visited four or five temples. And have you tried the hamburgers at Cloud 9?'

All the authors rave about those burgers, but I am sorry to say that because my mission has always been to go native in the widest sense, I can't review them as I only eat and drink what is genuinely Bhutanese. Like most tourists to Bhutan, all I knew about its cuisine was that chillies are the most eaten vegetables, for unlike elsewhere in the world, here chilli isn't considered a spice. The national dish emadatsi, for example, is 250 g chillies cooked with a smaller quantity of cottage cheese (serves two). Therefore, I do realise that I might not have any intestines left at the end of this book, people warned me of bum burns, that my undies might turn into ashes if I fart... but as Shakespeare once pointed out, 'it is the baseness of thy fear that makes thee strangle thy propriety.' And so (as I believe that in his day the word 'propriety' meant true nature), I fearlessly proceed according to my true nature, avoiding the dining options suggested in the guidebooks and instead sneak into all the cook shacks where I check what Bhutanese customers eat, order the same, and if it means overdosing on chillies, then...well, so be it.

Helpful people who felt I was heading for disaster tried

to steer me towards other more easily digestible thrills of Thimphu. For such a small town it offers a surprising array of cuisines ranging from Indian to Far Eastern, Mediterranean and even Mexican, to American-style bagel cafés.

I ignore all these and, at the northern end of the main street Norzin Lam, I find an eatery called Apy's. The lady running it explains that she hails from the town of Phuentsholing, so she'll cook a south Bhutanese meal. She asks which meat I prefer and says she'll make a datsi of it (with cheese and chillies), and also serve the local lentil curry, fresh salad and the staple maaso (red rice).

In case the food turns out insufficiently spicy, she takes out homemade pickles—one with mangoes from her own garden in Phuentsholing, another with cocktail-cherry-sized chillies grown in Sikkim. While she's in the kitchen, for my entertainment, her uncle connects a video call on his smartphone to Phuentsholing and I get to wave to all their relatives back home and tell them how happy I am to be in Bhutan—they are excited that foreigners eat at Apy's and ask me how I like it. I do a thumbs up and to prove how much fun I'm having, I pop one of the innocuous-looking Sikkimese chillies into my mouth. It's oh, so juicy, and I swallow it only to suffer a thousand deaths as it releases its bombastic fury. Hot burps shoot up my throat. Throughout the video call, puffs of chilli smoke erupt from my mouth and every other word I speak is an oral volcano. How do the Bhutanese handle this? Later, reading local novelist Chador Wangmo, I realise that toddlers are fed chillies as soon as they open their eyes (or mouths). '"Dechzangmo, come, eat your breakfast!" my mother yelled...It was red rice with beef emadatsi. My mother's special dish always had me licking my fingers. She cooked small chunks of dry beef with a lot of green Indian chillies and datsi,' opens the fifth chapter of Wangmo's novel *La Ama: A Mother's Call.*

Spicy enough to nuke curry-hardened tummies, Bhutanese food also differs from Indian (and Chinese for that matter), in its cautious approach to oil. In fact, it can be made without any oil at all—emadatsi, for example, is chillies basically boiled with water and cheese for ten minutes. Other varieties have fall-in-love-with names such as kewadatsi, which is like a potato-au-gratin and quite mild; saagdatsi of stir-fried greens; and several types of meat datsi—usually either sikam (pork) or shakam (beef)—and then there's shamudatsi which is cheesy chillies with mushrooms.

Regarding this 'shamu' phenomenon, Bhutan has at least one hundred species of edible wild mushrooms (and 250 inedible ones, so one must choose wisely) among which the finest varieties include matsutake and chanterelles. I am a total cheese and mushroom fanatic—even my writing, as you may have noticed, combines cheesiness with a mushy mentality—and as soon as I get into the habit of ordering shamudatsi, in which the mushrooms cushion the chillies as it were, I'm at ease in Thimphu.

My best meal is a total chance experience at the Dorji Trotzey that a random man points me to. The eatery is otherwise impossible to find as it is hidden in a back alley and not at all aimed at tourists. Kind of cool in a Bhutanese way: Low benches and tables, lunch menu comprising staples written on a whiteboard and as they run out, the names are removed from it. I have shamudatsi again (mushrooms stir-fried in you-know-what sauce), pork ribs with chilli, and shakam paa—after datsi, paa is the second most common dish, usually involving sun-dried chewy meat such as beef, pork or weird intestines. Refreshing jaju (riverweed soup), unlimited chilli pickles and a cooling whey beverage are complimentary, as is the Himalayan red rice.

After returning home I try to recreate the shamudatsi. It appeared so simple, but turned out to be trickier in one's own kitchen. I experiment with different cheeses and mushrooms, including yak's cheese and dried mushrooms imported from the Himalayas, but it isn't anything like it was in Bhutan. The only thing that tastes about right is the pickles I brought with me—homemade shakam ezzay and fishy ayzey.

As a matter of fact, genuine Bhutanese food is next to impossible to get outside the country's borders. I've heard of one joint called Ema Datsi in New York and I've had emadatsi in certain Tibetan settlements in south India. That's about it.

Yet what I sampled in Bhutan was always perfect, once my tastebuds had been sufficiently adjusted…meaning, numbed. This left me wondering whether Bhutan might become the next secret gourmet pilgrimage destination. The combination of exclusivity—ain't easy to get there—and accessibility, once you do get there, good cheap food can be had everywhere. In one word? Yum-yum-yum. Anything to add? Yum.

Before I forget, one must also try all the different beers that are brewed in the hills from the purest mountain waters. On a surprisingly sunny monsoon day, I'm walking about with my shirt soaked and I can't tell whether it is the natural perspiration shooting out through the pores on my back, or the emadatsi I had for lunch clawing its way out of my body, or a bit of both. My life instantly takes a turn for the better when I spot a handful of downmarket bars north of the Chubachhu Roundabout. They are…how should I put it…the most beautiful things I have ever seen. Not only because I'm thirsty, but the row of tumbledown houses look incredibly inviting—wooden structures with about two drinking dens each, wall to wall. Each of them stares back at me as if they have been waiting a truly long time for my arrival.

It's a mind-altering moment.

We fall in love. It helps that the first I step into (no obvious name on the outside) is run by a couple of ladies and now and then a Buddhist monk drops in to down a can of super-strong beer. For me it takes a six-pack to get accustomed to the yeastiness of Red Panda—a fresh beer which is apparently unfiltered and brewed without preservatives—but by and large, my philosophy is that anything that is drinkable is probably drinkable. I sit quietly, meditate and read Bhutanese newspapers, acting Buddhistic.

When a drizzle cools the air outside, I move on to the next sensation that turns out to be another bar—it may be too early to have more beer, but I must get indoors since it starts pouring. This bar (again, no name on the outside) is in an alley by Clock Tower Square in the centre of town and looks like it could date back 500 years, but from a purely scientific perspective, I know it can't be older than from the 1960s—when Thimphu was built. A princess-like girl with sharp features mans the bar, while lads sleep on mattresses on the floor, and one aunty sips on her grog. They seem all to be part of a family living in the bar. I order a Druk, a soothing lager type of beer made from pure Himalayan spring-water, and something of the country's flagship alcohol.

From there on it is downhill. To clarify, I mean that I walk down towards the weekend market by the river running through town, which is known to be a haven of vice. Not that shoppers notice the supposed drug and flesh trade (I certainly don't) as it is one of the tidiest markets in South Asia. Nevertheless, it appears to be a good idea to sample momos at a shady bar in a dilapidated corner building, which has a menu hanging on the outside wall, suggesting the by far cheapest rates in town. It's the first bar that has a name, so as I'm downgrading to the city's supposed underworld haunts, it feels as if I'm upgrading as I step into Rignam Bar.

For the third time in a row, here's yet another of the finest dives of the world. I could easily write a novel about it. There's a rack of intriguing bottles on a wall behind the glass counter, a variety of interesting snacks, and some four tables. At one, a girl of about ten sits and chops green chillies. She turns out to be the bartender—I kid you not—and she calls out to her daddy who is a bald wrestler-type operating the kitchen, to steam me a plate of momos. She then brings me a sample of the strongest beer of the country, brewed by Kinjore Breweries that specialise on extra-strong beers. Their Thunder 15,000 has a slogan claiming 'Happiness for All' and is way ahead of all the others in punch. Their momos are extra-salty and hyper-chillified, as if made to keep one thirsty for more. So, I have another Thunder 15,000 to verify that the quality is consistent.

Other bar nibbles I encounter in town, as I go on scientifically exploring the scene, include fried yak skin chips and what looks like a sausage but turns out to be black pudding. It is so spicy that it's inedible. When I try to slip my plate to a stray dog that drifts in, pretending to be a customer, the stern lady who runs the bar admonishes me that I must not share the food with non-paying quadrupeds. She pours a mug of water on the dog that until then has been leisurely gobbling leftovers under the tables and I'm forced to eat up the unpalatable pudding alone—and it doesn't help that the only accompaniment is volcano-hot chilli sauce. More drink is needed to wash it down and luckily the bars in Bhutan are well stocked not only with ales and stouts, but grainy lagers brewed from rice and sweet wines fermented from peaches.

An interesting story I hear about the many practical uses of alcohol in Bhutan—though I'm not sure how factual it is—goes that until 1970 when the country got its own currency, taxes were collected in kind. It could be farm produce such as dried meat or rice wine, the latter being a smoky, potent cousin of sake distilled from various types of fermented grains. Because meat, as one might expect, got infested with maggots when stored for too long in the treasury, booze was preferable. This caused another problem, as taxmen were frequently found dead drunk in the royal vault. The unavoidable decision was that Bhutan must begin using money and hence the local currency Ngultrum was born, and still today, 10 Ngultrum (which equals Rs 10 or $0.13) buys me a cup of booze in dive bars.

According to drinking etiquette, it might be good to know that whenever you've had enough of whatever you've had, rotate your hand before your mouth clockwise murmuring, '*me zhu, me zhu*' and they'll put you either in a taxi or in an ambulance depending on your physical condition. If you are sober enough to walk out on your own legs, say '*kardrinchhey*' and pay your bill. If you find that you must spell out the Bhutanese word letter by letter, or cannot find your legs anywhere nearby, then revert to the previous alternative and ask for the nearest hospital by saying, '*Menkhang ga tey in na*?' And all will end well.

The End?

Acknowledgements

No book is just a book, to paraphrase an old saying, and especially in the case of a travel memoir like this, lots of people and places obviously contributed to it finding its shape. First of all, I would like to extend my heartfelt thanks to all—whether named or nameless—chefs, barkeepers and hoteliers who enriched my travels beyond the imaginable.

So many really nice real humans populated this book's path but probably more than by anybody else, it has been virtually co-authored by my constant companion, fellow foodie and wonderful wife Anjum Hasan, who taught me how to cook and eat like an Indian, to like chilly chicken, chilly pakoras, chilly pancakes, chilly pickles, chilly chillies...until I got completely chilled out. Spice is nice! Adds love to life and life to love.

The phenomenal foodie Mita Kapur and her hospitable husband Rahul frequently crossed my path during the 2010s when I wrote this book, so it owes a lot to their seemingly limitless *joie de vivre*—you'd not be reading this without the two of them and the beers Rahul would hand me whenever Mita, who eventually became my literary agent, graciously looked the other way.

Moreover, I thank all the collegial writers I've encountered over my travels in India—novelists, poets and others too numerous to mention but who all shared their precious time—

as well as fellow booklovers, who offered ideas and suggestions, often over too many beers.

And last but not least, it must be acknowledged that Indian culinary culture is great—no, let me rephrase that: overwhelming—and so to make it possible to fit so much of it into this book I sincerely thank, for their feedback and suggestions on various things to add or cut or simply understand better (in alphabetical order) Aditi De, Aditi Sengupta, Amit Dixit, Amitav Ghosh, Amrita Dutta, Anders Mathlein, Anders Paulrud, Ann Ighe, Avtar Singh, Basav Biradar, Dave Besseling, Ishita Chatterji, James Brunner, Jan Ekholm, Johan Lindskog, Johan Mikaelsson, Jonas Eklöf, Kareena Gianani, Lakshmi Sankaran, Michael Dwyer, Mukund Padmanabhan, Nandini Nair, Neha Dara, Nina Solomin, Paul Fernandes, Per Styregård, Pradeep Sebastian, Ramachandra Guha, Renuka Chatterjee, Robin Walsh, Sanjukta Sharma, Shreevatsa Nevatia, Soity Banerjee, Stellan 'the Kitchen Obelisk' Wahlström, Vaishna Roy, Veena Venugopal and Vineetha Mokkil. Anything great that I've written in this book is thanks to them, while all that appears flawed is obviously my own errata, not theirs, because I am not as intelligent as they are.

As I'm still trying to digest India, let this book—which may be a big leap for a gluttonous bibliophile like me but hopefully less painful than a sprained foot (or upset tummy) for its readers—be a first tiny step towards my optimal and ultimate karmic enlightenment.

Notes

1 Note to readers: In this book the word hotel doesn't necessarily imply a place where one sleeps, but rather where one can eat or buy (or 'parcel') food that isn't home-cooked. The places where one gets rooms are usually called lodges, guesthouses or boarding houses—at least in my budget range. In recent times, some of these have rebranded themselves as hotels to be more in tune with globalisation, but as one travels across India one still comes across hotels where, if you ask for a room rather than food, they'll think you illiterate. So for example, Kamat Hotels, which is a restaurant chain dating back to the 1950s, does not usually let you stay overnight unless it is explicitly stated that rooming facility is available.

2 This was not the first time that Bengaluru was lampooned in an international bestseller. One of the first occasions that comes to mind is 'the military station of Bundlegunge, in the Madras division of our Indian empire' in *Vanity Fair* (1848) by the Kolkata-born William Thackeray, where we encounter, amongst others, a caricature of a British colonel: 'Time has dealt kindly with that stout officer, as it does ordinarily with men who have good stomachs and good tempers and are not perplexed over much by fatigue of the brain. The Colonel plays a good knife and fork at tiffin and resumes those weapons with great success at dinner. He smokes his hookah after both meals and puffs as quietly while his wife scolds him as he did under the fire of the French at Waterloo.'

3 IPA incidentally translates as Indian Pale Ale and the story goes that it was brewed stronger so that it would survive the transportation from England to India. In modern England, IPA generally denotes a very strong beer but earlier IPA was medium-strong; it has been brewed in England for more than 200 years and hence predates Indian beer manufacturing.

4 The bar bill was eventually written off as 'irrecoverable' in 1899. Interestingly, Churchill later confessed in his memoir, *My Early Life*, about his youthful habits when he was living in Bengaluru, that he 'liked wine, both red and white, and especially champagne; and on very special occasions I could even drink a small glass of brandy.' After his hasty departure, when Churchill swapped his army career for a journalistic one (to cover some war or the other), he didn't carry more luggage than he could lift onto the train and hence Churchill's library with his scribbled opinions on the margins of the pages ended up in Bengaluru's second-hand bookshops (where lucky collectors may come across them occasionally even today).

5 The dubious but oft-repeated quote from Pliny's encyclopaedic work reads: 'This ant excavates gold from holes, in a country in the north of India, the inhabitants of which are known as the Dardæ. It has the colour of a cat, and is in size as large as an Egyptian wolf. This gold, which it extracts in the winter, is taken by the Indians during the heats of summer, while the ants are compelled, by the excessive warmth, to hide themselves in their holes. Still, however, on being aroused by catching the scent of the Indians, they sally forth, and frequently tear them to pieces, though provided with the swiftest camels for the purpose of flight; so great is their fleetness, combined with their ferocity and their passion for gold!' This would suggest that Pliny did not at all refer to Kolar, which is situated in the deep south and where camels are rare, but that rather these mines (if at all they existed) must have been in the north in the regions between erstwhile Hindustan and the Tibetan plateau. Scholars have suggested that this references the Punjabi river Sutlej's banks.

6 Food conundrums run like red threads through Narayan's writings and in his autobiography he describes the hatred that the Lutheran Mission School teachers displayed against Hindu students: 'Among the non-Christians in our class I was the only Brahmin boy, and received special attention; the whole class would turn in my direction when the teacher said that Brahmins claiming to be vegetarians ate fish and meat in secret, in a sneaky way, and were responsible for the soaring price of those commodities.' It was not just vegetarianism that bothered, for even when a Malgudian goes to north India in a rare geospatial shift, as in *Waiting for the Mahatma*, he finds himself starved: 'He yearned for coffee, his favourite, like a true South Indian, but coffee could not be had here.' When he is longing for something to eat, he is told: 'You can't expect all our South Indian stuff,' and then instructed matter-of-factly that he would have to learn to eat chappati, and vegetable and curd and fruit, and 'not ask for rice or sambar.' As he works his way through the meals, he 'longed for the taste of the pungent South Indian food and its sauces and vegetables, but he suppressed the thought.' This might be an echo of Narayan's troubles to find homely food abroad where most Indian restaurants serve Punjabi food.

7 The vada is 100 per cent indigenous and was mentioned in sutras in the centuries BCE. Known to foreign tourists as curried donuts, 'vadē' are scientifically defined by food scholar Achaya as a 'disc with a hole in the centre, soft and elastic inside and crispy brown on the outside' and is, obviously, my top candidate for the UNESCO world heritage list. The oldest known Indian snack, the vada is also the likely ancestor of that quintessentially Newyorkish bagel. It must have travelled from India to the eastern Mediterranean along with the people previously labelled as gypsies who left Rajasthan around 1,000 years ago to adopt Europe's roads as their home. Interestingly, a traditional breakfast dish of theirs is the iconic Turkish *simit* consisting of savoury-crispy bread rings sprinkled with sesame seeds and estimated

to have become popular 500 years ago. And as its Latin name indicates, *Sesamum indicum* had its origins in India. Other proto-bagels can be found in Kashmir, where the 'desi donut' called czochworu (also topped with sesame seeds) is eaten. Even the westernmost provinces of China have varieties of vada–suggesting that vadai are as global as they are round, so there is nothing unusual about them being the origin of bagels. In medieval Italy, those Mediterranean bread rings became a Jewish staple that subsequently through migration turned into a popular street-food in Germany, which is where it eventually came to be known as bagel (from *bent* in German). It travelled to America in the nineteenth century and then even beyond earth on space missions—as comfort food for Jewish astronauts, bagels have been approved as suitable space grub.

8 In *The Man-Eater of Malgudi*, a brass food container found in a dead man's room is examined despite the fact that the man obviously had his head smashed with a blunt instrument and his tiffin box was unopened—and once opened the 'smell of stale food hit the ceiling—a strong-smelling, overspiced chicken pulav, brown and unattractive and stuffed up to the lid.' In *Waiting for the Mahatma* a character gets pukey at the sheer mention of chicken crying out, 'Chicken! Chicken! Oh! I can't stand the thought of it!'

9 In the Malnad area of Karnataka the name 'doddamane' was traditionally a generic term for stately bungalows or small palaces owned by a particular district's biggest landlord; they often doubled as administrative centres where village meetings were held.

10 The fact that Malgudi has no palace is the main difference between the fictional city and R.K. Narayan's hometown. Another intriguing detail regarding the books, now that we are analysing their veracity, is that they form a loose autobiographical arch should one read them with that in mind: *Swami and Friends* is on Narayan's childhood, *The Bachelor of Arts* is about his student years up to his marriage, *The English Teacher* deals with his early

working life and the premature death of his wife (he himself tells us so in his autobiography) while in other novels, he uses his experience of writing for cinema, his attempts at launching a periodical and so on.

11 Apparently, the fictional Raju's real name was Keshav. A trivia footnote for the cultural tourist: the Metropole has hosted every literary celebrity that has set foot in Mysuru, from Somerset Maugham...to myself. Author of *The Sheltering Sky*, Paul Bowles, noted that 'in places like the bar of the Hotel Metropole at Mysore, or at the North Coorg Club of Mercara, one may still come across vestiges of the old colonial life'. This hotel is also where cult director Alejandro Jodorowsky stayed during the shooting of his film *Tusk*, a psychedelic feminist version of *The Jungle Book*, in nearby jungles. It was originally the maharaja's guesthouse for foreign visitors while the century-old heritage hotel Lalitha Mahal—allegedly modelled on Saint Paul's Cathedral in London—was the guest accommodation for viceroys, royalty and state guests.

12 Incidentally, the more urban locations of the TV series *Malgudi Days* seem to be recognisable as places in Mysuru. In one episode I spot, for example, what is now the Green Hotel (part of Premier Studios from 1954 to 1989). The regal century-old building has a Malgudi café, staffed by Dalit women, and there I find myself drinking the nicest *café au lait* in town. I suspect that Narayan, who was fussy about coffee and constantly chasing the perfect blend, may have enjoyed a sip of it too.

13 In case you wonder, like I did, what all this GI-tagging is about, it's a Geographical Indication that suggests that something belongs somewhere—for example whiskey must be Scotch where it is distilled laboriously (never mind that India consumes more Scotch than Scotland has produced since whiskey was invented in 1494). It seems parmesan is only real if the cheese is from the vicinity of Parma in Italy (even if high-quality parmesan is produced near Puducherry in Tamil Nadu). And champagne

that is not made in France is nothing but bubbly white wine. The decision is finalised by the World Trade Organization in Switzerland which, considering how many GI-tagged products originate in Mysuru, perhaps ought to shift its headquarters here.

14 If any reader is desperate to sample a dosa similar to what the author would have eaten, try Dasaprakash Paradise's 'dose dhamaka' platter—across the road from the R.K. Narayan Museum—where he used to go. Furthermore, in his autobiography, he notes regarding his dosa habit that during morning walks down Vani Vilas Road, he 'was trapped by the frying smell emanating from a little restaurant tucked away in a lane off the main road, where I ate a *dosai*, washed it down with coffee, and, lighting a cigarette, resumed my walk. I was careful with money, never spending more than a rupee a day. All morning I wandered. At every turn I found a character fit to go into a story.' It is hard to pinpoint this 'little restaurant', but in the same area today, between Agrahara Circle and the palace, one finds a Brahmins Dosa Point and a 'branch' of the branch-less Mylari Hotel. Take your pick.

15 Interestingly, potato, without which any dosa would be rather slim, is not native to the country, but was introduced by Englishmen and officially first enjoyed at a gala dinner in colonial Calcutta. Ditto tomatoes and chillies and capsicums that nowadays form the basis of so many Indian dishes, not to mention cashew nuts, corn and fruits ranging from papaya to pineapples. Whether curried like the bhaji that is served with puris, sautéed with cumin into a main course such as aloo jeera, or simply tandooried, or stuffed into parathas, samosas and dosas, potatoes have become more than a cornerstone of Indian cuisines, especially in Bengal where the per capita consumption—in the form of poshto and shukto or added to biryanis—is second only to that of Ireland.

16 For those unaware, idlis are not merely dull 'rice cakes' as often referred to scornfully in English. In the south, the disk-shaped delicacy holds a status akin to the tandoori chicken in the north.

Even if it is suspected by scholars to be an Indonesian or Arabian import, according to Achaya, idlis were first mentioned in the oldest literary work in Kannada, *Vaddaradhane*, in about 930 CE; here, a monk begging for alms receives an idli from a kind lady. So whether idlis came from the East or the West, the ingenious fermented low-calorie high-nutrition rice roundels, if we may call them so, have been adorning plates hereabouts for more than a 1,000 years.

17 In his travelogue *The Gentleman in the Parlour: A Record of a Journey from Rangoon to Haiphong*, Maugham describes seeing his Indian chef 'nimbly shin up a tree in the compound and shake down the fruit he needed for some sauce. Like many another artist his personality was more interesting than his work; his cooking was neither good nor varied, one day he gave me trifle for my dinner and the next cabinet pudding; they are the staple sweets of the East,' Maugham infers before adding that his 'own knowledge of these matters is small, but I made so bold as to teach my Telegu [*sic*] how to make a corned beef hash. I trusted that after he left me he would pass on the precious recipe to other cooks and that eventually one more dish would be added to the scanty repertory of Anglo-Eastern cuisine.'

18 I obviously tried cooking rum-rasam at home by mixing Old Monk with takeaway thali leftovers, but it tasted like hand-sanitiser boiled with those pink things they put in urinals. French fusion is perhaps an acquired taste?

19 Amazingly, the low-profile is one of India's greatest culinary exports popular from China to Europe. In Portugal *canja de galinha* is a traditional chicken soup thickened with rice gruel. In Hong Kong, restaurants such as Trusty Congee King even get listed in Michelin-guides for their slow-stewed seafood-flavoured gourmet permutations of kanji.

20 I feel slightly bad about my Swedish fellow countrymen once having tried to colonise India. However, a small consolation is that it was an utter failure and lasted only for a month—

September 1733 to be precise. A Swedish ship disembarked some twenty sailors and despite being badly afflicted by scabies and scurvy they managed to build a shop at the place which became known as Parangipettai ('foreign market'). Between them, they had fifteen firearms and were unable to protect themselves when the French attacked with the assistance of British troops a few weeks later. Subsequently, Porto Novo also harboured Dutch traders. The adjacent Danish settlement at Tranquebar lasted longer—from the 1620s, the Danes clung on for centuries until they sold their fort in 1845.

21 The son of a pork butcher, Grimod de la Reynière published the *Almanacs des gourmands* from 1803 onwards, a calendar for gluttons who loved eating excessively, ranking restaurants and other food outlets in post-revolution Paris where the former private chefs of executed noblemen were in the process of giving birth to the French food scene; hence he has been labelled the first restaurant reviewer in culinary history.

22 The dum-pukht, known as dumb-poked in English or, in the language of Persia, *dampukht* (meaning 'slow-baked') became a staple in 1784 when a Nawab in Lucknow noticed that day or night his labourers ate tastier food than he himself. He sent his cooks to learn from the construction workers' wives, who buried a potful of rice and meat under coals for hours at end, thus uplifting their practical dum-pukht to an elaborate dish fit for kings by using the finest basmati rice, mutton and the most aromatic spices such as cardamom, cinnamon, mace and saffron. Unless that's an apocryphal story (since food critics believe the dum-pukht legend originated at a Delhi restaurant in 1998), it triggered a biryani revolution in India that spread to the eastern and southern regions too—reflecting local preferences such as the addition of potatoes in Kolkata or sour tomatoes in Chennai.

23 Even if vada-pav is sold at stalls in my hometown Bengaluru, they're not at all the same as what Mehta describes: 'The crispy batter, the mouthful of sweet-soft pav tempering the heat of

the chutney, the spices of the vada mixture—dark with garam masala and studded with whole cloves of garlic that look like cashews—get masticated into a good mouthful, a good mouthfeel.' However, people aren't as purist as I make them sound, because there's plenty of innovation in the field, to the extent that there nowadays are weird permutations like Schezwan vada-pav that may have been created to counter the foreign hand's attempt at cornering the vada-pav market with their McAloo Tikki®™ burgers.

24 The colour of raspberry soda is like an angry traffic light, but it gives a heritage high. These raspberry pops date way back to when Ardheshir & Sons soda factory was founded in 1884 (making it two years senior to Coca-Cola of the US) and their Pune plant still produces purely 'desi' sodas.

25 Interestingly, similar cooking methods are practised by the Romani communities in Europe among whom pigs and sheep roasted in hay-lined pits is a festive dish. As discussed in a previous footnote, they are believed to have reached Europe from Rajasthan some thousand years ago and were earlier referred to as gypsies, who may well have brought along this technique as a memory of an otherwise forgotten home.

26 Actually, in genuine Continental culinary art, fish is hardly ever topped with cheese nowadays (even though the ancient Romans may have done so), unlike in this wonderful Indian version of 'Conti'. But it tastes really good. Other dishes that Indian chefs have adopted creatively from Europeans include cutlets and chops that in their 'desified' versions are more often vegetarian than not, as is the chutney sandwich, whereas European sandwiches generally contain a slice of meat. In the other direction, Indian cookery has improved European eating habits in fundamental ways for example by showing how to make vegetarian food tastier in the form of veg curries. As we saw in Chapter V, Mahatma Gandhi was pleased to encounter theoretical vegetarianism among the 'isms' of the nineteeth-

century England when he moved there in 1888, but despite that it wasn't an evolved gastronomic art and Indian restaurants were rare (it is another matter that London, last I went, had six named after Gandhi). Regarding Indian influences, in certain cases such as with the vegetarian khichdi, the English turned it into non-vegetarian kedgeree in the 1790s and theirs is rather like a fish biryani–which was their interpretation of the Mughal way of eating khichdi. South Indian rasam became Mulligatawny Soup in its English avatar (believed to be a mispronunciation of the Tamil word *milagu-tannir*, 'black pepper water'), re-engineered with the addition of chicken, that on fancier menu cards was renamed as *potage de Madras*. The earliest mention of the soup is from 1784 when a Britisher imprisoned by Tipu Sultan lamented being fed more kanji and rasam than he could stomach: 'In vain our hard fate we repine, In vain our fortunes we rail; On Mullighy-tawny we dine, On Conjee, in Bangalore jail.' Although the colonials took to rasam, it was popular to make fun of—such as in this poem called 'The Police-Wallah's Little Dinner': 'First we had Mulligatawny soup,/ Which made us all perspire,/ For the cook, that obstinate nincompoop,/ Had flavoured it hot as fire.' Anglo-Indian fusion had already spread across the empire by then and entered the culinary vocabulary, although curry was spelled *currey* as in *Receipt To Make a Currey the Indian Way* by Hannah Glasse (1758). It is sometimes mentioned that the 1390s' book, *The Forme of Cury* by an English royal cook, is the first curry cookbook in English, but as it was written well before colonial days, it would seem unlikely—rather it is referring to health food, how the right diet can 'cure'. That stereotypical catchphrase for the diversity of Indian gravy items was first referenced in English in 1681, but even seventy years earlier Edward Terry had documented his foodie adventures in India that included lovely non-veg without specifying whether they were curries or not. The spicy relish *piccalilli*, known since the 1750s, is essentially a British version of Indian pickle, Worcestershire sauce was born out of a hilariously failed attempt to recreate a Bengali curry in Worcester, near Birmingham, at a time when restaurants in London were adding curries to their menus in the mid-1700s. Their insatiable craving for curried food became increasingly common when Englishmen retired from colonial service. A first full-fledged Indian-owned restaurant serving Mughal curries, the pioneering Hindostanee Coffee House opened, it is said by a gentleman from Patna, in about 1809 in London replete with bamboo recliners and hookahs. The compound 'curry powder' was coined the next year to denote 'a condiment consisting of several pungent ground spices' and perhaps unsurprisingly, by 1845, the curious Anglo-Indo-Italic dish 'curried macaroni' rewrote the pages of food history as India became an increasingly important colony—even Queen Victoria hired two fulltime Indian cooks to prepare curry *every* day for her luncheons. In spite of the fact that English food has traditionally been considered to be bland and dull, they did in their own bumbling way popularise Indian gastronomy. Perhaps it is because of this that culinary experts suggest western origins for various Indian gravies such as 'ishtoo'; the Mughal's classic slow-stewed meat with ghee and onions. But it's difficult to determine whether stew is a British version of curry or ishtoo is an Indian modified stew; anybody who wishes to pass judgement on the matter can pay a visit to the last Mughal's chef's descendants at Karim's in Delhi, and order their signature ishtoo, known as aloo gosht. Current curry houses have their roots in the Punjabi dhabas, whose owners migrated with the exodus that followed upon Indian independence. These post-Partition migrants set up affordable canteens across England, which is how the Hindi word tikka found its way into English dictionaries (in 1955) as an 'Indian dish of marinated meat cooked on a skewer'. Thus, what may have initially been perceived as *ethnic* food gained the status of a national dish once it was married with that legendary canned tomato soup, giving birth to Chicken Tikka Masala. Another similarly Anglicised dish which appears to be a product of a second wave of South Asian UK-bound migration following Bangladeshi independence, is Balti, that's actually a traditional Lahori chicken dish, woked in a *karahi* pan nicknamed 'balti' in which it is also served. It may be noted that during this process of Anglicising subcontinental foods, restaurant names too changed from stereotypical nomenclature such as Maharaja to things like Balti Brassiere that, in a purely geographical sense, disconnect their menu from its origins. Indeed, distinctly Indo-British dishes such as 'Birmingham Balti' (first attested in 1977) are considered part of British heritage worthy of GI-tagging.

27 To be precise, the fictional Chandrapore is based on Bankipur, the colonial parts of Patna. A guidebook from the time notes that the 'modern city contains nothing of much interest to the traveller, except a building called the Gola, which was built for a granary in 1783, but has never been used for that purpose,' but inside of which 'there is a most wonderful echo, the best place to hear which is in the middle of the building. As a whispering gallery there is perhaps no such building in the world. The faintest whisper at one end is heard most distinctly at the other.' This may well have inspired the sound phenomena that spooked the memsahib at Barabar.

28 The only time I went to Barabar (in 1992) I too found them unnerving—a fat man tried to kidnap me and another man had his throat slit—so understandably I haven't gone back. In the decades since, I have decoded Forster's novel as the story of...ah, well, I'll write about it in due time, but it is basically about cultural misinterpretation when somebody clueless goes where they misunderstand everything without realising that they haven't understood anything. It is a common phenomenon among tourists—sometimes causing the ecstasy that tourists feel in India, at other times the disappointment they come away with—but this delusional aspect of tourism has not yet been named by psychiatrists. But maybe *A Passage to India* is a book for India rather than about India, 'probably the best novel ever

written about the country by an Englishman,' to quote literature professor Harish Trivedi, 'an enduring literary monument of the 200 years of British rule in India. It preserves for us human feelings and attitudes from that fraught period as only literature can.'

29 'Where can a man get food? Calcutta is not rich in respect of dainty accommodation. You can stay your stomach at Peliti's or Bonsard's,' Kipling advises travellers, 'but in Lal Bazaar, not far from "The Sailors' Coffeerooms," a board gives bold advertisement that "officers and seamen can find good quarters." In evidence a row of neat officers and seamen are sitting on a bench by the "hotel" door smoking,' he says and describes the boozy '*tâble d'hôte*. The fare is substantial and the regulation "peg"—every house has its own depth of peg if you will refrain from stopping Ganymede—something to wonder at. Three fingers and a trifle over seems to be the use of the officers and seamen who are talking so quietly in the doorway.'

30 In China, where tea may also be said to be (as in India) the national drink, it is drunk without milk or sweeteners, very light—except in former colony Hong Kong where it is had the English way. The Chinese swill cup after cup and the tea houses tend to provide unlimited refills, whereas in India it is common to share the cup 'by-two' (in Bengaluru parlance) or 'cutting-chai' (in Mumbai) so for obvious reasons there's no free refill policy. The Chinese tea habit dates much further back, presumably to the T'ang dynasty, at which time it became known as *cha* which is the origin of the word chai.

31 So-called 'Sino-Indian' cuisines can be broadly divided into four main styles, of which the original is the Bengali from Tangra. The other three consist of the Mumbai-style notable for Chinese bhelpuri, chicken lollipops and anything called manchurian, and the North Indian Chinjabi, a Punjabified version with its chili potatoes, chilly paneer skewers, Schezwan naans and of course tandoori momos, and last but not least the even more chillifed

Andhranese with its chilly chicken that is extremely popular in south India alongside the increasingly common Schezwan dosa. There are many other localised variations such as the Gujarati noodle-topped pizzas and dhokla manchurian while Instagrammers experiment with dishes such as 'chocolate manchurian'. As to how domesticated it has become, it's instructive to consider that 37 per cent of restaurants in India have 'Chinese' items on the menu while in a major city like Mumbai the figure jumps up to 53 per cent.

32 Regarding the potentially contentious issue of eating certain non-veg items deemed to be pets, the Chinese who are famous for their dog dishes, domesticated canines tens of thousands of years ago. But when I was living in China a decade ago, I only heard rumours of their so-called 'chow dogs' that were especially fattened for culinary use (tasted like chicken, I was told), never able to find these at restaurants. More recently, while travelling in Vietnam and Cambodia, I learnt that the once popular dog meat had virtually vanished from menus due to protest from European animal right's groups (which hurts tourism) and could only be had in rural backwoods villages or was sold discreetly in the form of dog salami in the big cities where I managed to score a portion—it is a rather gamey meat, by the way, although others compare it to chicken or mutton. Maybe they ate different dogs. It is true that my Viking ancestors also enjoyed canine barbecue before getting Christianised and like them I try my best to shrug off any Biblical dictates that claim hounds to be taboo, as the actual wording (*Leviticus 11:27*) goes that 'four-footed animals that walk on their paws are unclean; whoever touches their carcasses will be unclean until evening'. This suggests to me that dogs may be enjoyed for dinner after sunset. It is a little known fact that the explorer James Cook found roast puppy a delicious festive food. These Polynesian *kuri*-dogs resembling foxes with long bodies and short legs, were according to Cook one of the tastiest dishes 'next to an English lamb' (as retold by Anne Salmond in

The Trial of the Cannibal Dog: Captain Cook in the South Seas) served on Tahiti in 1769, so he got a doggy bag to bring along (or at least live dogs that provided fresh meat at sea) on his onward journeys, that ended a decade later in 1779, when Hawaiians cooked Cook. Previously, he had already lost crew members to cannibals who used to roast their feet, hands, heads, hearts and lungs. So the famous dog-meat market at Dimapur, the capital of the Nagas, suggests itself as a place all semi-professional foodies ought to sample at least once in their lifetimes. I'll go there in my next book if readers like this book. If not, then not.